CULTURE, RHETORIC, AND VOTING

CULTURE, RHETORIC, AND VOTING

THE PRESIDENTIAL ELECTION OF 2012

EDITED BY

DOUGLAS M. BRATTEBO
TOM LANSFORD
JACK COVARRUBIAS
ROBERT J. PAULY, JR.

The University of Akron Press
Akron, Ohio

All inquiries and permission requests should be addressed to the Publisher,
The University of Akron Press, Akron, Ohio 44325-1703.

20   19   18   17   16   5   4   3   2   1

LIBRARY OF CONGRESS CATALOGING-IN-PUBLICATION DATA

Names: Brattebo, Douglas M., editor. | Lansford, Tom, editor. | Covarrubias, Jack, editor. | Pauly,
   Robert J., 1967– editor.
Title: Culture, rhetoric, and voting : the presidential election of 2012 / edited by Douglas M.
   Brattebo, Tom Lansford, Jack Covarrubias, Robert J. Pauly.
Description: Akron, Ohio : The University of Akron Press, [2015] | Includes bibliographical
   references and index.
Identifiers: LCCN 2015038212| ISBN 9781629220383 (paperack : alkaline paper) | ISBN
   9781629220406 (epub) | ISBN 9781629220390 (epdf)
Subjects: LCSH: Presidents—United States—Election—2012. | Voting—United States. | Political
   campaigns—United States. | Presidential candidates—United States. | Obama, Barack. | Romney,
   Mitt. | Elections—United States. | United States—Politics and government—2009–
Classification: LCC JK526 2012 .C85 2015 | DDC 324.973/0932—dc23
LC record available at http://lccn.loc.gov/2015038212

The paper used in this publication meets the minimum requirements of American National
Standard for Information Sciences—Permanence of Paper for Printed Library Materials, ANSI
Z39.48–1984. ∞

Culture, Rhetoric, and Voting was typeset in Goudy with Avenir display by Amy Freels, printed on
sixty-pound natural, and bound by BookMasters of Ashland, Ohio.

In memory of James A. Garfield, Twentieth President of the United States

Contents

III. Voting

Acknowledgments

This book is the product of a conference, "The Presidential Election of 2012," held at Hiram College on November 16 and 17, 2012, as the dust was just starting to clear from Election Day (Tuesday, November 6). One hundred and thirty-two years earlier, in November 1880, Hiram College had seen one of its very own elevated to the presidency. James A. Garfield—who in 1851 commenced two years as a student at what was then the Western Reserve Eclectic Institute, returned to the school in 1856 as an instructor and soon thereafter became its principal, and left the school in 1861 to embark upon a career in the Union Army and in government—became the twentieth president of the United States. Appropriately, the conference participants enjoyed a private tour of the James A. Garfield National Historic Site in nearby Mentor, Ohio—an experience that fueled dinner conversation as nearly forty scholars from the United States and Canada enjoyed the music of a string quartet.

The high quality of the scholarly chapters contained in this volume speaks for itself. The editors are enduringly grateful for the creativity, diligence, and patience that each author brought to his or her contribution. Graduate assistant Charlie Carlee provided valuable editorial assistance in assembling the manuscript. The University of Akron Press has been a steady partner on this project, and we have benefited mightily from the wise counsel and good work of Amy Freels, editorial and design coordinator; Carol Slatter, coordinator of print manufacturing and digital production; and director Thomas Bacher. However, neither the conference nor the resulting book would have been possible without the superb efforts of several other estimable people. Brittany Jackson was indefatigable in handling a wide range of planning and logistical challenges associated with the conference. Anita Stocz and Mary Landries ensured that there would be suitable lodging for the participants, that the venues for the panel discussions and meals would be appropriate, and that transportation to and from airports and the historic site would be seamless. Todd Arrington, Chief of Interpretation and Education at the James A. Garfield National Historic Site, and his National Park Service colleagues epitomized professionalism and enthusiasm as they shared their knowledge of the Garfield family and the site with the conference attendees. Keynote speakers Shirley Ann Warshaw, Professor of Political Science at Gettysburg College, and Stephen Koff, Washington Bureau Chief of the *Cleveland Plain Dealer*, offered up insightful analysis of the Obama presidency and Ohio's role in presidential elections, respectively. And the Garfield Institute for Public Leadership provided generous support for the conference, underwriting nearly one-fifth of the conclave's budget.

The conference was a true team effort, so rewarding and productive that we surely will convene another such gathering in the future. Hiram College's new James A. Garfield Center for the Study of the American Presidency, whose mission is to cultivate in students a deep understanding of the institution of the presidency and the individuals who have held the office, is certain to be the locus of that effort. We hope President Garfield would be proud.

Introduction

Chapter 1

Introduction

Douglas M. Brattebo, Hiram College and
Robert J. Pauly, Jr., University of Southern Mississippi–Gulf Coast

When Barack H. Obama was elected in November 2008 and then inaugurated as the forty-fourth president of the United States in January 2009, he broke a significant cultural barrier as the first African American ever to hold that office. In his election campaign in 2008, Obama, then a one-term Illinois senator, was effective in drawing support from voters across a range of cultural, class, ethnic, and age groups in defeating Republican presidential nominee John McCain, a senator from Arizona. However, rather than bring Americans together as he had so confidently promised to do, Obama instead was quickly overcome by a political environment in which divisions grew ever sharper over the course of his first term. The Democratic-Republican divide was punctuated by rhetoric on both sides that often emphasized cultural barriers, whether related to ethnicity, race, religion, socioeconomic status, or, more often, a combination of these factors. Consequently, it is hardly surprising that the outcome of the 2012 presidential election—Obama's victory over former Massachusetts governor Mitt Romney—was driven largely by the extent to which each side succeeded in crafting the culturally driven rhetorical messages needed to motivate their respective supporters to cast their ballots in the election.

The interconnected roles of cultural factors, campaign rhetoric, and the resultant voter behavior demand thoughtful analysis from a range of academic disciplinary perspectives. The purpose of this volume is to provide precisely that type of analysis through the collaborative efforts of scholars from several academic disciplines and subdisciplines, including history, communication studies, political science, psychology, religion, and sociology. It is divided into three parts that focus, in turn, on the broad range of cultural aspects of the 2012 presidential election, the rhetorical approaches of the Obama and Romney campaigns during the election, and the ways the voters responded, which, of course, determined the ultimate outcome.

Part One consists of four chapters that focus on matters psychological, spiritual, and cultural. William D. Pederson explores the role of the outsider in American politics and argues that Obama and the other presidents with whom he identifies are outsiders, psychologically, who resolved their outsider origins positively by using the political arena as the domain in which to self-actualize by working on public policy issues. Pederson classifies these presidents as having in common a "rational democrat" leadership style, which often confounds critics because such presidents build on a rationalist legacy modeled by their heroes rather than offering extremist solutions. Max J. Skidmore examines the political philosophy of Roger Williams (1603–1683), who was English, an Anglican clergyman, a Puritan, and the founder of Rhode Island (where he also founded America's first Baptist church). Skidmore contends that the devout Williams, who was his age's most fervent opponent of coercion of conscience and also the figure who laid the groundwork for the traditional American principle of church and state separation, would be appalled at much of 2012's political rhetoric, particularly churches' explicit endorsement of purely political initiatives and the setting aside of theological and doctrinal concerns for brazen calculations of worldly self-interest. Luke Perry analyzes Mitt Romney's faith as a unique factor in the 2012 presidential election by examining public perceptions regarding the prospect of a Mormon president and related political dynamics, including the historical record of discrimination against Mormons, comparisons to John F. Kennedy's 1960 presidential campaign, the role of evangelical voters in the Republican Party, and the notable barriers to a

Mormon becoming president. Perry concludes that discomfort with Mormonism limited Romney's ability to utilize his faith as a means to connect with potential voters. Wrapping up the first section, Graham Dodds looks at the state of cultural politics and the "culture wars" in the 2012 presidential election cycle. Dodds reviews the history of the topic, considers the impact of four issue areas with a cultural valence (religion and the role of evangelicals, gender and women's issues, gay rights, and aspects of economic and tax policy), and suggests how we might best make sense of the culture wars right now.

Part Two offers four chapters that examine the rhetoric of the 2012 presidential election. Justin S. Vaughn undertakes an analysis of the two major parties' national conventions and contends that such spectacles have become part and parcel of the "postrhetorical" presidency in their deployment of distractions, lack of policy substance, and dishonest manipulation of information. Vaughn catalogs the normative consequences of this development and suggests a path for scholars who wish to research it in the future. Matthew R. Miles looks at the economic policy positions and rhetorical appeals of the two presidential campaigns to see whether the top priority was to attract independent voters or mobilize their core constituencies. Using a national survey experiment, Miles finds strong support for the base-mobilization thesis, which sometimes can convert partisan-leaners into stronger partisans and help to build a postelection policy coalition. Douglas Mock examines the three presidential debates of 2012 and finds, consistent with a great deal of research on presidential debates from 1960 to the present, a plethora of negative features that serve democracy poorly. Because attempts at witty one-liners, incessant squabbling over procedural matters, media coverage focusing on perceived "knock-out punches," and moderators inserting themselves into the proceedings and becoming the story were all prominent in the 2012 presidential debates, Mock proposes fundamental format changes for future election years. To round out this section, Casey Malone Maugh creates a rhetorical roadmap of President Obama's discourse on gay rights by analyzing his speeches and public comments on gay marriage. Maugh finds that Obama's decision to support gay marriage after years of opposition sheltered the president from the common flip-flopping narrative frequently exploited in modern-day politics, and it also strategically aligned Obama with disenfranchised left-leaning voters and young voters, reinvigorating their sense of Obama as a candidate for reelection.

Part Three is made up of three chapters that look at voting behavior in 2012. Using survey research, Lisa Hager examines the tactic, widely used by both 2012 presidential campaigns, of promoting early voting to boost turnout and stockpile votes before Election Day. Hager finds that older voters, more politically engaged voters, and voters living in states that do not require justification to vote early are more likely to do so, suggesting that less restrictive early voting laws and voters' ages matter more in the pre–Election Day turnout competition than the campaigns' strategies. Will Miller and Sean Foreman note that, as much as Obama ran a superior campaign in 2008, changing demographics played an equally important role, particularly the long-term decline in the percentage of white voters in the electorate. Miller and Foreman examine the 2012 presidential campaigns' efforts to court women, Hispanics, Catholics, young voters, and seniors as some of the key constituencies on the road to the White House to identify the most significant voting blocs in swing states that determined the outcome of Obama vs. Romney. Mark D. Brewer and Richard J. Powell examine the group-based appeals of the Obama and Romney campaigns, particularly those made to Democratic and Republican core constituencies, as well as to uncommitted voters. Brewer and Powell find that Romney tended to use broad economic appeals tailored to specific group concerns and delivered by surrogates identified with those groups, while Obama tended to utilize more conventional group appeals rooted in specific policy initiatives.

I. Psychology, Religion, and Culture

Chapter 2

Understanding Barack Obama's Leadership
Gamble of the "Rational Democrat"
William D. Pederson, Louisiana State University–Shreveport

America's forty-fourth president remains a puzzle to much of the public, and he still confounds many pundits and even political scientists. Extreme conservatives went out of their way to undermine his presidency during his first presidential term, as well as during his reelection campaign. Liberals have often been put off by Barack Obama's apparent aloofness from some of their favorite causes and his seemingly endless efforts to seek bipartisan compromise with those determined to defeat him. Yet he was reelected and his two successive popular-vote majorities puts him in the exclusive company of the only other Democrats, Andrew Jackson and Franklin Roosevelt, to accomplish this feat in American history. Moreover, the Gallup polls have found him the "most admired" man in the world for the fifth consecutive year, and he was selected as *Time* magazine's "Person of the Year" in 2012. The purpose of this chapter is to consider Obama's leadership in relation to other presidents who have demonstrated a similar style.

To accomplish this, the chapter is divided into four sections. The first section suggests that Obama most closely identifies with America's sixteenth president, Abraham Lincoln, not only because Lincoln is celebrated as the nation's greatest president but also because both are psychological outsiders in American politics. It is not only that Obama does this but that other presidents have done the same thing for essentially similar reasons. The second part of the chapter suggests that these presidents successfully resolve their "outsiderness" by going into politics. Several have used the Great Emancipator as a model to emancipate themselves from their outsiderness by self-actualizing through the arena of politics. They become policy wonks who help resolve public policy issues, whether borne of slavery and secession, the Great Depression and World War II, or a paucity of health care insurance and looming regional genocide. The third part of the argument is that these self-actualizers most closely fit into a "rational democrat" leadership style both at home and abroad. The Mount Rushmore presidents generally and Franklin D. Roosevelt specifically, as well as a variety of political leaders abroad, build on one another's legacies since they identify with them. Critics often fail to understand their leadership style since it is seldom extremist. The final section of the chapter offers tentative conclusions on Obama's future based on those who have practiced this leadership style in the past. The "rational democrats" enjoy politics so much they are willing to seek reelection despite facing heavy criticism. Abraham Lincoln and Franklin Roosevelt are perhaps the best example of this.

THE OUTSIDER PHENOMENON

It is not unusual for politicians to identify with earlier successful ones. Seemingly success might breed success. Yet frequently overlooked in this process is that it often has deeper psychological roots. As a Republican, Theodore Roosevelt naturally identified with Abraham Lincoln as the party's first successful presidential candidate. Yet TR was both a physical and social outsider—he suffered terrible problems with asthma as a youth, and he had a Confederate mother and a Yankee father who did not join the Union army. The young TR never seemed to understand that his father had stayed out of the Civil War in order to keep peace with his spouse. Similarly, Lincoln, himself Southern born, identified with George

Washington so much that he served two brief stints with the Illinois militia, and then he identified later with Henry Clay, "The Great Compromiser," who is typically ranked as America's best legislator (Porter 1987). Lincoln may be the presidency's prototype outsider: physically, he was too skinny, too tall, and perhaps too ugly; socially, he was born in the South but grew up on the frontier, becoming a hick lawyer; and intellectually, he had less than a year of formal schooling.

Franklin D. Roosevelt conveniently patterned his life after that of his distant uncle, serving in many of the same political positions. Though seemingly not an outsider, FDR never forgot his social rejection during his years at Harvard University, and after polio struck, FDR modeled his recovery on how his one-time "99-pound weakling uncle" had transformed his body. TR's identification with Lincoln allowed FDR to effectively co-opt Lincoln into the Democratic Party (Rietveld 2003). FDR became the Great Emancipator intent on averting the Nazis' intended worldwide concentration camp system, while Aaron Copland set America's war effort to music in the "Lincoln Suite" in 1942.

Post–World War II outsider presidents have followed a similar path. Harry Truman, an almost accidental president, suffered from poor eyesight growing up in Missouri but his service in World War I transformed the young captain. As a student of history without a college degree, he considered Lincoln a great president despite his Confederate mother-in-law. As a New Dealer he built on that immediate legacy by integrating the armed services and pursued a containment policy toward Communism as Lincoln had initially advocated against slavery. Gerald Ford learned belatedly as a teenager that he had been adopted. After college he gave up seeking approval through sports by instead earning a law degree as a means to enter politics. Though a Republican, he helped to restore Truman by putting his bust in the Oval Office. Until the Obama presidency, Bill Clinton was perhaps the best recent example of a regional outsider in American politics who publicly identified with Lincoln on his way to the White House. As the oldest son of a thrice-married Southern mother, Clinton was overweight and a band member in secondary school. He obtained a law degree like the Great Emancipator and hung Lincoln's portrait in the governor's office in Little Rock, Arkansas. Clinton is sometimes referred to as America's first "black" president, as he knew how to preach in different settings.

Yet America's first biracial rather than strictly "African American" president, Barack Hussein Obama, may be the best example of the largely forgotten role of the outsider in the American presidency. His running for president during the bicentennial of Lincoln's birth distracted public attention from a deeper story. Though his campaign in 2008 repeatedly emphasized the obvious link between him and the Great Emancipator (Alter 2010), Obama's identification with Lincoln likely runs deeper than that of any previous president. Obama knows Lincoln's story in terms of both his words and deeds. They are both classic outsiders.

The son of a white American mother from Kansas and an absent African father, his very name—Barack Hussein Obama—accentuates his outsiderness. Being born and reared outside the continental United States reinforced his apartness, and Obama even spent time in Indonesia as a youth. Similarly, Lincoln was born in a border state where he spent his first six years before moving to Indiana where he was reared through his teenage years. Like Obama, Lincoln "lost" one parent but had an "angel mother," in the form of a stepmother, who compensated for his loss much as Obama's maternal grandmother filled in for his father and often his own mother. Obama's intrepid maternal grandmother provided her grandson with the model of the Great Emancipator. She had learned it from a high school teacher in Kansas who was steeped in the Lincoln legend (Maraniss 2012). Lincoln would declare his independence from his father by traveling down the Mississippi twice to New Orleans, the largest port city in the Old South, and Obama would come to the mainland for his higher education and eventually establish roots in the "Land of Lincoln" where he married an African American and Lincoln had married an ambitious Southern belle. Both Lincoln and Obama were outsiders on the make.

The major difference between Obama's and Lincoln's backgrounds is seemingly in their educational experience. Lincoln only had a total of one year of formal schooling, so he was forced to become an autodidact in terms of developing into a lawyer. In contrast, Obama was intensively educated through attending an elitist prep school in Hawaii and later Harvard Law School. Yet even in terms of their extreme educational difference they are psychologically similar in Lincoln's lack of education and Obama's "overeducation." From opposite directions they became intellectual outsiders. The polished Edwin Stanton, whom Lincoln eventually made his second secretary of war, initially would have nothing to do with Honest Abe when the two men worked jointly on a railroad legal case. In fact, Stanton humiliated the future president for his obvious lack of "class." Similarly, Obama is criticized from the opposite direction for his aloof manner compared to Bill Clinton's "down-home" style. In fact, Obama initially was rejected by some African Americans for not being a genuine African American. To add insult to injury, some extreme conservatives insisted that Obama was not an American.

Outsiders tend to have an extraordinary amount of energy. These individuals are "on the make" and therefore restless and always on the move. They have "ants in their pants." They are driven to prove themselves. Most outsiders are cutting old social ties and seeking inroads into a new group that they aspire to join. Even if they find a means to join the aspirational group, they seldom feel they really fit in; they never feel completely "at home" in the new group. F. Scott Fitzgerald's *The Great Gatsby* may be the best fictional depiction of this condition. Most social outsiders simply overconform in an effort to gain acceptance. At the other extreme, a few rebel and may become perpetual revolutionaries. Psychologists tend to view these behaviors as "negative resolution" of one's marginality or outsiderness. These individuals are perpetually frustrated with identity issues and may engage in ego defense mechanisms, blaming others for what they are unable to resolve within themselves.

On the other hand, psychologists also recognize that some individuals are able to resolve this psychological tension "positively" through creative behavior. These individuals are "comfortable in their own skin" (Pederson 2012). The Mount Rushmore presidents are a good starting point to explore this idea.

SELF-ACTUALIZATION THROUGH POLITICS

Abraham Lincoln may be the ultimate prototype of an outsider who resolved his outsiderness positively through the arena of politics. After experimenting with a variety of jobs, he ran for the state legislature at an earlier age than all other future lawyer-presidents (Green and Pederson 1989). Though he lost, he had finally found his "calling." Lincoln lost in part because he had been serving in the Illinois militia rather than focusing on campaigning. Despite that, Lincoln made a credible showing and then spent the rest of his life either running for political office or seeking a political position (Hoftstadter 1948). The most memorable part of Lincoln's brief militia service had been his election as the company captain by his peers: he felt the rush of public acceptance for who he was, and so began his lifelong "political career." Lincoln used the law initially as the means to sustain his political interests and family, yet he did not become a lawyer until three years after his first successful election to the state legislature. Having directed his "little engine that knew no rest," Lincoln rapidly became the nominal leader of the Whigs in Illinois within four years. He was prepared for the slavery issue to the extent that he saw through extremists' panaceas—whether John C. Calhoun's illogical concept of "the concurrent majority," John Brown's revolutionary abolitionism, or Stephen Douglas's so-called "popular sovereignty." Initially, Lincoln merely advocated a "containment" policy of allowing slavery in the Old South as the Constitution permitted but refusing to extend it into the territories.

Similarly, FDR did not assume that democratic government was doomed during a totalitarian era. He rejected Huey Long's proto-fascist approach in Louisiana and Douglas MacArthur's militarism during the Great Depression. FDR bought time for preparing the nation's military capacity, while holding regular elections as Abraham Lincoln had done, which the British actually postponed during World War II. FDR built on Lincoln's successful Land Grant College Act with the "G.I. Bill" and used Lincoln's logic against southern planters to justify the Allied position opposing a worldwide Nazi slave system.

Obama fits into this same pattern. He may have been as unprepared as Lincoln in terms of executive experience, and even more so in terms of political experience in general, but as the community activist turned lawyer-professor he wanted to practice politics to fulfill himself as Lincoln, FDR, and others like them had. The country was ready for him.

From the start of his governing Obama pursued moderate policies while avoiding demagoguery. Rather than wage an ideological crusade against the evils of Big Business gone wild, he supported the taxpayer bailout of the auto and banking industries with loans despite the outrageous bonuses paid to the heads of the same firms that had caused the economic meltdown in the first place. Recognizing the plight of average Americans struggling against the greed of the financiers, Obama supported regulation with the Dodd-Frank bill in Congress (Kaiser 2013).

Obama soon turned his attention to national health care despite the pleas of his top staff members to at least wait until he was safely reelected. He allowed Congress to grapple with the issue until the time was finally ripe to achieve some kind of historic resolution. Though a bipartisan coalition failed to emerge during the agonizingly prolonged and intensely partisan debate, his party backed him in achieving a "first beginning" that had eluded Theodore Roosevelt at the beginning of the twentieth century, Franklin Roosevelt during the New Deal years, and the Clintons at the end of the century. Even when polls suggested that less than a majority of the public supported "Obamacare," the president was willing to make the issue a part of his reelection campaign. He had rejected the liberal "single payer" option while co-opting the Heritage Foundation's erstwhile conservative policy recommendation as something politically possible to accomplish in a divided Congress and nation. It worked.

Similarly, on other domestic human rights issues Obama slowly but steadily moved from ending the "Don't ask, don't tell" policy in the military to becoming the first president in American history to endorse same-sex marriage on the way to his reelection victory. Because of fierce opposition to immigration reform during his first term, he postponed pushing the issue. Yet like the other Mt. Rushmore and other outsider presidents who have self-actualized through the political arena, Obama supported a de facto amnesty in the name of justice (Pederson 1977; Noah 2012). The result was overwhelming Hispanic support for his reelection.

In terms of foreign policy, Obama acted to remove America troops from a combat role in Iraq and Afghanistan, signaling a retreat from the idealist neoconservative folly of changing traditional societies with military might. Though drone use became a controversial part of this change, he nonetheless backed, without any Cabinet support, the NATO-led intervention in Libya to prevent the likely slaughter of rebels and civilians by Muammar Qaddafi (Lewis 2012). Moreover, in April 2012, Obama took the initiative in setting up the Atrocities Prevention Board in the White House (Landler 2013). Preventing genocide is seemingly the bedrock of Obama's foreign policy.

OBAMA AS A "RATIONAL DEMOCRAT"

Political scientists, political psychologists, and organizational theorists have used a variety of labels for leaders who seemingly are the most admired ones ("lawmakers," "active-positives," "active-flexibles," "transforming," "craftsmen," etc.). They seemingly are different from the bulk of "passive" leaders, as well as from hyperaggressive leaders who damage themselves and others in an effort to accomplish their goals. In contrast, the self-actualizers who enjoy working on public policy issues in politics have resolved who they are and have the extra energy and time to work on political rather than personal issues. They seemingly enjoy others while the individuals who work for them find it equally enjoyable. These leaders stress reason in solving problems while promoting democratic values in their solutions.

The models for this type of leadership style are Abraham Lincoln and Franklin Roosevelt. Both were active and initially underrated by others until they faced the actual challenges of the presidency. Lincoln, in particular, was denigrated as a "dark horse" candidate who won the presidency with only a plurality of the popular vote. He was frequently dismissed as a frontier hick. In contrast, FDR was seemingly an aristocratic playboy who merely wanted the presidency as another toy. Nonetheless, both confounded the criticism while creatively addressing the major issues the nation confronted.

As noted earlier, rather than slipping into John C. Calhoun's illogical concept of "the concurrent majority," the abolitionist fanaticism of John Brown, or the sophistry of Stephen A. Douglas's "popular sovereignty," Lincoln initially favored a "containment" policy toward slavery—allowing it in the Old South since it was protected by the U.S. Constitution but prohibiting its spread. Lincoln's views would evolve further from voluntary "colonization" to compensated emancipation and finally the Emancipation Proclamation in response to secession and the Civil War. His position on slavery was reinforced in the long run by his economic and social policies that enlarged the middle class: the Homestead Act, the Land Grant College Act, and the Pacific Railway Act, all enacted in 1862. Though race-baited during the Lincoln-Douglas debates, Lincoln articulated—for the most part—the rationale for free labor and self-government. He was not a demagogue or an economic or racial elitist (a "Marx of the Master Class").

"No drama Obama" follows in Lincoln's rational democratic footsteps. Both are essentially moderates who prefer reason above ideology regardless of the issue at bar; both like to think more than talk when dealing with public policy issues. Most disconcerting to their critics and supporters alike, they seemingly want to encourage that mode of behavior in American society from schools to the nation's divided political institutions. Rational democrats promote political maturity in nations (Davies 1963).

TENTATIVE CONCLUSIONS

The argument of this chapter is that the best American presidents historically have been psychological outsiders who resolved that tension by self-actualizing through the political arena. They use their intellectual gifts to work on creative solutions to issues facing the nation rather than retreating from them or making them worse. Many of America's best presidents seem to have identified at least in part with its most psychologically marginal president. Lincoln had a burning aspiration due to his physical, social, and intellectual differences from the norm. Yet he was able to resolve these issues early on by finding what he most enjoyed doing in life—practicing politics. Similarly, Obama is an outsider who identified with both Lincoln personally and with Lincoln's rational and democratic approach to resolving public policy issues. Obama seems to share Lincoln's regard for history's ultimate judgment on his policies. Rather than remain content with short-term popularity, Obama is willing to sometimes go against fickle public opinion in the pursuit of democratic values at home and abroad. It is a gamble that rational democrats are willing to take.

Lincoln again may be the enduring model for rational democrats who illustrate a willingness to run for reelection based on the public policy positions they have taken. The Great Emancipator did this during an era of one-term presidents. Despite his near certainty that he would be defeated, Lincoln not only held the 1864 election (unlike the British who postponed their elections during World War II), he believed the Union and Emancipation deserved a public vote. Rational democratic lawmakers want their policies endorsed and are willing to risk defeat (Barber 1965). Similarly, Obama put himself and his policies before the public in 2012. It was a vindication of his leadership style and identity.

Curiously, other nations seemingly identify with this style of leadership. There are more streets, schools, and stamps abroad with Lincoln's name or image on them than any other American president. He is a universal symbol of a leadership style that he defined in action. The outsider careers of Mohandas Gandhi, Jawaharlal Nehru, Thomas Masaryk, Willy Brandt, and Nelson Mandela reflect in part the leadership style of the Great Emancipator. Barack Obama is part of this democratic legacy (Pederson 2014).

REFERENCES

Alter, J. 2010. *The Promise*. New York: Simon & Schuster.
Barber, J. 1965. *The Lawmakers: Recruitment and Adaptation to Legislative Life.*
     New Haven: Yale University Press.
Davies, J. 1963. *Human Nature in Politics*. New York: Wiley.
Green, T., and W. Pederson. 1989. "The Behavior of Lawyer-Presidents." In *The
     "Barberian" Presidency*, edited by W. Pederson. New York: Peter Lang.
Hofstadter, R. 1948. *American Political Tradition*. New York: Knopf.
Kaiser, R. 2013. *Act of Congress*. New York: Knopf.
Landler, M. 2013. "Work on Task Force Gives Insight." *New York Times*, June 23.
Lewis, M. 2012. "Obama's Way." *Vanity Fair*, October, 210–217, 259–264.
Maraniss, D. 2012. *Barack Obama: The Story*. New York: Simon and Schuster.
Noah, T. 2012. "Expand 'Stealth Amnesty.'" *New Republic*, December, 15–16.
Pederson, W. 1977. "Amnesty and Presidential Behavior." *Presidential Studies
     Quarterly* 7 (4): 175–183.
Pederson, W. 2012. "Obama's Lincoln: Image to ideology." In *Obama Presidency*,
     edited by R. Watson et al., 37–50. Albany, NY: SUNY Press.
Pederson, W. 2014. "Abraham Lincoln and Mohandas Gandhi as Outsiders."
     Anekaant 2: 21–25.
Porter, D. 1987. "America's Ten Greatest Senators." In *Rating Game in American
     Politics*, edited by W. Pederson, 110–130. New York: Irvington.
Rietveld, R. 2003. "Franklin D. Roosevelt's Abraham Lincoln." In *Franklin D.
     Roosevelt and Abraham Lincoln,* edited by W. Pederson and F. Williams,
     10–60. Armonk, NY: M. E. Sharpe.

Chapter 3

Church and State in America
What Roger Williams Might Say Regarding the 2012 Elections
Max J. Skidmore, University of Missouri–Kansas City

INTRODUCTION

Roger Williams was certainly the first person in America to advocate the complete separation of church and state, and arguably was one of the most important influences on the development of the United States as a secular country. As a founder of the Baptist Church in America, he inspired generations of Baptists who became the fiercest defenders of church-state separation. In recent years, however, American fundamentalists/evangelicals—including many Baptists—have come to reject separation, and have moved in the direction of theocracy. This reflects to a large extent the influence of the late Francis Schaeffer, who as indicated in the pages to follow, became America's "Anti-Roger Williams."

The results are what Williams feared: the corruption of the church when it becomes too close to politics. This chapter examines how this happened, and how it was that many fundamentalists/evangelicals by 2012 had come to take positions for political gain at the expense of theological purity. The elections that year illustrate how wise Williams was. If he had been able to observe American politics in 2012, he would undoubtedly have been disappointed by the Democrats, and dismayed by the Republicans.

ROGER WILLIAMS

Roger Williams, in common with all American colonists in the seventeenth century—in outlook, thought, and temperament—was more English than American. Over the next hundred years, assumptions, attitudes, and worldviews were to change considerably. Williams was every bit a Puritan, and thus his words sound strange to modern Americans, even to those familiar with the language of the Founders. Nevertheless, he was far in advance of his contemporaries with regard to such matters as coercion in religion and freedom of conscience.

Williams was intensely pious, which sets him apart from many advocates of religious freedom who are skeptics. The thrust of his many works was that conscience cannot be coerced, that those who attempt to do so are in error, and that diversity is compatible with civil peace. He wrote his greatest work, *The Bloudy Tenent of Persecution for Cause of Conscience*, in 1844, when he was in London seeking a charter to protect the colony that he had founded (subsequently to become "Rhode Island and Providence Plantation") against real threats from its neighboring colonies, Massachusetts Bay, Connecticut, and Plymouth. He described his treatise's arguments at its beginning. In paraphrased form they were: First, that the vast amount of blood that had been spilled in religious wars had not been "required nor accepted by Jesus Christ." Second, that one can prove by scripture that persecution for conscience or belief is unauthorized. Third, that arguments favoring persecution can be countered. Fourth, that the doctrine of persecution for conscience is guilty of unwarranted killing. Fifth, that no civil state has jurisdiction over spiritual matters. Sixth, that since the coming of Jesus, God commands that freedom of conscience be granted to all, including pagans, Jews, Muslims, or "antichristian consciences," that all should be free to worship as they believe, and that the only sword to be used against them should be a spiritual sword, not physical violence. (This was perhaps the most radical of all his assertions, going far beyond those that advocates of "toleration" would support, as it would have protected not only those adherents of all religions, but even atheists.) Seventh, that the scriptural government of Israel "is proved figurative and ceremonial, and no pattern nor precedent for any kingdom or civil state in the world to follow." Eighth, that "God requires not uniformity of religion to be enacted and enforced in any civil state," and that any attempt to do so "sooner or later is the greatest occasion of civil war, of the ravishing of conscience, of the persecution of Jesus Christ and his servants, and of the hypocrisy and destruction of millions of souls." Ninth, that requiring religious uniformity would "necessarily disclaim our desires and hopes of the Jews' conversion to Christ." Tenth, that attempting to enforce religious uniformity in a civil state "confounds the civil and religious," and denies "that Jesus Christ is come in the flesh." Eleventh, that acceptance of religious diversity brings civil peace, and makes possible the enforcement of "civil obedience from all sorts." "Twelfth and last," that "true civility and Christianity may both flourish" in a society that embraces "diverse and contrary consciences" (Williams 86–87).

Having died more than a century before the American Revolution, Williams can hardly be thought of as a Founding Father. Still, considering his pioneering role supporting unrestricted conscience, religious freedom, and actual separation of church and state, it may be appropriate to consider him as a Founding Grandfather (or Great-Grandfather), or perhaps at least as a Founding Godfather.

There would be resistance to bestowing such a title on Williams. Jefferson, it might be said, appropriately receives honor for being the Apostle of Freedom (his status as a slaveholder notwithstanding). Moreover, there is no evidence that he found inspiration from Williams. As the distinguished historian of American religions, Edwin Gaustad, tells us, the "most famous wall in American history belongs to Jefferson, not to Williams. With similar but not identical concerns, both men wanted a clear division between the civil and ecclesiastical estates. Williams spoke of it as 'the hedge or wall of separation between the garden of the church and the wilderness of the world.' Jefferson spoke of it as a 'wall of separation between church and state.' No evidence demonstrates that the latter statement was dependent on the former." Still, Gaustad does say that Jefferson's interests and those of Williams "could on occasion happily coincide" (Gaustad 1999, 207).

No less keen a historian of colonial America than Edmund Morgan says of Williams that his "defense of liberty of conscience would seem to have been somewhat more limited than that which a Thomas Jefferson or a James Madison offered in the next century." Williams, after all, had "honored conscience in any form," but he had "sworn eternal warfare not against every tyranny over the mind of man but only against compulsion in religion." His goal was freedom to find God, rather than freedom of thought for its own sake. Nevertheless, Morgan concedes, the difference between the view that "ultimately prevailed in the United States" and that of Williams is "easily exaggerated." Williams, like the Founders, was vindicating reason. To praise him for his support of church-state separation and for religious freedom is appropriate, but "it falls short of the man. His greatness was simpler. He dared to think" (Morgan 2007, 141–142).

Similar resistance inspired a recent exchange in the *New York Review of Books* ("Roger Williams on His Own" 2012, 73–74). John M. Barry's *Roger Williams and the Creation of the American Soul: Church, State, and the Birth of Liberty*, may be the closest thing to the definitive biography of Williams yet produced (Barry 2012). It inspired a complimentary review by Gordon Wood, who called Barry "one of the most talented of the distinguished nonacademic historians writing today," and stated that Barry's "is one of the best biographies of Williams that we have. And that's saying something, since Williams is surely the most written-about figure in seventeenth-century America" (Wood 2012).

Wood is one of the most justly heralded historians of early America, but Barry also brings powerful credentials to the controversy. He is a careful and thorough researcher, a thoughtful observer, and a superb writer. In 1992, *The Ambition and the Power: The Fall of Jim Wright: A True Story of Washington*, told the tale of a brash minority-party backbencher's unlikely toppling from power of one of the most formidable figures in Washington (Barry 1992). The relentless attack that Newt Gingrich launched upon the speaker reflected a slash-and-burn approach to politics that was to bring his party to power, free it of traditional restraints, and reshape it into a juggernaut devoted solely to winning.

Rising Tide: The Great Mississippi Flood of 1927 and How It Changed America analyzes one of the worst disasters in American history, and one that persisted month after month (Barry 1998). Barry deftly describes the politics of race and class, and the self-serving actions of prominent figures who made things worse, but nonetheless assured their political futures. Black workers were essential, and expendable. The thirty feet of water that inundated countless miles of land and drove more than a million inhabitants away, many permanently, made it clear that government must be stronger.

The Great Influenza describes in minute detail the horrors of the worst pandemic to infect the world in modern history, the influenza in 1918 that swept the globe in three successive waves (Barry 2005). Never had anything infected so many, and killed so many in such a brief period. The most recent estimate indicates that at least fifty million died, and perhaps as many as a hundred million (Johnson and Mueller 2002). In contrast to other forms of influenza, it struck young, healthy adults even harder than the elderly or the very young. The total number of deaths in America from the pandemic was as high as 675,000 (Taubenberger 2005, 73). "Nearly half of all deaths in the United States in 1918 were flu related" (Garrett 2005, 2).

These three books were all definitive works. Despite Barry's being a nonscientist, *The Great Influenza* brought him praise from the American Medical Association, and even led him to relevant academic appointments (for example, as visiting scholar, Center for Bioenvironmental Research, Tulane and Xavier Universities). And each of the three books dealt with matters now nearly forgotten outside of professional communities.

Thus, one might expect *Roger Williams* to bring equal praise to Barry. As indicated, Gordon Wood did praise it and found it to be impressive. Nevertheless, neither Barry's deep research nor his thoughtful conclusions were sufficient to insulate him from criticism. Wood wrote that Barry exaggerated the influences on Williams by "the great English jurist Sir Edward Coke" and by Sir Francis Bacon, "whom Coke hated." Moreover, Barry was "probably not" correct when he said that Williams is vital today, or that he might have been "a better source of the idea of separation of church and state than Thomas Jefferson." Williams, said Wood, was far too individualistic and too extreme "to have much relevance today" (Wood 2012).

Wood's words were too much for Barry. They sparked a controversy that only an academic can appreciate. Barry's rejoinder came a few months later ("Roger Williams on His Own" 2012). It began politely, and remained so. He said it was flattering to be called "'one of the most talented of the distinguished nonacademic historians writing today' by such a distinguished academic historian as Gordon Wood." Nonetheless, Wood's review, Barry said, required a response, and respond he did. He discussed the similarity of Williams's views on personal freedom and those of Coke, and conceded that evidentiary influence from Bacon had been less direct. Barry, though, pointed out that he had been careful to use words such as "seem," or "may have" in the relevant discussion. Moreover, he said, Williams knew Bacon and cited his work "conspicuously, if rarely, on the dedication page of his most important book." Finally, he said, he believed Wood simply to be mistaken when he rejected Barry's statement that Williams "could not be more relevant today" ("Roger Williams on His Own" 2012).

Without belaboring the point, Barry's book also said that "Bacon left a large mark on the world, and a large mark on Roger Williams as well" (Barry 2012, 34). In later passages, though, Barry wrote that "although Williams never explicitly stated that he derived his political ideas from Coke, the principles which Coke articulated clearly anchored Williams's thinking," and he mentioned that every man's home is his castle and the idea that the English constitution, including all its traditions, not merely the Magna Carta, "prohibited arbitrary power." Then, he said, Williams had rejected Bacon's views on royal prerogative and state power, "but Bacon may have influenced him in other, more fundamental ways. Bacon may have influenced the way in which Williams thought" (Barry 2012, 221).

Wood's reply seemed to express hurt feelings, and again, he complained that Barry had not been able to reconcile Williams's Puritanism with the principles either of Coke or Bacon, and reiterated that Barry could not document their influence. More important for this chapter is Wood's assertion that Barry could not demonstrate Williams's relevance today. Williams, Wood said, was largely ignored by his fellow colonists in the seventeenth century. Williams's reputation developed only gradually over the last 300 years. Curiously, however, in attacking Barry, Wood seems to provide support for Barry's argument. "Only in the late eighteenth century when Isaac Backus and the Massachusetts Baptists rediscovered Williams and used his beliefs on behalf of their dissenting cause in New England did this radical Puritan begin to acquire his modern importance," Wood wrote ("Roger Williams on His Own" 2012). This appears to be a clear acceptance of the idea that Williams does have "modern importance." Wood went on to say that he had "no doubt of Williams's importance in the West's long struggle for religious liberty," but argued that Williams was too individualistic, too devoted to radical separatism, too "eccentric to be, as Barry claims, the source of the American soul" ("Roger Williams on His Own" 2012). Far from damning Barry's book with faint praise, Wood appears unconsciously to be praising it with faint damns.

This becomes especially notable when reviewing Wood's original review. He wrote that, "actually, when all is said and done, neither Williams nor Jefferson was the source of America's religious freedom. The multiplicity of competing sects and denominations in eighteenth-century America was the real source." As Jefferson's bill for religious freedom was making its way through the Virginia legislature in 1785 and 1786 under Madison's guidance, the many sects backing it (including, among others, Baptists, Presbyterians, and Quakers) paid no attention to Jefferson's preamble that said "our civil rights have no dependence on our religious opinions." All that each one wanted, he said, was disestablishment of the Anglican Church in Virginia, and a guarantee that no other sect would gain control over it. "That," he said, "as Madison but not Jefferson came to appreciate, was a far more important source of America's religious freedom than the ideals of John Locke or Roger Williams" (Wood 2012). Recognizing the strength of influence from Baptists, along with others, considering Williams's influence on the Baptist tradition, raises at least the possibility that Williams may have contributed more than Wood conceded.

Gaustad, for example, wrote that both New England and Virginia had "a strong libertarian Baptist voice during the Revolution and after," and that they "waved the banners of religious liberty with vigor and effect," leading in the popular support for Jefferson's Bill for Establishing Religious Freedom (Gaustad 1999, 204). Jefferson's rhetoric, Gaustad said, "required neither earlier documents nor earlier champions of religious liberty," but his bill did "echo language of both Rhode Island's and Pennsylvania's charters" (Gaustad 1999, 205). Madison, Gaustad said, learned of the great concern for separation of church and state from conversations with many people, including "John Leland, a Baptist itinerant preacher of great force and great conviction." Leland agreed with Madison that "church establishments had done far more harm than good," and remarked that "state establishment of religion, like a bear, hugs the saints but corrupts Christianity" (Gaustad 1999, 206–207). Williams, even if there were no direct connection to Leland, certainly influenced that Baptist belief Leland expressed, and which was to become influential. Moreover, the principle that Jefferson's Virginia bill incorporated became in 1791 a part of the U.S. Constitution with the ratification of the First Amendment. Gaustad distinguishes twentieth-century scholarship treating Williams as primarily a theologian, rather than a political philosopher, from his influence in "the broader culture." Gaustad's conclusion is that recent "American society has become noisily and notoriously pluralistic. This," he said, "has made Roger Williams more relevant, for he had strong opinions about what government should do about religious pluralism: leave it alone. Turks, Jews, infidels, papists: leave them alone. By 1990 the list had grown much longer, but the principle remained the same" (Gaustad 1999, 217–219).

James Calvin Davis, writing some years before Barry, comes down strongly on the side that credits Williams with significant influence—and with continuing relevance. He notes the many great scholars (Perry Miller and others) who dismiss any effect Williams may have had on the Founders, but argues that "the lack of serious attention paid to Williams obscures the important contribution he made—and continues to offer—to the legacy of religious freedom in the United States" (Davis 2008, 38). True, it is unlikely that the Founders sought inspiration from *The Bloudy Tenent*, Davis says, but he argues that a good case can be made that Williams's influence "on the codification of religious liberty in the United States was more than symbolic. Eighteenth-century evangelical Baptists, themselves given insufficient credit for their role in establishing religious freedom in America, considered Williams to be their denominational forefather and their inspiration on the subject of religious liberty" (Davis 2008, 39). These Baptists "were influential enough to have the ear of presidents, including Thomas Jefferson, who wrote to assure the Danbury (Connecticut) Baptist Association of his commitment to religious freedom when he penned his famous 'wall of separation' metaphor. But unlike their Enlightenment-indebted counterparts, the Baptists offered a tradition of theological justification for religious freedom, and for this they had Williams's influence to thank. In fact," he said, "the most prominent Baptist spokesman of the eighteenth century, Isaac Backus, appealed directly to Roger Williams in his protest of the religious establishment of Massachusetts" (Davis 2008, 39). Davis even argued that Williams had an influence on the Enlightenment thinkers themselves, albeit in a more roundabout way, through Locke. "Locke," he said, "matured in the context of the English parliamentary debates over toleration to which Williams contributed significantly" (Davis 2008, 40). Many of Williams's arguments, Davis noted, appear almost verbatim in Locke, and he cites several authorities who believe that Locke actually read Williams. Regardless, Davis makes the case that "Williams's importance to religious freedom in the United States extends beyond his anticipation of, or even influence on, the arguments of later thinkers" (Davis 2008, 40–41). He said, bluntly, "Roger Williams may not have sat at the table on which the First Amendment was drafted, but his fingerprints are all over the tradition of religious freedom in America" (Davis 2008, 45). And thus, Baptists were in at the beginning of religious freedom in America, and long were among its most ardent defenders.

CHURCH-STATE SEPARATION AND THE ELECTION OF A CATHOLIC PRESIDENT

In 1960, Baptists were skeptical of John F. Kennedy's candidacy because of his Roman Catholic religion. On the twelfth of September, Kennedy spoke forthrightly to the Greater Houston Ministerial Association on the subject of church and state:

> I believe in an America where the separation of church and state is absolute—where no Catholic prelate would tell the President (should he be Catholic) how to act, and no Protestant minister would tell his parishioners for whom to vote—where no church or church school is granted any public funds or political preference—and where no man is denied public office merely because his religion differs from the President who might appoint him or the people who might elect him.
>
> I believe in an America that is officially neither Catholic, Protestant nor Jewish—where no public official either requests or accepts instructions on public policy from the Pope, the National Council of Churches or any other ecclesiastical source—where no religious body seeks to impose its will directly or indirectly upon the general populace or the public acts of its officials—and where religious liberty is so indivisible that an act against one church is treated as an act against all.

Kennedy proceeded to ask that he be judged on his record of fourteen years as a member of Congress. That included opposition to the appointment of an ambassador to the Vatican, "against unconstitutional aid to parochial schools, and against any boycott of the public schools," which, he said, he had attended himself. As he neared the end of his brief remarks, he took issue with press coverage that called him the Catholic candidate for president:

> I am not the Catholic candidate for President. I am the Democratic Party's candidate for President who happens also to be a Catholic. I do not speak for my church on public matters—and the church does not speak for me.
>
> Whatever issue may come before me as President—on birth control, divorce, censorship, gambling or any other subject—I will make my decision in accordance with these views, in accordance with what my conscience tells me to be the national interest, and without regard to outside religious pressures or dictates. And no power or threat of punishment could cause me to decide otherwise.
>
> But if the time should ever come—and I do not concede any conflict to be even remotely possible—when my office would require me to either violate my conscience or violate the national interest, then I would resign the office; and I hope any conscientious public servant would do the same.[1]

Kennedy's talk received extensive praise and helped to reassure skeptical Protestants about the prospect of his presidency. Catholics, of course, had mixed reactions. Writing a retrospective fifty years later, conservative Catholic George J. Marlin (publisher of a blog called "Street Corner Conservative") said: "While the secular media and Kennedy's followers declared the speech a triumph, his statements on the relation of church and state did not sit well with everyone. Some members of the hierarchy, particularly New York's Francis Cardinal Spellman, were not pleased that—by re-inventing himself and currying favor with liberals— Kennedy had discarded federal issues important to the Church, such as aid to parochial schools." He also remarked that Kennedy's vow to keep his religion private "opened a can of worms that haunts American Catholics to this day," and said that Catholic politicians who argue that one's religious views should have no place in the public square are arguing the absurd. He complained that officials who accept the guidance of the

church have since been branded "public villains." Marlin quoted historian William Miller, who, he said, concluded that the joke was that
Kennedy turned out to be anticlerical, and to be "our first Baptist president, one, that is, who defended a thorough-going separation more characteristic of that group than of his own church" (Marlin 2010). Despite
the fact that there actually were Baptist presidents previously, including
Harry Truman, Marlin's comment is indicative of just how ardently Baptists were known to be defenders of church-state separation. Then came
the dramatic change to American evangelical Protestantism.

THE ANTI–ROGER WILLIAMS: FRANCIS SCHAEFFER (AIDED AND ABETTED BY FRANK)

Traditionally, American evangelicals/fundamentalists had followed
the biblical admonition to separate from the world, and thus generally had
refrained from participating in politics. In the 1930s and the decades
immediately to follow, those who voted were likely to follow their economic
interests as working-class Americans and to support the New Deal and its
successors in the Truman and Kennedy-Johnson administrations. In the
1970s and 1980s, though, there was a new Great Awakening, of sorts, which
whirled around the rekindled Calvinist teachings of a conservative Presbyterian, Francis Schaeffer, and his son Frank. They were Americans who
had lived for years as expatriates, conducting in Switzerland a retreat for
both the religious and nonreligious, which became well known as L'Abri.
Francis Schaeffer, himself, had for much of his life been apolitical. It was
only later that he turned to engage the world politically.

"Schaeffer's new stance reflected some of the philosophy of Rousas
John Rushdoony, a twentieth-century Christian philosopher" (Broomfield 2012, 40) and the most extreme of the evangelicals/fundamentalists.
He combined quasi-anarchist economics with a stark theocracy and was
the father of "Dominionism," or "Re-constructionism." Broomfield
writes that "Schaeffer is considered by some scholars to be a dominion-
ist, as are Pat Robertson and even Sarah Palin," and he goes on to describe
some of Rushdoony's ideas. Rushdoony called for the creation of a Christian United States that will subdue the world, with a huge expansion of
the death penalty. Capital offenses would include not only those of today,
but also adultery, blasphemy, homosexuality, the practice of astrology,

incest, the striking of a parent, or "in the case of women, un-chastity before marriage." These, Broomfield says, "were a bit much for Schaeffer and Robertson," but he suggests that they may to some extent have remained disciples who managed to make Rushdoony's doctrines "more palatable for the mainstream" (Broomfield 2012, 40). Nevertheless, Broomfield says that, according to Frank, his father thought Rushdoony to be "clinically insane" (Broomfield 2012, 45), which seems to be a reasonable interpretation of one who, among other things, would put children to death for showing disrespect to their parents.

Frank writes that he and his father were the major force encouraging American fundamentalist/evangelical leaders to become politically active and to unite with those whom they had considered theological enemies. Specifically, Frank was the first to seize upon abortion as an important political topic that might energize evangelicals. Previously, American Protestants had tended to dismiss it as a "Catholic issue." He described the making with his father of "a new Christian documentary titled *How Should We Then Live?*—a film that became a huge success "with the burgeoning religious right in America" (Broomfield 2012, 56). As the younger Schaeffer described it, "When we started making *How Should We Then Live?* Dad had not wanted to mention abortion in the series. . . . If it hadn't been for me, Dad's reputation as an evangelical scholar would have remained intact. As it was, my absolutist youthful commitment to the pro-life cause goaded my father into taking political positions far more extreme than came naturally to him" (Schaeffer 2007, 260; quoted in Broomfield 2012, 56).

According to Frank, the elder Schaeffer said that he didn't "want to be identified with some Catholic issue. I'm not putting my reputation on the line for them!" he shouted. "What does abortion have to do with art and culture? I'm known as an intellectual, not for this sort of *political thing*" (Broomfield 2012, 56–57). Nevertheless, the father gave in. They changed the documentary, and with it, they changed history. The 1977 film was a sensation. Through the years it has sold millions of copies, and "it became a staple of evangelical/fundamentalist" teachings for Protestants and Catholics as well (Broomfield 2012, 57–58). Abortion became the key issue uniting the religious right as they rage not only against the modern world, but even against the U.S. government. The Schaeffers had

overcome the traditional enmity between Protestants (especially Baptists) and Catholics.

Frank now admits with regret that the group that he and his father
worked with and influenced so strongly, including "such evangelical/
fundamentalist luminaries as Jerry Falwell, Pat Robertson, Franklin
Graham, James Dobson and John Hagee" were, in fact, a "hate-America
group," and that he and his father crossed the line into open sedition. He
and his father not only were part of this group, but were leaders. "We were
very anti-American," Frank said (Broomfield 2012, 58).

The Schaeffers had become openly political, and therefore were eager
to spread their influence beyond explicitly religious circles. In the 1970s
and 1980s they met frequently with such powerful political figures as
Ronald Reagan, George H. W. Bush, Gerald Ford, Jack Kemp (who was
the Republican candidate for vice president in 1996), and former Surgeon
General C. Everett Koop. Frank said that "the evangelical antiabortion
movement that Dad, Koop, and I helped create seduced the Republican
Party" (Broomfield 2012, 76). Before the Schaeffers, Frank said speaking
of politicians, "nobody paid any attention to Jesus" until "Kemp, Koop,
and Reagan realized that they could pry off Catholics' and evangelicals'
votes from the Democratic Party." As it is now, he said, "Religion in
America is politics…big-time politics" (Broomfield 2012, 9).

Melding the evangelical and political communities, the Schaeffers
became "evangelical/fundamentalist royalty" in America. Jerry Falwell
helped spread their writings throughout the religious right. They "were
invited constantly to speak at churches, on Christian radio, and on television shows across the country. "Frank speaks at length in *Crazy for God*
about their many personal experiences with Falwell, Robertson, Ralph
Reed, [Tim] LaHaye, Dobson, and many others" (Broomfield 2012, 75).

Francis Schaeffer's final book, *A Christian Manifesto* (Schaeffer 1981),
was among his most thorough and influential statements. It was here, and
in his sermon the following year, 1982, at the Coral Ridge Presbyterian
Church in Fort Lauderdale, Florida, where he cast aside any pretense of
moderation. In his lengthy sermon, he contrasted the "Christian world
view" with that of the "humanist," who allegedly saw man as the measure
of all things. The latter grew from "Darwin's theory of evolution, which
fundamentalists had hated since Darwin proposed it in 1859." He railed

against the wrongs that he and other fundamentalists saw in America, "permissiveness, pornography, the public schools, the breakdown in the family, and finally abortion." He saw recent Supreme Court rulings—dealing with prayer in public schools, religious symbols on public property, and abortion—as stripping Christians of their "freedoms." "It was Schaeffer who led the way for evangelical/fundamentalist Christians to begin thinking that American democracy had been established by Christians and that the Declaration of Independence and the Constitution had been written" by the Founders deliberately to establish a "nation based on the Judeo-Christian ethic" and a literal interpretation of the Bible (Broomfield, 2012, 43). Only one word, he thundered, could describe the United States of today: "TYRANNY! TYRANNY!" he roared (Broomfield 2012, 44).

EFFECTS OF ERODING CHURCH-STATE SEPARATION

Frank Schaeffer rejected, and now regrets, his past and his role in inciting American political extremism. He describes his awakening in *Crazy for God: How I Grew Up as One of the Elect, Helped Found the Religious Right, and Lived to Take It All (or Almost All) Back* (Schaeffer 2007). He had come "to recognize that the forces he unleashed were deadly." Among the most extreme were the Christian Reconstructionists of the late R. J. Rushdoony mentioned above and Rushdoony's son-in-law, Gary North—many of the Reconstructionists, including North, have ties to the right-wing extremist John Birch Society—and it was the Reconstructionists who began the Christian homeschooling movement. They also have adherents among the "C Street Group," or "The Family," in Washington, D.C., that includes powerful politicians, predominantly Republican but also some Democrats. The younger Schaeffer noted the violence in the antiabortion movement, and the "anti-government rhetoric on the right that at least flirts with revolution and secession." Regardless of the "flag-waving veneer of patriotism" there was a "stark hatred for America, for democracy, and for the American political system. His journey away from fundamentalism began when he was startled to recognize that, in the land that his followers hoped to create, he would be among the first to be eliminated (Skidmore 2012, 198–199; Sharlet 2008).

Frank Schaeffer recognized a core influence that he perceived in all fundamentalisms of the world, "whether Jewish, Islamic, Christian, or some other: a hatred of women, and of sex, all under the guiding motivation of fear (among Christians, producing 'Jesus victims')." Hence, his subtitle: "How the Bible's Strange Take on Sex Led to Crazy Politics—and How I Learned to Love Women (and Jesus) Anyway." He draws an indirect "but deadly connection between the 'intellectual' fig-leaf providers and periodic upheavals like the looney American Right's sometimes-violent reaction to the election of people like Barack Obama." He states that, of course, "your average member of some moronic gun-toting Michigan militia is *not* reading Francis Schaeffer." What the religious right's "Roman Catholic and Protestant enablers" did do was to raise questions of validity and invalidity that sought to create doubt about "the very legitimacy of our government" (Skidmore 2012, 198–199).

Roger Williams was committed to freedom of conscience for two reasons. Bringing the church too close to the state led directly to corruption in the church. Moreover, mingling of church and state inevitably stifled human freedom and discouraged thought. Frank Schaeffer pointed out in 2011, just as the campaigns for the 2012 elections were becoming heated, that much of the agenda of the religious right had come to reflect little if anything to do with religion, and much to do with politics and of the political ideology that almost completely took over the Republican Party after Reagan's 1980 nomination.

"In the scorched-earth era of the 'health care reform debates' of 2009 and beyond," Schaeffer said, "Evangelicals seemed to believe that Jesus commanded that all hospitals (and everything else) should be run by corporations for profit, just because corporations *weren't* the evil government." Additionally, "the right even decided that it was 'normal' for the state to hand over its age-old public and patriotic duties to private companies—even for military operations ('contractors'), prisons, health care, public transport, and all the rest" (Schaeffer 2011).

When fundamentalists/evangelicals turned to Francis Schaeffer, they turned away from Roger Williams. The result was that in their attempts to manipulate, they became the ones manipulated. Williams had written of religion as "the garden," as distinct from government, which was "the wilderness." Williams had no doubt that churches participating actively in politics were permitting government to encroach upon the garden. To the extent that the churches continued to "honor their fundamental tenets of love, humility, and justice" they nevertheless were being "manipulated by politicians for less than honorable political ends. To the extent that churches attempt to use political power to force their beliefs on others, they violate their fundamental tenets by becoming manipulators themselves." Moreover, when human beings—whether in religion or government—attempt to use "God to accomplish their temporal ends," in Williams's view they place themselves above God, and commit "the most deadly of all sins—pride" (Fishman 2007).

THE ELECTIONS OF 2012

The campaigns of 2012 were filled with incidents such as to cause sadness or outrage to a Roger Williams, had he been here to observe and criticize, but these incidents were not unique to 2012. Their roots certainly went at least to the furious rejection by the religious right of President Jimmy Carter. Carter, of course, made much of the fact that he was a born-again Baptist, but one who accepted what had long been the Baptist position supporting separation of church and state. The religious right nevertheless flocked to the banner of Ronald Reagan, a divorced former Hollywood actor who, as president, overturned Carter's ban and returned hard liquor to the White House. Fundamentalists/evangelicals, recent converts to fervently right-wing Republicanism, remain true to the myth of Reagan as the political savior. And as Frank Schaeffer graphically pointed out in 2011 just as the races for the next year's elections were becoming heated, fundamentalists/evangelicals had in fact adopted positions that were based more on politics than theology.

On the Democratic side—goaded by Republican vice presidential candidate Paul Ryan's gibe that he found it "rather peculiar" that the Democratic platform made no reference to "God"—the Democratic National Convention rushed to remedy the "defect" and include a mention of God. The railroad was off and running when the convention's presiding officer gaveled the resolution of change through on a voice vote—a vote that listeners at the convention, as well as those following it on radio or television, agreed had been shouted down. Ryan had said that failing to mention God was "not in keeping with our founding documents, our founding vision," and added (on Fox News) that "you would have to ask the Obama administration why they purged all this language from their platform" (Walshe 2012). According to all reports, it was the White House that rushed to ensure that the change would indeed make it into that platform.

It was the Republican side, though, that would have offended Williams the most. The many Republican primary debates were marked by a startling adherence to ideology. Each candidate—instead of arguing that he or she would be more competent, make wiser choices, ensure better government, be more efficient, or provide better service to the country or its people—repeated over and over that he or she would be "more conservative" than the others, and "more like Ronald Reagan" (never mind the fact that modern Republicans would view a resurrected Reagan as the worst of all figures, the dreaded "RINO"—Republican In Name Only). The ultimate nominee, Mitt Romney, boasted that he had been a "severely conservative" governor of Massachusetts.

Former senator Rick Santorum, with politically suicidal candor, condemned Kennedy's famous speech on church-state separation. It made him "want to throw up," Santorum said. "I don't believe in an America where the separation of church and state is absolute" (Barbaro 2012, 1). Of course, Santorum was speaking as an ultra (or perhaps "severely") conservative Roman Catholic. He had never been shaped by a Protestant preference for church-state separation.

Fundamentalists/evangelicals represented a long tradition of hostility toward the Roman Catholic Church, but their reaction toward Mormonism had been even harsher, if possible. They typically considered the Latter-day Saints to be a cult and rejected their sect's claims to be Christian. So binding have the fundamentalist/evangelical ties to the Republican Party become, however, that the party came to embrace (albeit with varying degrees of enthusiasm) and actively support a political ticket headed by a Mormon and including a Catholic—a Catholic, paradoxically, whose views were shaped by the militantly atheist, sexually unconventional, and aggressive apostle of selfishness, Ayn Rand.

This would be praiseworthy if it were an expression of ecumenism or lessening of religious prejudice. Williams, though, almost assuredly would see it as a subordination of theological concerns to political advantage. In the early phases of the 2012 nomination process, many evangelicals expressed opposition to Romney's candidacy, saying they could not vote for a Mormon. However, as the other candidates saw their fortunes crumble—Rick Perry's ineptitude, Rick Santorum's hostility to the modern world, including contraception, Ron Paul's sometimes engaging but often bizarre views, Michele Bachmann's less-than-winning combination of innocence and venom, Newt Gingrich's being Newt Gingrich, and so on—it became conventional wisdom that Governor Romney would have the best chance to defeat President Obama. Quickly, the Republicans fell in line, including fundamentalist/evangelical leaders, whose adherence to the party trumped their suspicion of a Mormon. There remained some evangelical opposition to Romney, but it was overwhelmed.

Romney tirelessly courted evangelicals. Some Americans, Romney told them, have carried church-state separation much too far, and "well beyond its original meaning." We are a "nation under God, and in God, we do indeed trust" (Romney 2012). The Founders, of course, used neither phrase.

In May 2012, stepping into a lion's den as JFK had done earlier before the Dallas Protestants, Romney gave the commencement address at Falwell's Liberty University. Some students and alumni protested a Mormon's appearance, but evangelical leaders welcomed his efforts to make peace with the non-Mormon elements of the religious right. His talk, like that of Kennedy before him, promised that he would make his own decisions and would follow no church leader's dictates (E. G. 2012).

An official of the Southern Baptist Church, Richard Land, who had long been hostile to Mormonism and had never before endorsed a candidate, announced just before the elections that he would endorse Romney. He said he feared Obama, because he believed the president sought to "remake America in the model of a European welfare state" (E. G. 2012). This is certainly a political statement, not a religious judgment. Earlier, Land had favored Texas Governor Rick Perry, had compared Mormonism to Islam, and said that Romney was "not a Christian" (Schulzke 2012). Land had long been an active Republican, but had always pledged not to endorse a candidate. Also, he recently had been fired from his radio program because he made on-air comments that brought allegations of plagiarism and racial insensitivity (Gibson 2012).

It would seem intuitive, considering basic Christian beliefs, that Christian groups would favor regulations to reduce the prevalence in the United States of gun violence. Many mainstream religious groups in fact do favor gun control. "The push for a faith-based action for gun control," though, is complicated. "Gun ownership and opposition to gun control are part of the religious worldview of many Christians, especially evangelicals and Pentecostals in the South and West. Southern Baptists and Mormons, in particular, are influential voices opposing restrictions on gun ownership"

("Guns and God," 2012). This is not a question of individual Christians and their positions on gun control, but rather of churches. In 2002, when Richard Land was "the chief public policy spokesman for the Southern Baptist Convention," he "decried what he called 'a long-term assault on your Second Amendment rights to keep and bear arms'" ("Guns and God," 2012). Rich Scarborough, a fellow Southern Baptist minister, in Lufkin, Texas, criticized efforts at gun control immediately after the shootings at a movie theater in Aurora, Colorado. "It's not about guns, but sin," he charged, blaming "liberals" who "refuse to recognize the existence of evil." He said "the answer isn't gun control but revival" (Cook 2012). If he were thinking more of the Christian message and less of political talking points, he might have conceded that, until achieving revival, somewhat greater control of guns might help.

Baptist voices in support of church-state separation continue to exist, but they are less likely to be found among fundamentalists/evangelicals. The Baptist Joint Committee for Religious Liberty says that "the separation of church and state, or the 'wall of separation' talked about by Colonial Baptist Roger Williams, Thomas Jefferson, and the U.S. Supreme Court, is simply a shorthand metaphor for expressing a deeper truth that religious liberty is best protected when church and state are institutionally separated and neither tries to perform or interfere with the essential mission and work of the other." The BJC echoes Williams when it notes that "Baptists became champions of religious liberty and church-state separation in large measure because we are a people of the book. For many Baptists, religious liberty is well grounded in scripture" ("Church-State Separation," 2012). For many others, though, politics has come to supersede religious considerations, which Williams would see as corruption.

On November 4, 2012, the Sunday before Election Day, the Billy Graham Evangelistic Association ran a full-page advertisement in the *New York Times* and numerous other metropolitan newspapers. "Vote Biblical Values Tuesday November 6," it proclaimed over a picture of the aged Baptist evangelistic star, Billy Graham. Graham had once been close to one American president after another. Then, he felt that he had been used by Richard Nixon and announced that he would stay away from politics. He also had been embarrassed when selections from the "White House diaries of key Nixon aide H. R. Haldeman came out in 1994." They quoted conversations in which Nixon and Graham spoke of "satanic

Jews" and condemned Jews for being pornographers and injecting "left-wing bias" into the news media. Graham vehemently denied the accounts, but when the National Archives released the relevant White House tapes in 2002, they verified Haldeman's account (Skidmore 2004, 292).

Be that as it may, however, Graham's public statements through the years have tended to be moderate in relation to those of other evangelicals. The recent comments in the *Times*, as he approached his ninety-fourth birthday, do to be sure have a Graham ring, but the tone is more of a Franklin, rather than a Billy, variety. The comments call, among other things, for choosing "candidates who base their decisions on biblical principles and support the nation of Israel," who protect "the sanctity of life and support the biblical definition of marriage between a man and a woman," and plead that readers will pray with Graham "that America will remain one nation under God."

Shortly before releasing this strategically timed—if ultimately futile—ad, Graham had come under fierce criticism from other religious conservatives. Not only had he met with Republican presidential candidate Mitt Romney, telling him that he would do "all I can to help you" according to a Romney aide (Banks 2012), but the Billy Graham Evangelistic Association removed the mention of Mormonism from among its list of "cults" on its website (Burke 2012), thus facilitating the presidential candidacy of Mr. Romney, a Mormon. It is genuinely praiseworthy to see barriers of religious prejudice come down, but in this instance, it seems to have resulted not from brotherhood, but from politics trumping religion. The Rev. Samuel Wynn, a long-time Graham admirer, says that because of the association's removal of Mormonism from its list of cults, he will never again "support anything by the Billy Graham Evangelistic Association." Wynn has accused Graham of "putting politics above piety," and asked "what's more important for the kingdom of God: politics or the message of Jesus Christ?" (Burke 2012).

CONCLUSION, WITH SOME (INDIRECT) ASSISTANCE FROM ROGER WILLIAMS

As luck would have it, just as this chapter was being completed, there came an echo from Roger Williams himself—well, at least from a descendant. A religion writer, Becky Garrison, published an article in the *Wash-*

ington Post, "Roger Williams Goes Baptist on Legendary Evangelist Billy Graham." Franklin, she remarked, earlier had "questioned if Romney and [even] Obama were Christians," but in February declared that it now would be appropriate for evangelicals to "vote for a Mormon." She said to those who sense "Franklin Graham's more strident approach to faith and politics" in this strongly rightward political thrust that Billy's spokesman, A. Larry Ross, "assures us repeatedly that the elder Graham is truly involved with these statements" (Garrison 2012).

The important part of Garrison's article for the purposes of this chapter, though, is that she is a descendant of Roger Williams. She suspects, she says, that one person who would not join in prayer with the Grahams that America remain one nation under God would be her "ancestor Roger Williams, the founder of the Baptist church in America where Billy Graham serves as an ordained minister." She said pointedly that the founder of Rhode Island, who "created the first charter granting religious liberty" to all, would in no way "align himself with any Christian entity that sought to sit at the right hand of the president of the United States." She said, in fact, that her illustrious and pious ancestor "would be appalled at the sight of Billy Graham, Jerry Falwell, and other Baptists draping the cross of Christ with the American flag as they advance the notion of American exceptionalism." She described an outraged Williams, who would charge into the National Prayer Breakfast "and turn over the tables— temple style." In a rousing conclusion, Garrison dissected the arguments of the Schaeffer-inspired fundamentalists, pointing out that Williams was a pioneer of inclusion, regardless of religious views, and of protecting the right of anyone to worship as he or she chooses. Williams even included American Indians, whom most of "the elect" saw as "damned" and as subhuman savages. "Regardless of how he might feel personally about a particular controversial issue like marriage equality," she said, "he would be at the forefront in fighting against those who refuse to grant equal civil rights to anyone marginalized by the established church" (Garrison 2012).

Of course, Americans do not have an established church. One of the reasons we do not is Roger Williams. Without the tradition that he established, our freedom from such a church could be in great danger—and in fact might never have existed. In President Obama's 2012 victory, the country turned back the strongest contemporary forces that have been working to depart from the ideas of freedom bequeathed to us, not only by Jefferson and Madison, but by their predecessor, Roger Williams—and by the Baptists for whom he was the inspiration (at least until recently).

REFERENCES

Banks, A. M. 2012. "Why Is Billy Graham So Involved in the 2012 Elections?" Religion News Service, *Huffington Post,* October 23.

Barbaro, M. 2012. "Santorum Makes for Religion in Public Sphere." *New York Times*, February 27.

Barry, J. M. 1992. *The Ambition and the Power: The Fall of Jim Wright: A True Story of Washington.* New York: Viking.

Barry, J. M. 1998. *Rising Tide: The Great Mississippi Flood of 1927 and How It Changed America.* New York: Simon and Schuster.

Barry, J. M. 2005. *The Great Influenza: The Story of the Deadliest Pandemic in History.* New York: Penguin.

Barry, J. M. 2012. *Roger Williams and the Creation of the American Soul: Church, State, and the Birth of Liberty.* New York, Viking.

Broomfield, C. S. 2012. "Francis A. Schaeffer: The Force Behind the Evangelical Takeover of the Republican Party in America." M.A. thesis, University of Missouri, Kansas City.

Burke, D. 2012. "Billy Graham Faces Backlash over Mormon 'Cult' Removal." Religion News Service, *Huffington Post,* October 25.

Church-State Separation. 2012. Statement of the Baptist Joint Committee for Religious Liberty. Retrieved September 15, 2012 from http://bjconline.org /index.php?option=com_content&.

Cook, J. 2012. "Answer to Aurora Shootings Isn't Gun Control but God-Connection." Christian News Wire, *Washington Post.* Retrieved November 4, 2012 from http://www.christiannewswire.com/news/5010920256.html.

Davis, J. C. 2008. "Introduction." In *On Religious Liberty: Selections from the Works of Roger Williams.* Cambridge: Belknap Press of Harvard University Press.

E. G. 2012. "An Unnecessary Speech." *The Economist,* May 14.

Fishman, E. 2007. "Unto Caesar." *The American Scholar* (Autumn).

Garrett, L. 2005. "The Next Pandemic?" *Foreign Affairs* 84 (July/August).

Garrison, B. 2012. "Roger Williams Goes Baptist on Legendary Evangelist Billy Graham." *Washington Post,* November 2.

Gaustad, E. S. 1999. *Liberty of Conscience: Roger Williams in America.* Valley Forge, PA: Judson Press.

Gibson, D. 2012. "Land Breaks Pledge, Endorses Romney." *The Baptist Standard,* November 1.

"Guns and God: Faith Groups and the Politics of Gun Control." 2012. *Religion Link.* Retrieved November 4, 2012 from http://www.religionlink.com/tip_080603 .php.

Johnson, N., and J. Mueller. 2002. "Updating the Accounts: Global Mortality of the
    1918–1920 'Spanish' Influenza Pandemic." *Bulletin of the History of Medicine* 76
    (1): 105–115.
Marlin, G. J. 2010. "JFK's Houston Speech at 50: Three Views." *The Catholic Thing*,
    September 9. Retrieved October 28, 2012 from http://www.thecatholicthing
    .org/columns/2010/jfks-houston-speech-at-50-three-views.html.
Morgan, E. S. 2007. *Roger Williams: The Church and the State*. New York: W. W.
    Norton.
"Roger Williams on His Own." 2012. An exchange of letters between John M. Barry
    and Gordon S. Wood. *New York Review of Books*, October 25, 73–74.
Romney, M. 2012. Interview in Washington Cathedral's *Cathedral Age*. "Church
    State Separation Taken Too Far by Some." *Huffington Post Politics*, August 21.
Schaeffer, F. 1981. *A Christian Manifesto*. Westchester, IL: Crossway.
Schaeffer, F. 2007. *Crazy for God: How I Grew Up as One of the Elect, Helped Found
    the Religious Right, and Lived to Take It All (or Almost All) Back*. Cambridge:
    Da Capo Press.
Schaeffer, F. 2011. "Debt Ceiling Chaos Is a Born-Again Religion Problem."
    Huffington Post, July 15.
Schulzke, E. 2012. *Deseret News*, November 3.
Skidmore, M. J. 2004. *Presidential Performance*. Jefferson, NC: McFarland.
Skidmore, M. J. 2012. Review of *Sex, Mom, and God*. *Journal of American Culture*
    35 (2): 198–199.
Sharlet, J. 2008. *The Family: The Secret Fundamentalism at the Heart of American
    Power*. New York: Harper.
Taubenberger, J. K. 2005. "Chasing the Elusive 1918 Virus: Preparing for the Future
    by Examining the Past." In *The Threat of Pandemic Influenza: Workshop
    Summary. Washington: National Academies Press/Institute of Medicine*.
Walshe, S. 2012. "Paul Ryan Hits 'God' Absence from DNC Platform." *ABC News:
    The Note*, September 5. Retrieved November 4, 2012 from http://abcnews.go
    .com/blogs/politics/2012/09/paul-ryan-says-god-omission-at-odds-with
    -founding-documents-that-dont-mention-god/.
Williams, R. (1644) 2008. *The Bloudy Tenent of Persecution for the Cause of
    Conscience*. London: J. Haddon, (1644) 1848. Excerpted in *On Religious
    Liberty: Selections from the Works of Roger Williams*, edited by James Calvin
    Davis. Belknap Press of Harvard University Press.
Wood, G. S. 2012. "Radical, Pure, Roger Williams." *New York Review of Books*, May
    10.

NOTES

1. Text of remarks widely available, including at: http://www.americanrhetoric.com
/speeches/jfkhoustonministers.html; retrieved October 28, 2012.

Chapter 4

Perceptions of Mormonism
Romney's Faith-Based Challenges
Luke Perry, Utica College

PROPHECY, PERSECUTION, AND THE U.S. PRESIDENCY

In 1830, Joseph Smith founded the religious order that would become the Church of Jesus Christ of Latter-day Saints (LDS or Mormons). Smith's prophecies produced the Book of Mormon, which is understood by Mormons as an additional volume of Christian scripture. The LDS church has grown from twenty-six thousand at the time of Smith's murder in 1844 to six million members in the United States and fourteen million abroad. Mormons are the fourth largest church in the United States and the wealthiest relative to size. Conventional accounts have suggested that contemporary Mormons in America are experiencing a unique moment of national prominence and acceptance. The cover of *Newsweek* on June 13, 2011, pictured Mitt Romney posing as a missionary from the critically acclaimed musical *Book of Mormon* behind the headline, "A Mormon Moment: How the Outside Faith Creates Winners." Indeed, two Mormons competed in the Republican presidential primary, Romney and former Utah governor and U.S. ambassador to China Jon Huntsman. Harry Reid of Nevada, a Democratic Mormon, was the Senate majority leader. The widespread prominence of other Mormons was undeniable. Political pundit Glenn Beck was a national media personality. Stephenie Meyer was a best-selling author of the *Twilight* novels, the basis of the five-movie series entitled *The Twilight Saga*. Mormons filled the television airwaves in the HBO mini-series *Big Love* and the reality program *Sister Wives*. Mormons were equally visible as prominent businessmen, having founded companies such as Marriott, Oakley, Sorenson Media, Hollywood Video, and Huntsman Chemical, and leading many more, including Kodak, Dell, American Motors, Fisher Price, Black and Decker, Nationwide Insurance, and Jet Blue. Yet many Americans wondered whether the country was truly ready to elect a Mormon president.

Remarkably, both presidential nominees in 2012 came from groups that were historically persecuted. Few Americans, however, were aware of the plight of Mormons. Early Mormons lived in theocratic communities and drew the ire of neighbors because of their mysterious and charismatic practices, increasing numbers, and expanding control of surrounding lands. Mormons originally had little interest in politics. This changed as Mormons were persecuted by vigilantes, local governments, and state governments (Perry and Cronin 2012). Critics believed no one would convert to Mormonism out of his or her own free will. Smith was viewed as a menacing charlatan. Mormons were harassed, threatened, beaten, tarred and feathered, arrested, and ultimately expelled westward from central New York during the fourteen years of Smith's life as the Mormon prophet.

The low point of Mormon persecution was the 1838 executive order issued by Missouri Governor Lilburn Boggs that expelled Mormons under the threat of extermination without regard to age or gender. The Haun's Mill Massacre, the climax of the Mormon Wars, followed shortly thereafter. Missourians ambushed and killed seventeen Mormon men and boys as women and children fled into the woods. This prompted Smith and other Mormons to comply. The men were treated as prisoners of war and forced to surrender all their belongings under the supervision of the state militia. These experiences prompted Mormons to think of themselves as a persecuted people, and "memories of hardship, suffering, and the opposition of a hostile world became a large part of Mormon identity" (Bushman 2008, 42).

Federal lobbying on behalf of Mormons began the following year. After five years of effort garnered disappointingly little support, Joseph

Smith decided to run for president in 1844. The LDS church developed a campaign pamphlet, *General Smith's Views of the Powers and Policy of the Government of the United States*, which was distributed to prominent members of the federal government and the news media. Smith "reserved his deepest scorn for those who asserted that federalism prohibited the federal government from intervening on behalf of citizens who were denied their rights as American citizens" (Hickman 1968, 23). Smith wanted to grant the president full power to use the army to suppress mobs without needing a formal request from a state governor, which was a common prerequisite at the time. Mormon leaders called for volunteers "to preach the Gospel and electioneer" (Poll 1968, 20). Smith's assassination by an angry mob in June 1844, a rarity for U.S. religious leaders, makes it very difficult to ascertain his specific motivations and expectations for the presidency aside from overcoming religious persecution.

Mormons fled the country after Smith's death only to find themselves under its boundaries once again after the Mexican War. Brigham Young became the Mormon patriarch of the State of Deseret, which became the Utah territory and later, the state of Utah. Mormon persecution was undertaken by the federal government in the second half of the nineteenth century. The issue was plural marriage. Mormons believed that God wanted them to recreate the marital order of the Old Testament. Smith had secretly informed fellow Mormon leaders of his plural marriage revelation in 1841. Twenty-nine other men took at least one additional wife under Smith's authorization. Smith typically asked permission to marry from a father or uncle of the desired bride. Wives were not gathered in one household. Smith occasionally spent nights with different wives. The 1852 public announcement of plural marriage doctrine was carefully orchestrated. The church called a conference, where the practice was defended religiously as a divine commandment, and socially, permitting only sanctified men to have multiple wives. Salvation was assured to husbands and wives who followed the practice. Plural marriage was a "vital symbol of early Mormon sectarian identity" that "allowed Mormons to embody the radical 'peculiarity' of the church's charismatic origins." An estimated 5 to 20 percent of nineteenth-century Mormons participated in plural marriages (Elisha 2002, 45).

For many Americans, plural marriage exemplified Mormon depravity and subversion. Non-Mormon politicians and businessmen used this perception to undermine Mormon influence in Western territories. In the decades that followed, news of the practice spread and a public backlash emerged. Some likened the practice to slavery. Mormons vigorously defended plural marriage until 1890 when faced with highly aggressive federal antipolygamy legislation. Domestic relations were typically local concerns at the time. The people of Utah favored plural marriage and the state legislature supported them. This created a firm legal basis until the federal government intervened. Congress first established a series of family laws for residents of Utah, including rules for divorce, for adultery, for incest, for alimony to women who wanted a divorce, and for unlawful cohabitation, which prohibited a man from living with more than one woman, even if they were not legally married. These laws essentially applied relevant legal architecture from other states to the Utah territory. Legal violations resulted in nearly three thousand separate criminal prosecutions, an extraordinary number at the time. During the 1880s, Congress added political disfranchisement to criminal punishments and imposed a new governing structure on the Utah territory.

Mormon opposition to plural marriage ended when Congress attacked the church's economic power and went after church property, including temples, which are sacred and private places to Mormons. In 1887, Congress directed the attorney general to seize all church property worth more than $50,000. Some of these funds were to be used for a new public education system in the territory. *Late Corporation of the Church of Jesus Christ of Latter-day Saints v. the United States* (1890) deemed these actions constitutional. Mormon centrists were prompted to press for the abandonment of plural marriage. There was no public support nationally and declining support within Utah. The LDS church publically encouraged followers not to engage in plural marriage. This was insufficient for federal agents. Mormons had to change their theology, which took the form of the 1890 Manifesto, by which LDS president Wilford Woodruff recommended that Mormons refrain from any form of marriage forbidden by law. The manifesto was a clear concession to the federal government and halted aggressive antipolygamy efforts.

Utah became the forty-fifth state of the Union six years later. American perceptions of Mormons began to shift from hostility to neutrality as the religion transformed "from a remote, disreputable sect to a more assimilated regional religion" (Mauss 1984, 440). Troubles surrounding plural marriage resurfaced, however, as Utah Mormons were elected to the U.S. Congress. In 1903, the Utah legislature elected Reed Smoot to represent that state as a U.S. senator. Smoot was the first native-born Utahan to undertake a career in national politics and the only Mormon apostle to serve in the Senate. The Quorum of the Twelve Apostles is the second highest leadership group in Mormonism, second only to the First Presidency, which consists of the prophet and two of his advisors. Smoot's election created controversy because of his position in the church, unease surrounding Mormon religious practices (particularly plural marriage), and fears that Smoot would be given political directives from the LDS prophet. A four-year effort to oppose Smoot's seating was orchestrated by a coalition of Protestant churches. All five of the major Protestant denominations were involved, including Episcopalian, Presbyterian, Congregationalists, Baptists, and Methodists.

Smoot's opponents did not accuse him of any legal violation. Smoot's perceived ineligibility for the Senate was based on his participation in a religious organization in violation of the law that corrupted family norms and exercised a disproportionate control over Utah politics and commerce, to the alleged detriment of the nation as a whole. Protestant activists had previously been successful in denying a U.S. House seat to B. H. Roberts, a high-ranking church official who, unlike Smoot, was a polygamist, a Democrat, and had upset Mormon leaders by entering the political arena without church approval. The 56th Congress voted not to seat Roberts after six weeks of discussion. The Senate seated Smoot before scrutinizing his qualifications. This shifted the terms of debate to why Smoot should keep his seat, not obtain it. The inquisition began two days after Smoot was seated.

The hearings produced 3,500 pages of testimony by a hundred witnesses on various aspects of Mormonism, including polygamy, family structure, ritual, worship, secret oaths, economic communalism, and theocratic politics. One major issue was the dramatic revelation that four of Smoot's fellow apostles took additional wives after the 1890 Manifesto and a minimum of two apostles continued to perform plural marriages. This blatant disregard for federal law generated animosity nationally and fueled suspicion about other mysterious and illegal activities in which Mormons were engaged. A second major issue was the intense loyalty of Mormons to the church. Smoot's opponents believed that Mormons put the welfare of the church and their desire to build the kingdom of God ahead of the national interest. Some thought Mormons eventually sought to rule all of the country through the theocratic structure established in the Utah territory. The second concern was the degree to which the living Mormon prophet would dictate Smoot's political behavior. Mormon president Joseph F. Smith, nephew of Joseph Smith, was repeatedly asked during his Senate testimony if Smoot would be obligated to follow his orders on political matters. Smith consistently replied that Smoot should follow his own conscience and his obligation to his constituency, not church leadership. Importantly, Mormons entered the national political scene under the condition that LDS leaders would refrain from interfering with public elected government officials who were Mormon. A third major issue was the hope of Republicans and Democrats to use Smoot's seating for partisan political advantage. Both parties believed that Mormons could wield influence in national politics, both within the Electoral College and also in elections of U.S. senators by state legislatures.

Smoot was ultimately seated in 1907 and his three decades of work in the Senate significantly enhanced the acceptance of Mormons in national politics. Mormon identity significantly changed as a result of the Smoot hearings, as Mormons conformed to national terms of acceptance. Smoot, rational and soft-spoken, became the embodiment of Mormonism for many Americans, replacing Brigham Young, the bearded patriarch with multiple wives. Smoot became a leading voice of conservative morality and explained Mormonism as a civil religion, in Protestant terms, to the aggravation of some Mormons. Smoot's travel to Europe as an American political representative enabled him to meet with aristocratic, ecclesiastical, and democratic leaders. His work abroad was a turning point in the internationalization of Mormonism.

The impulse of Mormons to gather as one lessened throughout the twentieth century. Zion had always been an expansive concept in the eyes of Joseph Smith, who had "dreamed of an array of cities, initially in the United States and then in all of the Americans, extending Zion to the rest of the world" (Bushman 2008, 48). Mormon leaders encouraged new converts to develop the church in their home areas. Mormonism spread to Latin America in the 1970s, Asia in the 1980s, and Africa in the 1990s. By century's end, the Mormon Church was organized in 149 nations and territories. Over two million copies of the Book of Mormon are now published annually in over fifty languages (Bushman and Bushman 1999). Calling Mormonism an American religion is increasingly inaccurate, as more Mormons now reside abroad than in the United States.

MORMONS' CHOSEN SON

The remarkable contrast between America's first Mormon presidential candidate (a martyred religious, political, and economic dissident) and Mitt Romney (patriotic defender of political, social, and religious conservatism) is one of the most interesting subplots in the 2012 election. The Romneys have deep roots within the Mormon tradition. Miles Romney, an Englishman, converted to Mormonism in 1837 after encountering a missionary and moved to Nauvoo, where Mitt Romney's great-grandfather, Miles Park Romney, was born six years later. The Romneys headed west after Smith's assassination and Miles helped to settle towns in Utah and Arizona, prior to fleeing to Mexico after being pursued by local authorities for being a polygamist. Mexican law did not prohibit polygamy as American law did. Mitt stated that his ancestors took additional wives to help build the church as they were ordered to, but he described the practice as "awful." George Romney, Mitt's father, was born in Mexico to Anna and Gaskall Romney, who deviated from precedent and did not engage in plural marriage. The Romneys left Mexico to escape the 1912 revolution and eventually settled in Salt Lake City (Kranish and Helman 2012).

George Romney was the president of General Motors before entering politics and becoming a three-term Republican governor from Michigan during the 1960s. His decade in the public eye gave him "as recognizable a national profile as perhaps any Mormon since Brigham Young" (Haws 2013, 13). Romney sought the Republican presidential nomination in 1968 and was briefly a frontrunner until his campaign was done in by his position on the Vietnam War. Romney was a supporter turned critic. He explained this shift as the result of "brainwashing" he received from American generals during his 1965 visit to Vietnam. This, coupled with his support of civil rights for African Americans, made it difficult for him to establish sufficient support from state and local party elites. Thus, "Romney's religion was mostly a nonfactor in his fall from popular grace" (Haws 2013, 13). Romney went on to become secretary of Housing and Urban Development under Richard Nixon.

Mitt Romney was viewed as a miracle baby by his mother, Lenore, whose doctor believed she was unable to get pregnant again. Mitt was raised by a leading Mormon family in the affluent suburbia of the 1950s. Romney began his college career at Stanford in the San Francisco Bay Area during the heart of the counterculture movement. Romney was exempted from the draft because he was considered "a minister of religion" after accepting a call to serve a two-year mission in France. In France, Romney experienced a near-fatal automobile accident in which he sustained serious injuries, including fractured ribs, a broken arm, and a concussion. Romney recovered quickly and assumed significant leadership responsibilities in the French mission when the director returned to America to bury his wife, who died in the accident. The mission reached its goal of baptizing two hundred people in 1968, the first time it had met its mark in nearly a decade. Romney returned to the United States with a newfound confidence after a life-changing experience.

Romney completed his undergraduate studies at Brigham Young University to be closer to his wife, Ann, whom he married in 1969. Romney then earned a dual graduate degree from Harvard Law School and Harvard Business School. Mitt and Ann raised five sons in Belmont, Massachusetts, where Mitt served as bishop, and was later promoted to stake president, responsible for approximately twelve congregations. In 1984, Romney was enticed by his mentor and eventual boss, Bill Bain, to run Bain Capital, a new venture capital company. Venture capital is typically a risky business, but Romney negotiated a deal with Bain that would allow him to return to his previous position at Bain and Company if Bain Capital went under. Bain Capital launched and reshaped hundreds of companies, including Staples and Domino's Pizza (Kranish and Helman 2012). This was lucrative for Romney, who had accumulated an estimated net worth of over $250 million by the time he launched his first presidential candidacy in 2007.

Romney entered politics in 1994 when he sought to defeat incumbent Massachusetts senator Ted Kennedy. Romney supported some traditional Republican policies while staking out more moderate positions in a state where GOP candidates had achieved some success by being fiscally conservative and socially liberal. Romney was more guarded and calculating than his father, George, who "admonished Mitt to loosen up, stop listening to consultants, and trust his gut" (Swidley and Ebbert 2007, 6). Romney easily won the Republican primary, but lost badly in the general election. Romney told his brother after the loss, "I never want to run for something again unless I can win" (Swidley and Ebbert 2007, 9).

Romney ran for governor of Massachusetts in 2002 and sought to model himself after Bill Weld, the moderate Massachusetts Republican who served as governor during the 1990s. Romney defeated Democratic nominee Shannon O'Brien, the former state legislator and treasurer, by five points. At the time, Democrats in Massachusetts outnumbered Republicans by nearly three to one. Romney portrayed himself as an agent of change who would reform Beacon Hill by courting independent voters; indeed, he rarely referred to himself as a Republican. The Massachusetts state Republican party retained its small base in Massachusetts, swept wealthier towns in the Interstate 495 crescent, and limited Democratic margins in urban areas. Mitt won his first election forty years after his father had won his first election as governor of Michigan. Both men were fifty-five years old at the time of their first political victories.

After one term as governor, Romney sought the Republican nomination for president. Romney was "telegenic, bright, independently wealthy, articulate, a proven businessman, and by most accounts, a successful governor," who had "'saved' the 2002 Salt Lake Winter Olympics and thereby become the favorite son of the business and government elites within the Republican Party" (Medhurst 2009, 196). Romney's faith, however, was an obstacle for his candidacy. No Mormon had ever gained a party nomination for president. Twenty-nine percent of voters in February 2007 viewed Mormonism as a turnoff and stated they were less likely to vote for a Mormon presidential candidate (Cohen and Agiesta 2007). This was very different from what George Romney experienced in politics. Romney's religion first came up during the governor's race in 1962. His opponent quickly remarked that the topic was out of bounds (Haws 2013, 16). George emerged on the national stage after John F. Kennedy and before the religious right. "The denominational mood of the day was one of ecumenism" (Haws 2013, 14). Furthermore, the 1960s were a period of Mormon ascendance in American culture. Church membership grew rapidly after World War II and became international-ized with the intensification of the missionary process. The church was largely associated with the Tabernacle Choir, which served as a vital public relations tool. The predominant image of Mormons was that of wholesomeness. Their patriotic and family-centered norms were a sharp contrast to the hippie counterculture movement.

Mitt faced an unexpected challenge early in his initial presidential bid. Mike Huckabee, former governor of Arkansas and Baptist preacher, climbed in the Iowa polls in October 2007, particularly among evangel-ical Christians, who constituted nearly half of Republican voters in the state. By December, Romney and Huckabee were virtually tied. The cam-paign had planned on addressing Romney's faith, but not under these circumstances. Romney's "Faith in America" speech was designed to elevate Mormonism to a legitimate expression of religious values. The speech was given on December 6, 2007, at the George Bush Presidential Library in College Station, Texas.

Romney sought to connect his candidacy with that of John F. Kennedy, both in the location of the speech and the selected content. Kennedy had addressed the issue of his religion before the Greater Houston Ministerial Association in 1960. Like Kennedy, Romney stated that he did not define his candidacy by his religion. Romney stated his belief that "a person should not be elected because of his faith nor should he be rejected because of his faith." Romney also asserted that every faith draws its adherents closer to God and that Americans "share a common creed of moral convictions," even though theological differences exist between churches. "No candidate should become the spokesman for his faith" because "if he becomes President he will need the prayers of the people of all faiths" (Romney 2007).

There were several important differences between Romney's speech and Kennedy's speech, including the timing, the audience, and the content. Kennedy's Catholicism had posed a greater challenge among the general electorate than among primary voters. The situation was reversed for Romney, who was trying to convince fellow Republicans that he was worthy of the opportunity to compete in the general election. Romney's audience consisted of political supporters who were not able to ask questions, whereas Kennedy's audience was made up of Protestant ministers who were allowed to ask questions. Romney discussed his religious convictions in the speech. Kennedy, in contrast, viewed religion as a private matter and had not discussed his religious views. "Kennedy hoped to persuade Americans not to vote against him simply because of his faith," in contrast to Romney, who "tried to gain votes because of his faith" (Kaylor 2011, 499). For example, Romney used the occasion to advocate social conservative viewpoints, including criticism of a perceived overreach of secularism in American society. Romney argued that separation of church and state recently had been taken "well beyond its original meaning" as some sought "to remove from the public domain any acknowledgement of God." Romney would "take care to separate the affairs of government from any religion," but not separate Americans from "the God who gave us liberty" or America's religious heritage (Romney 2007).

Other aspects of the speech explicitly addressed concerns about the influence of the LDS church on Romney's political behavior. Romney assured Americans that "no authorities of my church, or of any other church for that matter, will ever exert influence on presidential decisions" because "their authority is theirs, within the province of church affairs, and it ends where the affairs of the nation begin." Romney referenced his governorship as evidence of his ability to serve as a chief executive in a manner that did not confuse church teachings and professional obligations. Still, Romney acknowledged that his word and experiences would not be sufficient for some Americans who would prefer him to distance himself from his religion. "That I will not do," Romney stated, because "I believe in my Mormon faith and I endeavor to live by it. My faith is the faith of my fathers—I will be true to them and to my beliefs." Romney explained that others "believe that such a confession of my faith will sink my candidacy," but "Americans do not respect believers of convenience" and "tire of those who would jettison their beliefs, even to gain the world." This statement was particularly intriguing given the flexibility of Romney's political beliefs during his time as governor and up through his 2012 campaign for president. For example, Romney shifted from championing health care reform at the state level in Massachusetts to heavily criticizing the 2010 Affordable Care Act during the subsequent Republican presidential primaries to embracing parts of the bill in debates prior to the general election.

As a whole, Romney's speech more closely resembled the rhetoric of Mike Huckabee, George W. Bush, and Jimmy Carter than that of John F. Kennedy (Kaylor 2011). The comparison of Romney to Kennedy "is more complicated for Latter-Day Saints" because Kennedy was a lay member of the Catholic Church, where "most Mormon men serve in Church leadership positions, and many of those in Congress have also served at one level or another in the Mormon hierarchy" (King and King 2000, 20). Defenders of Romney's speech stated that no serious person of faith could in good conscience make a declaration of absolute rejection of religious influence on governance. Romney climbed between two to five points in the polls immediately after his "Faith in America" speech. Sixty-two percent of Americans were aware of the speech; 49 percent held a favorable view; and 39 percent held a negative view (Medhurst 2009).

Still, concern surrounding the prospect of a Mormon president remained strong. Seventeen percent of Americans stated that they would not vote for a well-qualified presidential candidate who was Mormon, which was no better than popular views during George Romney's candidacy in 1967 (see Table 4.1).

Table 4.1 Voting for a Well-Qualified Presidential Candidate Who Is Mormon

If your party nominated a generally well-qualified person for president who happened to be Mormon, would you vote for that person?			
	Yes	No	No Opinion
Americans at large	80%	17%	3%
Trend on Willingness to Vote for a Mormon for President			
	Yes	No	
April 1967	75%	17%	
February 1999	79%	17%	
February 2007	72%	24%	
March 2007	77%	19%	
December 2007	80%	17%	

Gallup Poll conducted from December 6 to December 9, 2007. Retrieved from http://www.gallup.com/poll/103150 /percentage-unwilling-vote-mormon-holds-steady.aspx.

Twenty-two percent of Americans viewed being Mormon as an undesirable characteristic for the next president to have. Forty-six percent of

Americans held an unfavorable opinion of the Mormon religion, with 30 percent "somewhat unfavorable," and 16 percent "very unfavorable" (see Table 4.2).

Table 4.2 Public Opinion on Mormonism and a Mormon President

Being Mormon as a characteristic for the next president to have	
Desirable	6%
Undesirable	22%
Doesn't matter	78%
Opinion of the Mormon Religion	
Very favorable	9%
Somewhat favorable	33%
Somewhat unfavorable	30%
Very unfavorable	16%
No opinion	11%

Gallup Poll conducted August 23–26, 2007. Retrieved from http://www.gallup.com/poll/103150/percentage-unwilling-vote-mormon-holds-steady.aspx; Gallup Poll conducted February 22–25, 2007. Retrieved from http://www.gallup.com/poll/103150/percentage-unwilling-vote-mormon-holds-steady.aspx.

Romney lost both the Iowa and New Hampshire nominating contests. His campaign ended in February 2008 after a disappointing performance in the Super Tuesday primaries.

A MORMON NOMINEE IN 2012

Polls surrounding Romney's presidential candidacy in 2012 revealed continued popular misunderstanding and skepticism about Mormons. A majority of Americans knew little to nothing about the Mormon religion (see Table 4.3).

Table 4.3 Knowledge of Mormonism among Americans at Large

Know about Mormon religion . . .		
	2007	2011
Great deal/Some	48%	49%
Not very much/Nothing	52%	50%
Don't know/Refused	1%	1%

"Romney's Mormon Faith Likely a Factor in Primaries, Not in a General Election," November 9–14, 2011. Pew Research Center; Forum on Religion and Public Life. Retrieved from http://www.pewforum.org/Politics-and-Elections/Romneys-Mormon-Faith-Likely-a-Factor-in-Primaries-Not-in-a-General-Election.aspx.

Polygamy most frequently came to the minds of Americans in thinking about the LDS church (see Table 4.4). Mormons were perceived as
unusual because of the relatively small size of the faith and the fact that
the teachings were new (Bowman 2012). For example, Mormonism was
theologically controversial because of its restoration of lost scripture and
the role of prophecy and revelation. A slight majority of Americans
understood Mormonism as Christian compared to over 30 percent who
did not and 17 percent who did not know. At the same time, two-thirds
of Americans believed Mormonism was very different from their own
religion, and just over 20 percent of Americans believed their religion
had a lot in common with Mormonism (see Table 4.5).

Table 4.4 What Comes to Mind When Americans Think about the LDS
Church

2007 Feb. 22–25	All respondents %	Favorable view of Mormon religion %	Unfavorable view of Mormon religion %
Polygamy	18	17	20
Salt Lake City/Utah	10	14	6
Good people/Kind/ Caring/ Strong morals	7	13	3
Dislike their beliefs/ Don't agree with their doctrine/ False teachings	6	1	13
Door-to-door evangelizing	6	7	6
Weird beliefs/Strange/ Cult-like	6	2	10
Big families/Family- oriented/ Community family	5	10	2
Just another religion	5	8	2
Secretive/Closed society	5	2	8
Devout in their beliefs/ Strict/Structured	4	5	4
Mitt Romney	3	6	*
Don't believe in Christ	3	*	6
Good religion	3	5	1

Frank Newport, "Americans' Views of the Mormon Religion," *Gallup News Service*, March 2, 2007. Retrieved from
http://www.gallup.com/poll/26758/americans-views-mormon-religion.aspx.

Table 4.5 American Perceptions of Mormonism as Christian

Is Mormonism Christian?		
	2007	2011
Yes	51%	51%
No	31%	32%
Don't know/Refused	17%	17%
Compared with own religion . . .		
	2007	2011
Mormonism has a lot in common	23%	22%
Mormonism very different	64%	65%
Don't know/Refused	13%	13%

"Romney's Mormon Faith Likely a Factor in Primaries, Not in a General Election," November 9–14, 2011. Pew Research Center; Forum on Religion and Public Life. Retrieved from http://www.pewforum.org/Politics-and -Elections/Romneys-Mormon-Faith-Likely-a-Factor-in-Primaries-Not-in-a-General-Election.aspx.

Perceptions of Mormonism created electoral challenges for Mitt Romney, particularly among evangelicals who constituted over 40 percent of Republican primary voters in 2007 and over half in 2011. A majority of white evangelical 2011 Republican primary voters did not consider Mormonism a Christian religion. This was over 30 percentage points higher than among mainline Protestants and white Catholics who were Republican voters. Only 35 percent of white evangelical Republican primary voters viewed Mormonism as Christian. This was much lower than among white mainline Protestants (67 percent) and white Catholics (63 percent) (see Table 4.6). Those who viewed Mormonism as unchristian were less likely to support Romney during the primary and to view his candidacy less favorably. White mainline Protestants and white Catholics preferred Romney as their candidate by eight percentage points compared to white evangelicals (see Table 4.7). Romney was still the top preference of registered GOP voters in November 2011 with 23 percent support, narrowly edging out Herman Cain, and well ahead of Newt Gingrich, Ron Paul, and Rick Perry (see Table 4.8).

Table 4.6 Perceptions of Mormonism among Republican Primary Voters

The Mormon religion . . .	All Rep./ Leaning R	White Evangelicals	White Mainliners
Is Christian	54%	35%	67%
Is not Christian	33%	53%	21%
Don't know	13%	12%	12%

"Romney's Mormon Faith Likely a Factor in Primaries, Not in a General Election," November 9–14, 2011. Pew Research Center; Forum on Religion and Public Life. Retrieved from http://www.pewforum.org/Politics-and -Elections/Romneys-Mormon-Faith-Likely-a-Factor-in-Primaries-Not-in-a-General-Election.aspx.

Table 4.7 Preferences by Religion in 2012 Republican Primary

	White Evangelicals	White Mainliners	White Catholics
Mitt Romney	17%	26%	26%
Herman Cain	26%	17%	23%
Newt Gingrich	19%	15%	19%
Ron Paul	7%	8%	8%
Rick Perry	12%	7%	5%
Michelle Bachman	5%	2%	4%
Rick Santorum	3%	3%	2%
Jon Huntsman	1%	1%	0%

"Romney's Mormon Faith Likely a Factor in Primaries, Not in a General Election," November 9–14, 2011. Pew Research Center; Forum on Religion and Public Life. Retrieved from http://www.pewforum.org/Politics-and -Elections/Romneys-Mormon-Faith-Likely-a-Factor-in-Primaries-Not-in-a-General-Election.aspx.

Table 4.8 Preferences of All Republicans and Leaning Republican Registered Voters

Mitt Romney	23%
Herman Cain	22%
Newt Gingrich	16%
Ron Paul	8%
Rick Perry	8%
Michelle Bachman	5%
Rick Santorum	2%
Jon Huntsman	1%

"Romney's Mormon Faith Likely a Factor in Primaries, Not in a General Election," November 9–14, 2011. Pew Research Center; Forum on Religion and Public Life. Retrieved from http://www.pewforum.org/Politics-and -Elections/Romneys-Mormon-Faith-Likely-a-Factor-in-Primaries-Not-in-a-General-Election.aspx.

A central question surrounding Mormons and presidential politics in 2012 was whether Mitt Romney, if elected president, would face politically related requests from the Mormon prophet Thomas Monson, and if so, what Romney would do. Much of this concern emerges from the logic of revelation. Nonbelievers tend to think that believing in a prophet that speaks for God requires unquestioning submission. However, not all believers follow this logic, as with Catholics who do not follow directives of the pope. Furthermore, the Mormon Church is heavily withdrawn from national politics in the twenty-first century compared with the nineteenth century, though Mormons remain heavily entangled in Utah politics. The church occasionally takes positions on issues viewed as central to Mormon doctrine, such as same-sex marriage, but bishops typically do not excommunicate Mormons for holding political positions contrary to predominant Mormon views. It is highly unlikely that LDS president Thomas Monson would have made direct policy requests to Romney if he had been elected president because the church is more interested in fostering national acceptance, given its long and violent history of persecution, than in immediate policy gains. LDS leaders are well aware that a politically active prophet would be very damaging for public relations, a major focus of the contemporary church.

The current LDS policy of political neutrality was evident in the 2012 election cycle with a relevant statement provided by the LDS Newsroom on the church's website. The statement began with the assertion that "the Church's mission is to preach the gospel of Jesus Christ, not to elect politicians" and that the church is "neutral in matters of party politics" in all nations where the church exists. The Mormon church does not: (1) "endorse, promote, or oppose political parties, candidates or platforms"; (2) "allow its church buildings, membership lists or other resources to be used for partisan political purposes"; (3) "attempt to direct its members as to which candidate or party they should give their votes to"; or (4) "attempt to direct or dictate to a government leader." The church does: (1) "encourage its members to play a role as responsible citizens in their communities including becoming informed about issues and voting in elections"; (2) "expect its members to engage in the political process in an informed and civil manner"; (3) "request candidates for office not to imply that their candidacy or platforms are endorsed by the Church";

and (4) "reserve the right as an institution to address, in a nonpartisan way, issues that it believes have significant community or moral consequences or that directly affect the interests of the Church (The Church of Jesus Christ of Latter-day Saints)."

Prior to national elections Mormon authorities typically issue a letter to be read aloud to each American congregation that encourages members to vote and emphasizes the church's neutrality in regard to partisanship and electoral outcomes. The First Presidency also issues guidelines for political participation among church leaders, which occurred in June 2011 in advance of the 2012 election cycle. General Authorities and general officers, as well as their spouses, are restricted from personally participating in political campaigns. Part-time church officers, such as area seventies, stake presidents, and bishops, can participate in political campaigns provided they do not speak for the church, use church resources, or engage in fundraising efforts that specifically target fellow Mormons

There were 2,286 delegates up for grabs in the Republican nominating process. Romney needed 1,144 delegates and won 1,522. This was significantly more than Santorum (255), Paul (158), Gingrich (138), and Huntsman (1), the other candidates who won delegates. Romney started slowly by winning just 5 out of a possible 28 delegates in Iowa, but did secure 8 out of 12 delegates in New Hampshire. Romney then won just 5 delegates out of 25 in South Carolina. Romney's important win in Florida at the end of January earned him all 50 delegates in the winner-take-all contest. Romney went on to win Nevada and Colorado, lose Minnesota and Maine, and work toward securing the nomination at the end of May by picking up several big delegate victories in states throughout the country. These wins included several Southern states (Virginia, Maryland, North Carolina, Arkansas, and Kentucky), several Midwestern states (Ohio, Illinois, Wisconsin, and Indiana), a few Northeastern states (Massachusetts, New York, and Pennsylvania), and a few Western states (Arizona, Washington, and Idaho). Romney was very competitive in the South, where many white evangelicals reside. There was no evidence to suggest that Romney's faith would prevent the party at large from coalescing around him in the general election. Importantly for Romney, white evangelical Republicans were strongly opposed to President Obama. Nine out of ten white evangelical Republican voters expressed a willingness to vote for Romney over Obama in the general election, and nearly eight of ten expressed strong support for Romney (see Table 4.9). Thus, white evangelical Republicans preferred other nominees in the primary but strongly preferred any Republican nominee to the prospect of Obama serving a second term.

Table 4.9 Opposition to Obama among GOP Voters

	Rep./Rep. leaning voters %	Is the Mormon religion Christian?	
		Yes %	No %
View of Romney			
Favorable	56	61	51
Unfavorable	29	25	36
Don't know	15	14	13
View of Obama			
Favorable	13	18	6
Unfavorable	85	81	92
Very unfavorable	49	44	58
2012 Election			
Romney	87	86	89
Strongly Romney	71	69	73
Obama	9	10	7
Other/Don't know	4	3	4

"Romney's Mormon Faith Likely a Factor in Primaries, Not in a General Election," November 9–14, 2011. Pew Research Center; Forum on Religion and Public Life. Retrieved from http://www.pewforum.org/Politics-and -Elections/Romneys-Mormon-Faith-Likely-a-Factor-in-Primaries-Not-in-a-General-Election.aspx.

This played out electorally in the general election, when 79 percent of white, born-again, evangelical Protestants voted for Romney. This was up from 73 percent who voted for McCain in 2008 and matched Bush's support in 2004. Evangelicals comprised 26 percent of the electorate, three points higher than in 2004. Romney won Protestants as a whole 57 percent to 42 percent. This margin was slightly larger than McCain's edge in 2008 and slightly less than Bush's edge in 2004. Obama received less support from Catholics as a whole than in 2008, but still edged out Romney, 50 percent to 48 percent. Romney won 7 percent more of the white Catholic vote than McCain did, but 5 percent less of the Hispanic

Catholic vote. Romney did gain more of the Jewish vote than both Bush and McCain did. Jewish support for Bush grew from 19 percent in 2000 to 25 percent in 2004. This dropped to 21 percent for McCain and grew to 30 percent for Romney. Religious voting patterns in 2012 were relatively similar to 2008 with a slight decrease in support for President Obama, particularly among Jews, white Catholics, and white, born-again evangelicals (see Table 4.10).

Table 4.10 Presidential Vote by Religious Affiliation and Race

	2000		2004		2008		2012	
	Gore %	Bush %	Kerry %	Bush %	Obama %	McCain %	Obama %	Romney %
TOTAL	48	48	48	51	53	46	50	48
Protestant / Other Christian	42	56	40	59	45	54	42	57
White Protestant	35	63	32	67	34	65	30	69
Born-again / Evangelical	n/a	n/a	21	79	26	73	20	79
Non-evangelical	n/a	n/a	44	55	44	55	44	54
Black Protestant	92	7	86	13	94	4	95	5
Catholic	50	47	47	52	54	45	50	48
White Catholic	45	52	43	56	47	52	40	59
Hispanic Catholic	65	33	65	33	72	26	75	21
Jewish	79	19	74	25	78	21	69	30
Other faiths	62	28	74	23	73	22	74	23
Religiously unaffiliated	61	30	67	31	75	23	70	26
Mormon	n/a	n/a	19	80	n/a	n/a	21	78

"How the Faithful Voted: 2012 Preliminary Analysis," November 7, 2012, Pew Research Center, Retrieved from http://www.pewforum.org/Politics-and-Elections/How-the-Faithful-Voted-2012-Preliminary-Exit-Poll-Analysis.aspx.

Romney also had a decisive advantage among the religiously active. This included a 20 percentage point edge among people who attend worship services weekly or more often, a 27 percentage point edge among those attending "more than weekly," and a 17 percentage point edge among those attending "once a week." Each of these margins was higher than what McCain had attained in 2008 and rivaled Bush's support among the religiously active in 2000 and 2004. Obama retained his edge among people who infrequently attend worship services. This included a 12 percentage point edge among voters who attend a "few times a month" and a 14 percentage point edge among voters who attend a "few times a year." Obama fell five percentage points among voters who never attend worship services, but he still experienced a commanding 28 percentage point advantage. Once again, these voting patterns were relatively consistent with past trends, though Obama lost ground in nearly every category compared to 2008 (see Table 4.11).

Table 4.11 Presidential Vote by Religious Attendance

	2000		2004		2008		2012	
	Gore %	Bush %	Kerry %	Bush %	Obama %	McCain %	Obama %	Romney %
TOTAL	48	48	48	51	53	46	50	48
Attend worships services . . .								
Weekly or more	39	59	39	61	43	55	39	59
More than weekly	36	63	35	64	43	55	36	63
Once a week	40	57	41	58	43	55	41	58
Monthly/ yearly	53	43	53	47	57	42	55	43
Few times a month	54	42	54	45	59	39	56	42
Never	61	32	62	36	67	30	62	34

"How the Faithful Voted: 2012 Preliminary Analysis," November 7, 2012, Pew Research Center, Retrieved from http://www.pewforum.org/Politics-and-Elections/How-the-Faithful-Voted-2012-Preliminary-Exit-Poll-Analysis. aspx.

There was remarkably little change in public attitudes regarding Mormons between Romney's 2008 and 2012 campaigns. Sixty-eight percent of Americans in 2011 stated that someone being Mormon would make no difference in terms of voting for a presidential candidate, which is comparable to the percentage of people who would be no less likely to vote for a candidate with a past history of using marijuana (Doherty 2011). Still, 2012 voters were much less comfortable with a Mormon presidential candidate than all other religious groups except Muslims. Nineteen percent of voters were "somewhat uncomfortable" with Mormonism as the faith of a presidential candidate. Seventeen percent were "entirely uncomfortable." Just one-third of voters were "entirely comfortable" with a presidential candidate who is a Mormon. This is much lower than comfort levels with Catholics and Jews, but higher than with atheists and Muslims (see Table 4.12).

Table 4.12 Comfort among Registered Voters with the Religion of Presidential Candidates

	Entirely comfortable %	Somewhat comfortable %	Somewhat uncomfortable %	Entirely uncomfortable %
Catholic	60	23	8	5
Jewish	55	25	9	6
Evangelical Christian	43	24	14	12
Mormon	35	25	19	17
Atheist	24	13	16	44
Muslim	21	17	23	36

Quinnipiac University Poll of 1,946 registered voters from May 31 to June 6, 2011. Retrieved from http:// www.mcclatchydc.com/2011/06/08/115445/poll-romney-leads-but-mormon-religion.html.

Education is one important factor in understanding the unwillingness of American voters to vote for a Mormon presidential candidate. People without college education are more resistant to voting for a Mormon. In June 2011, 12 percent of people with a college education would not vote for a qualified Mormon presidential candidate compared to 20 percent of people with some college and 31 percent of people with no college. Partisanship is another important factor. Twenty-seven percent of Democrats stated an unwillingness to vote for a Mormon president compared to just 19 percent of independents and 18 percent of Republicans. Romney's candidacy likely influenced the perspective of Democrats. Unwillingness by age and gender categories was relatively consistent at just over 20 percent (see Table 4.13).

Table 4.13 Willingness to Vote for a Mormon for President by Subgroup

	Yes, would vote for	No, would not vote for
By party		
Republican	80%	18%
Democrat	71%	27%
Independent	79%	19%
By education		
College graduates	86%	12%
Some college	79%	20%
No college	66%	31%
By gender		
Men	76%	21%
Women	75%	23%
By age		
18 to 34 years	73%	25%
35 to 54 years	77%	21%
55 and older	76%	22%
By region		
East	78%	17%
Midwest	72%	26%
South	74%	23%

"In U.S., 22% Are Hesitant to Support a Mormon in 2012," Gallup Poll conducted from June 9 to June 12, 2011. Retrieved from http://www.gallup.com/poll/148100/Hesitant-Support-Mormon-2012.aspx.

Romney's faith did not appear to hinder him significantly in the outcome of the primary election or general election, but it was a factor. America's tradition of civil religion provides a social context for national politicians to potentially connect with the electorate. Romney clearly limited public discussion of his faith because he was concerned that this would hurt him electorally. Romney loosened some during the Republican National Convention, when fellow Mormons discussed in detail how

Romney helped them in times of need, but this was after several months of the Obama campaign consistently attacking Romney's perceived economic credentials by demonizing and dehumanizing his work at Bain Capital. Romney potentially could have sought to lessen these blows in the context of his faith by highlighting his experiences as a local and regional leader in the LDS church, whereby Romney often prayed for the suffering, comforted the grieving, helped those in need, taught scripture, and annually tithed over 10 percent of his income. This type of narrative would have helped to reframe public perceptions of Romney as a heartless capitalist who really enjoyed firing people and making money.

In June 2012 Americans were more willing to vote for someone who is black (96 percent), a woman (95 percent), Catholic (94 percent), Hispanic (92 percent), and Jewish (91 percent) than someone who is Mormon (80 percent). This suggests that the likelihood for historic barriers to be broken in future presidential elections is greater with women, Hispanics, and Jews than with Mormons, gays or lesbians (68 percent), Muslims (58 percent), or atheists (54 percent) (see Table 4.14).

Table 4.14 Willingness to Vote for Persons of Various Characteristics

Between now and the 2012 political conventions, there will be discussion about the qualifications of presidential candidates—their education, age, religion, race, and so on. If your party nominated a generally well-qualified person for president who happened to be _____, would you vote for that person?		
	Yes, would vote for	No, would not vote for
Black	96%	4%
A woman	95%	5%
Catholic	94%	5%
Hispanic	92%	7%
Jewish	91%	6%
Mormon	80%	18%
Gay or Lesbian	68%	30%
Muslim	58%	40%
An atheist	54%	43%

"Atheists, Muslims See Most Bias as Presidential Candidates," Gallup Poll conducted from June 7 to June 10, 2012. Retrieved from http://www.gallup.com/poll/148100/Hesitant-Support-Mormon-2012.aspx.

Willingness to vote for a Mormon or an atheist jumped four and five percentage points, respectively, between 2011 and 2012. Long-term trends point to a significant net increase from 1937 to 2012 in willingness to vote for a woman (+62 percentage points), someone who is black (+58 percentage points), someone who is Jewish (+45 percentage points), or someone who is gay or lesbian (+42 percentage points) (see Table 4.15). Given this data, a woman and/or Hispanic president is quite possible, depending on the field of candidates in the next several election cycles, but a gay or lesbian, Muslim, or atheist president is relatively unlikely in light of public opinion toward a member of these subgroups assuming the powers of the presidency. For Mormons, the election outcome suggests that if Mormons are experiencing a moment of acceptance, sizeable concern still exists about the prospect of a Mormon president. In the absence of other nationally prominent Mormon politicians, it is unlikely these attitudes will be tested again in the near future.

Table 4.15 Percentage Who Would Vote for Presidential Candidate by Subgroup over Time

	1937	1958	1978	1999	2012
Woman	33%	54%	76%	92%	95%
Black	n/a	38%	77%	95%	96%
Jewish	46%	63%	82%	92%	91%
Gay/Lesbian	n/a	n/a	26%	59%	68%
Atheist	n/a	18%	40%	49%	54%
Catholic	60%	67%	91%	94%	94%

"Atheists, Muslims See Most Bias as Presidential Candidates," Gallup Polls compiled and posted on June 21, 2012. Retrieved from http://www.gallup.com/poll/148100/Hesitant-Support-Mormon-2012.aspx.

REFERENCES

Bowman, M. 2012. *The Mormon People: The Making of an American Faith*. New York: Random House.

Bushman, R. 2008. *Mormonism: A Very Short Introduction*. New York: Oxford University Press.

Bushman, C., and R. Bushman. 1999. *Building the Kingdom*. New York: Oxford University Press.

The Church of Jesus-Christ of Latter-day Saints. 2012. "Political Neutrality." LDS Website. Retrieved from http://www.mormonnewsroom.org/official -statement/political-neutrality

Cohen, J., and J. Agiesta. 2007. "Race, Gender Less Relevant in '08." *Washington Post.* Retrieved February 27, 2007 from http://www.washingtonpost.com /wpdyn/content/article/2007/02/27/AR2007022700283.html.

Doherty, C. 2011. "Are Republicans Ready Now for a Mormon President?" *Pew Research Center.* Retrieved July 5, 2011 from http://www.people-press. org/2011/07/05/are-republicans-ready-now-for-a-mormon-president/.

Elisha, O. 2002. "Sustaining Charisma: Mormon Sectarian Culture and the Struggle for Plural Marriage, 1852–1890." *Nova Religio: The Journal of Alternative and Emergent Religions* 6 (October): 45–63.

Haws, J. B. 2013. *The Mormon Image in the American Mind.* Oxford: Oxford University Press.

Hickman, M. 1968. "The Political Legacy of Joseph Smith." *Dialogue: A Journal of Mormon Thought* 3 (Autumn): 22–27.

Kaylor, B. 2011. "No Jack Kennedy: Mitt Romney's 'Faith in America' Speech and Changing Religious Political Environment." *Communication Studies* 62 (5): 491–507.

King, R., and K. A. King. 2000. "Mormons in Congress, 1851–2000." *Journal of Mormon History* 26 (2): 1–51.

Kranish, M., and S. Helman. 2012. *The Real Romney.* New York: HarperCollins.

Mauss, A. 1984. "Sociological Perspectives on the Mormon Subculture." *Annual Review of Sociology* 10: 437–460.

Medhurst, M. 2009. "Mitt Romney, 'Faith in America,' and the Dance of Religion and Politics in American Culture." *Rhetoric and Public Affairs* 12 (2): 195–222.

Perry, L., and C. Cronin. 2012. *Mormons in American Politics: From Persecution to Power.* Santa Barbara, CA: Praeger.

Poll, R. 1968. "Joseph Smith's Presidential Platform." *Dialogue: A Journal of Mormon Thought* 3 (Autumn): 17–36.

Romney, M. 2007. "Romney's 'Faith in America' Address." *New York Times.* Retrieved December 6, 2007 from http://www.nytimes.com/2007/12/06/us /politics/06text-romney.html?pagewanted=print&_r=0.

Swidley, N., and S. Ebbert. 2007. "Romney Determined to Make Mark Early." *Boston Globe.* Retrieved July 4, 2007 from http://www.deseretnews.com /article/680196334/Romney-determined-to-make-mark-early.html?pg=1.

Chapter 5

The Culture Wars in the 2012 Presidential Election

Graham G. Dodds, Concordia University (Canada)

INTRODUCTION

In trying to make sense of the enormous chaotic contest that is a presidential election, scholars generally focus on a particular aspect of U.S. politics and ask how it has changed from previous presidential elections. In this way, political scientists and others regularly debate the impact by and on macro-economic conditions, changing demographics, political parties, and a variety of specific policy issues. Over the last several decades, this list has usually included culture, as cultural politics and the "culture wars" have been a prominent feature of presidential elections and even U.S. politics more broadly. This is because although electoral politics is ultimately about votes, towards that end it is also concerned with culture, as candidates, political parties, and interest groups regularly make cultural appeals intended either to foster sympathy or to arouse antipathy. As one author recently explained it on *Salon.com*, "At its heart, culture war politics isn't about issues; it's about identity. The culture war has always boiled down to a simple idea: Our party is with you, and the other party is alien and threatening. They're just a different kind of people, people who don't share our values, see the world in the same way you do, or want what you want" (Waldman 2012). Not surprisingly, scholarly attention to the culture wars has produced a body of literature that is extensive and growing.[1] This chapter examines the state of cultural politics and the "culture wars" in the 2012 presidential election. Its analysis proceeds in three parts: (1) it briefly reviews the history of the topic; (2) it considers the impact of four issue areas with a cultural valence, namely religion and the role of evangelicals, gender and women's issues, gay rights, and aspects of economic and tax policy; and (3) it considers how we could best understand the overall state of the culture wars now.

PART 1
Historical Background

Many people trace the culture wars to Pat Buchanan's (in)famous speech at the 1992 Republican National Convention. Buchanan declared, "There is a religious war going on in our country for the soul of America. It is a cultural war, as critical to the kind of nation we will one day be as was the Cold War itself" (Buchanan 1992). Buchanan's evocation of an American *kulturkampf* was highly controversial, and columnist Molly Ivins famously quipped that it "probably sounded better in the original German" (Ivins 1992).

However, America's culture wars predated Buchanan's 1992 speech. Arguably, the antebellum divide between North and South was largely cultural, and the conflict over Prohibition was an early chapter in the culture wars (Dionne 2006). Some scholars trace the advent of the contemporary culture wars to the societal upheavals of the 1960s, the women's movement and the push for the Equal Rights Amendment (ERA) in the 1970s, gay rights legislation in Florida in 1977, and court cases against school prayer in the 1960s and racial discrimination in conservative religious schools in the 1970s and 1980s.[2] Other scholars point to the entry into mainstream politics by the religious right in 1979, when Paul Weyrich and Rev. Jerry Falwell founded the Moral Majority, which helped elect Ronald Reagan. After Reagan's presidency, religious conservatives continued to exert a strong pull on electoral politics with Rev. Pat Robertson's presidential run in 1988 and his subsequent creation of the Christian Coalition in 1989.

Although the religious right was central to political-cultural conflicts of the 1980s, the culture wars soon came to explicitly address culture itself, or at least the arts and government support of them via the National Endowment for the Arts (NEA). In 1989, social conservatives decried the use of tax dollars to subsidize allegedly blasphemous and obscene art by Andres Serrano and Robert Mapplethorpe. Similarly, in 1990, they criticized Annie Sprinkle and the so-called "NEA Four" of Karen Finley, Tim Miller, John Fleck, and Holly Hughes. In 1995, conservative critics forced the cancellation of a Smithsonian Institution exhibit on the fiftieth anniversary of the *Enola Gay*'s dropping of an atomic bomb on Hiroshima, Japan. And in 1999, Falwell complained that the character Tinky Winky from the BBC TV show *Teletubbies* was likely gay and hence a poor role model for American children.

The controversial 2000 presidential election was arguably a pivotal point in the culture wars, as the image of a country sharply divided into Democratic blue states and Republican red states was burned into the national consciousness. Previously, the culture wars had largely concerned competing political claims about cultural or moral issues, but now they were perceived as rooted in completely different cultures that were geographically distinct. David Brooks famously described the two cultures as follows:

> People in Blue America...tend to live around big cities on the coasts. People in Red America tend to live on farms or in small towns or small cities far away from the coasts.... Different sorts of institutions dominate life in these two places. In Red America churches are everywhere. In Blue America Thai restaurants are everywhere. In Red America they have QVC, the Pro Bowlers Tour, and hunting. In Blue America we have NPR, Doris Kearns Goodwin, and socially conscious investing. In Red America the Wal-Marts are massive, with parking lots the size of state parks. In Blue America the stores are small but the markups are big. (Brooks 2001)

Under George W. Bush, the culture wars continued, even if they were overshadowed by 9/11, the "war on terror," the Iraq war, and the financial collapse of 2008. For example, evangelicals and other social conservatives lauded Bush's appointment of Sen. John Ashcroft as attorney general and Bush's creation of the White House Office of Faith-Based and Community Initiatives. In the 2004 presidential election, many observers claimed that Bush's victory over Senator John Kerry was due to Karl Rove's outreach to evangelicals, even though the percentage of evangelicals in the electorate in 2004 was about the same as in 2000 (Brooks 2004).

Religious and cultural themes continued in the lead-up to the 2008 presidential elections. On the Republican side, former Arkansas governor Mike Huckabee's appeal to evangelicals evoked the political themes and strength of the old religious right. On the Democratic side, Illinois senator Barack Obama offered a new take on the culture wars. As a presidential candidate in 2007 and 2008, part of Obama's appeal was his promise to help move beyond stale political divisions and bring together Americans of different backgrounds. And part of that promise was—implicitly, if not explicitly—to end the culture wars. This potential was perhaps rendered most compellingly in Obama's keynote speech at the 2004 Democratic National Convention:

> The pundits . . . like to slice and dice our country into red states and blue states: red states for Republicans, blue states for Democrats. But I've got news for them. ... We worship an awesome God in the blue states, and we don't like federal agents poking around our libraries in the red states. We coach little league in the blue states, and we've got some gay friends in the red states. ... We are one people, all of us pledging allegiance to the stars and stripes. ...

Obama's first presidential campaign and his first term as president were by no means free from the culture wars, but that unifying ideal nevertheless remains part of his appeal.[3]

PART 2

In order to assay the state of contemporary American cultural politics, or more specifically, the role of cultural politics in the 2012 presidential election and also the impact of the election on cultural politics, this section examines four broad issue areas that have often been at the center of cultural politics, which I have loosely but alliteratively entitled God, Gals, Gays, and Growth.

God

Religion has long figured prominently in the culture wars, from the rise of the religious right as an organized political force several decades ago, to criticisms in 1988 by conservative columnists Rowland Evans and

Robert Novak of Governor Michael Dukakis's membership in the Greek Orthodox Church and his wife Kitty's Judaism (*Los Angeles Times* 1988), to charges that Obama is secretly a Muslim. In the last election cycle, religion was very much a factor. For example, in late 2011, the Republican-controlled House passed a resolution reaffirming "In God We Trust" as the official motto of the United States, as if the nation's religious heritage were under secular threat. Religion was also prominent in the Republican primaries, especially in the campaigns of Minnesota representative Michele Bachmann, Texas governor Rick Perry, and former Pennsylvania senator Rick Santorum. Indeed, the overt religiosity of the Republican primaries led a prominent progressive blogger to declare in February 2012 that "the culture wars have returned with a vengeance" (Konczal 2012). In large part, this was due to the surprisingly strong campaign of Santorum, who was often a figure in cultural controversies during his sixteen years in Congress. In February 2012, Santorum charged that Obama's political agenda was based on "some phony theology...not a theology based on the Bible" (Oppel 2012). Later that month, Santorum criticized John F. Kennedy's famous 1960 speech supporting the separation of church and state, which Santorum said made him "want to throw up" (Mak 2012).

When Santorum's candidacy fell to that of Mitt Romney, the Republican Party's traditional base faced a challenge, as Romney's membership in the Church of Jesus Christ of Latter-day Saints (LDS, or Mormons) did not sit well with many evangelicals. While evangelicals and fundamentalists appeared willing to embrace a staunch Catholic in Santorum, it was not clear that they would accept a Mormon as the Republican standard-bearer. Evangelicals might share Romney's opposition to abortion rights and same-sex marriage, and they might be willing to support individual Mormon politicians, but a Mormon president would arguably render Mormonism mainstream, something many evangelicals opposed.

The issue of accommodating different faiths has at times been a difficult one for the religious right, which was created by cobbling together groups that might not quite agree about theology but which did agree about social issues. Yet the old religious right never fully succeeded in reaching beyond Baptists and a few other denominations to conservative Jews and Catholics, let alone Mormons. And suspicion of Mormons was not limited only to the traditional religious right, as a Pew survey from

January 2012 found that one-third of American adults did not believe that Mormonism was a Christian faith (Chozick 2012).

Romney was acutely aware of public suspicion of Mormonism, and he sought both to downplay the issue and to assure voters that he shared evangelicals' commitments. For example, in May 2012 he gave a speech at Falwell's Liberty University. In early September, Democrats were essentially forced to change their party's official platform to include a mention of God, after they were criticized for having omitted it. Speaking on Fox News, Romney said, "I think their having removed purposefully God from their platform suggests a party which is increasingly out of touch with the mainstream of American people.... I think this party is veering further and further into an extreme wing that Americans don't recognize" (Boghani 2012). Several days later, Romney invoked the Pledge of Allegiance to underscore his commitment to God and to question Obama's commitment. These efforts helped to assuage evangelicals' concerns about Romney's religion. And the acceptance of Mormonism almost became official in mid-October, when the televangelist Rev. Billy Graham removed Mormons from a list of cults on his website, accepting Romney's faith as a legitimate form of Christianity.

In the end, even though the Romney-Ryan tandem was the first Republican ticket without a Protestant, it did well among evangelical voters. According to a Pew survey released one week before the 2012 election, white evangelical voters favored Romney over Obama by 76 percent to 17 percent, while Protestant voters favored Romney over Obama by 54 percent to 39 percent. In terms of actual votes, 78 percent of white evangelicals voted for Romney, compared with 74 percent for Senator John McCain four years ago. And white evangelicals made up 26 percent of the electorate in 2012, the same percent as in 2008 (Boorstein and Clement 2012). Thus, even though this important part of the Republican base remained large and engaged, and Romney managed to overcome early doubts and do better among evangelicals than the previous Republican nominee, it was not enough to win the election.

Gals

The role of women, both in society and in electoral politics, has often been an issue in the culture wars. For example, in 1992 Vice President Dan

Quayle criticized the TV character Murphy Brown for choosing to be a single mother. And in 2008, issues of gender and sexism greatly influenced the campaigns of New York senator Hillary Clinton and Alaska governor Sarah Palin. Additionally, over the past few decades, some groups of swing-voting women have been a much sought-after part of the electorate, from so-called "soccer moms" in 1996, to waitress moms, Walmart moms, and most recently Panera women (Helderman 2012).

Obama devoted significant attention to so-called women's issues during his first term, for reasons of both principle and politics. Early in his presidency, he issued unilateral directives to reverse Bush-era policies on abortion restrictions, and he signed into law the Lilly Ledbetter Fair Pay Act, extending the statute of limitations for filing a lawsuit for gender discrimination in pay. After the 2010 midterm elections, conservatives sought to put their own stamp on women's issues. In 2011, some members of Congress tried to eliminate federal funds for Planned Parenthood, which is the primary source of family planning for millions of women. This led to a major breast cancer charity, the Susan G. Komen Foundation, deciding to sever ties with Planned Parenthood, a move that it reversed after public pressure. Then conservatives in Congress tried to overturn the requirement in "Obamacare" that employer health plans cover contraception. And in February 2012, Obama publicly supported Georgetown University law student Sandra Fluke, who sought to testify about insurance coverage for contraception and was derided by Rush Limbaugh as a "slut" and a "prostitute" (Torregrosa 2012). In April 2012, the Senate voted to reauthorize the 1994 Violence Against Women Act and to broaden its protections to include LGBT women, illegal immigrants, and Native Americans. The vote split GOP senators, as many opposed it, while others were willing to accede in order to blunt the charge that the party was hostile to women.

These events combined to greatly animate cultural politics. Writing in April 2012 about the political clash over women's issues, one journalist proclaimed "the revival of the culture wars" (Torregrossa 2012). Some Democrats charged that there was a Republican "war on women." And in May 2012, the Obama campaign sought to capitalize on the matter by creating an online slide show entitled "The Life of Julia," showing how Obama's policies would help a fictional middle-class woman throughout her entire life.

The issue of abortion has often been at the center of the culture wars, and it returned to that prominent role shortly before the 2012 national party conventions. In August 2012, Missouri Senate candidate Representative Todd Aiken defended his opposition to abortion in all circumstances, claiming, "If it's a legitimate rape, the female body has ways to try to shut that whole thing down" in order to prevent pregnancy, such that an abortion ban need not have an exception for rape (Redden 2012). Two months later, in October 2012, Indiana Senate candidate and Tea Party favorite Richard Mourdock claimed that when rape does result in a pregnancy, "that is something God intended to happen" and should therefore be accepted (Redden 2012). Also in October, Illinois representative Joe Walsh claimed that technology had negated the need for exceptions to antiabortion limitations for the "health of the mother" (Redden 2012).

Each candidate's set of remarks was controversial in its own right, but altogether they seemed to add up to something more, as it seemed that Republican men had little understanding of, let alone sympathy for, women's reproductive health and choices. And the comments did not merely reflect poor word choice by individual candidates, as they highlighted many social conservatives' opposition to abortion in most if not all instances. Indeed, the GOP platform endorsed a constitutional ban on abortion and made no exceptions for rape, incest, or the health of the mother. This led to a heightened public role for abortion in the presidential campaign. Romney sought to distance himself from the congressional candidates' controversial remarks while not alienating evangelical voters (Cooper 2012). He did not join the calls to ban abortion even in cases of rape, nor did he oppose contraception, but he did call for an end to federal funding of Planned Parenthood.

Romney's difficulties with women and women's issues were soon compounded by his own poorly worded remarks. In the second presidential debate, he responded to a question about pay equity by saying that as governor he had tried to hire women and reviewed "binders full of women" job candidates. He then said, "if you're going to have women in the workforce…" and mentioned a woman who wanted to be home in time to make dinner for her family. The "binders" phrase was instantly mocked, and Romney's critics contended that he simply did not appreciate the difficulties that women routinely face.

The cultural debate about women was related both to specific policy issues and to electoral concerns, particularly the "gender gap," or the difference in men's and women's voting patterns. This gap has been a fact of American politics for the last few decades, with men preferring Republicans and women preferring Democrats. Exact numbers for 2012 vary from report to report, but it is clear that the gender gap was considerable in the election. Nate Silver predicted that it would be eighteen points, or just below the record level of twenty points from 2000, while Gallup found that it was actually twenty points in 2012, which made it the biggest gender gap since the organization started to compile voting data by major groups in 1952 (Silver 2012; Jones 2012). This gap was no doubt driven in part by the controversial remarks about abortion, and that may have strengthened pro-choice sentiment, as exit polls found that 59 percent of voters in 2012 felt abortion should be always or mostly legal, compared to 55 percent in 2008 (Enten 2012).

Gays

Beyond religious arguments and controversies about women and their reproductive choices, perhaps no other issue has so inflamed the culture wars over the years as gay rights. According to a recent journalistic account, gay rights is "perhaps the defining issue of the culture wars" (Enten 2012). Indeed, a local ordinance about gay rights in Dade County, Florida, in 1977 was arguably one of the causes of evangelicals entering into mainstream politics. And in the 2003 case of *Lawrence v. Texas*, Supreme Court justice Antonin Scalia complained in his dissent that by striking down an antisodomy law, "the Court has taken sides in the culture war." Recently, advocates for gay rights have consciously emulated the mid-twentieth-century push for civil rights for African Americans, invoking the language of expanding freedom and respect for difference (Douthat 2009). This argument has found increasing support among the American public, and the last several years have seen significant legal and political gains for gays and lesbians.

For example, in 2009, Obama signed a hate crime bill that was named in part to commemorate Matthew Shepard, who was killed in 1998 because he was gay. In 2009 and 2010, Obama issued presidential memoranda to unilaterally extend benefits to the same-sex partners of federal employees. In 2010 and 2011, Obama persuaded Congress to end the "Don't ask, don't tell" policy that had excluded gay Americans from military service. In 2011,

Obama directed the Justice Department to stop defending the Defense of Marriage Act (DOMA), a 1996 federal law that barred federal recognition of same-sex marriages, even when states recognized them. And in May 2012, Obama declared his own personal support for same-sex marriage, shortly after Vice President Joe Biden did so.

Beyond executive action, the judicial branch also acted to advance the cause of gay rights. For example, starting in 2010, federal courts overturned California's Proposition 8 banning same-sex marriage. The Obama administration announced in 2011 that it would no longer defend the DOMA in court, and the Supreme Court partially struck it down in 2013 in the case of *United States v. Windsor.* In terms of electoral gains for gay rights, in Wisconsin, Tammy Baldwin waged a successful campaign to become the first openly gay or lesbian senator. And voters in Maine, Maryland, and Washington approved referenda permitting same-sex marriage, while voters in Minnesota rejected a constitutional amendment against it.

These changes did not please many Republicans. Social conservatives have long resisted the movement toward equal rights for gays and lesbians, and they continued to do so in the 2012 primaries and general election. For example, in December 2011, Governor Rick Perry called homosexuality a sin. In May 2012, Richard Grennell, who had served as Romney's foreign policy spokesperson, despite being openly gay and an advocate of same-sex marriage, was forced to resign after Christian conservatives complained. In July 2012, the head of Chick-fil-A restaurants, Dan Cathy, publicly spoke out against the growing public acceptance of gay marriage. In response, the mayors of Boston and Chicago indicated that they opposed any new Chick-fil-A restaurants in their cities. Thus, the culture wars now even influence people's fast-food preferences. And in late August the Republican Party released its official platform, which called court decisions supporting same-sex marriage "an assault on the foundations of our society" and endorsed both DOMA and a constitutional amendment banning gay marriage.

Growth

One might think that fundamental economic issues would take precedence over more seemingly ancillary social issues, but this is not always the case, and the culture wars may rage even during difficult economic times. As Ross Douthat noted, "even amid downturns and deficits, the culture wars are still inevitably significant" (Douthat 2012a). Still, Romney's campaign sought to keep its focus on the economy, rather than on contentious social issues. Its model seemed to be Bill Clinton's 1992 campaign, which was predicated largely on the idea that poor economic conditions provided the rationale for supporting a challenger over an incumbent president, per the slogan, "It's the economy, stupid."

But that sort of economic focus often eluded the Romney campaign, which struggled to keep social issues at bay. Indeed, as the previous sections on religion and women and gays have indicated, social issues were often front and center during the 2012 contest. In late August, a popular political website mused over "Mitt Romney's Culture War Distraction" and noted, "The Campaign was supposed to be a referendum on President Barack Obama's stewardship on the economy. Instead, the past few weeks have been dominated by continuous eruptions of the debate over social policy" (Stein and Terkel 2012). While some Republicans worried that attention to social issues took time away from more politically promising economic matters, other Republicans "expressed confidence that this current bout of culture war nostalgia wouldn't trip up the presidential ticket" (Stein and Terkel 2012). Similarly, a headline in early September captured this dynamic as follows: "Even as culture fight dominates, Team Romney insists focus is still the economy" (McMorris-Santoro 2012).

Even when the campaigns did focus on economic issues, those issues often had a cultural slant. Americans had seen this before. Even though cultural politics can at times concern narrow or rarified issues that seem to be far removed from basic issues of political economy, economic issues have at times been a part of the culture wars. For example, in 2000 and 2004, a group called "Billionaires for Bush" staged protests to satirically support Bush's campaign, drawing attention to his support for policies that allegedly helped only the wealthy. More recently, writing about the effort in Wisconsin in early 2011 to balance the budget via sharp spending cuts and limiting workers' right to collective bargaining, David Brooks said, "See how quickly budget issues turn into culture wars?" (Brooks and Collins 2011). And in the first of the three presidential debates, Romney seemed to channel Ross Perot's moralistic deficit politics of two decades ago when he said of the federal debt, "I think it's not just an economic issue. I think it's a moral issue" (Bourgeois 2012).

Although the weak economy should have been an easy issue for Romney to exploit, his image as an experienced businessman who could improve Obama's economy and make it work for regular Americans was hurt by several developments. First, Romney refused to release most of his past tax returns, contrary to the norm for presidential candidates. This led to charges that he was secretly placing his considerable wealth in offshore accounts or had something else to hide. Second, the Obama campaign spent tens of millions of dollars on political advertisements over the summer portraying Romney as a rapacious capitalist out to benefit himself at the expense of regular people. For example, the TV ad "Stage" helped paint Romney as a cold-blooded executive at Bain Capital, as a worker at a paper plant recounted how he was paid to build a stage, on which Bain executives then announced that the workers would be fired.

Third, in September, a private recording was released of Romney saying that "47 percent of Americans are dependent on government" and "believe they are victims." The resulting media coverage fed into the caricature of Romney as an out-of-touch elitist who would neglect the poor and middle class while showering the wealthy with greater riches. David Brooks responded to Romney's comments in uncharacteristically caustic language: "Romney doesn't know much about the culture of America.... Romney doesn't know much about the political culture." Brooks further said, "Romney's comment is a country-club fantasy. It's what self-satisfied millionaires say to each other. It reinforces every negative view people have about Romney" (Brooks 2012). Indeed, Romney was subjected to a variety of unflattering comparisons to fictional wealthy characters: Thurston Howell, Richie Rich, Montgomery Burns, Daddy Warbucks, Ebenezer Scrooge, Mr. Potter, Gordon Gecko, and the Monopoly Man (Ostermeier 2012a). Shortly after the election, Romney reinforced his image as an instrumental politician uninterested in the needs of many Americans when he explained his defeat by claiming that Obama's campaign gave "extraordinary financial gifts from the government" to groups within the Democratic party's base, as if their votes were bought (Little 2012).

In previous elections, Democrats were often deterred from pushing issues of economic justice, such as progressive taxation, by conservative criticisms that they were engaging in "class warfare." For example, conservatives made that point in 2008, after Obama told "Joe the plumber" that progressive taxation was good because it helps "spread the wealth around" (Rohter and Robbins 2008). However, in 2012 this old polemic did not dissuade Obama from campaigning for higher taxes on wealthy Americans. Indeed, as Jonathan Chait put it, "If there is a single plank in the Democratic platform on which Obama can claim to have won, it is taxing the rich. Obama ignored vast swaths of his agenda, barely mentioning climate change or education reform, but by God did he hammer home the fact that his winning would bring higher taxes on the rich. He raised it so relentlessly that at times it seemed out of proportion. ... But polls consistently showed the public was on his side" (Chait 2012). This issue continued to be significant after the election, as Obama battled with the Republican House over tax increases to avoid the "fiscal cliff."

PART 3

As the foregoing brief discussion of four broad issue areas indicates, cultural politics and indeed the culture wars were a significant part of the 2012 presidential election cycle. Controversies about religion, women, gays, and the economy all had their own dynamics and particular issues, but they often had a cultural cast or were debated in the long-standing terms of the culture wars. But beyond the collection of vignettes discussed above, how can we best make sense of the overall nature of culture politics and the culture wars in the 2012 elections? Several possible conceptions or competing narratives suggest themselves. The following four accounts are multifaceted and are not mutually exclusive, nor are they exhaustive, but they offer plausible or perhaps persuasive ways of comprehending the contemporary condition of the culture wars.

More of the Same?

In some respects, it seems that the culture wars are now a regular part of American politics. And in part, this is because the themes of the culture wars tend to recur over time. Indeed, in the most recent election cycle, there were several flare-ups in the culture wars that seemed directly taken from the pages of history, or that at least had very close analogues from previous election cycles.

For example, during the GOP primaries, Newt Gingrich repeatedly called Obama the "food stamp president," as a record forty-six million

Americans participated in the Supplemental Nutrition Assistance Program. Gingrich's comments echoed those repeatedly made by Governor Ronald Reagan during his unsuccessful presidential campaign in 1976 about a "welfare queen" in Chicago who allegedly lied to receive generous benefits. Both politicians were trying to link governmental dependency and wasteful social spending to failed liberal policies (Bjerga and Oldham 2012). More controversially, they were both engaging in the old practice of using coded appeals to subtly utilize racism to appeal to working-class white voters.

In another repeat of old culture wars episodes, in December 2010 fears of a backlash from congressional Republicans forced the Smithsonian to cancel part of an exhibit on gay and lesbian themes. In fact, the artist in question, David Wojnarowicz, had been the target of nearly identical religious complaints back in the 1980s: in 1989 the American Family Association had complained to members of Congress about NEA support of his allegedly profane art, while in 2012 it was the Catholic League that articulated similar complaints to members of Congress. As an art reviewer in the *New York Times* bemoaned, "history is repeating itself" (Cotter 2010).

A third instance of a recurring culture war meme concerned the popular *Sesame Street* character Big Bird. In the first presidential debate, Romney indicated his desire to cut funding for PBS as part of a broad effort to reduce government spending, even though he professed his love for Big Bird. This remark echoed nearly identical episodes in the mid-1990s, when Bill Clinton repeatedly invoked the public's love for Big Bird to argue against House Republicans' plans to defund public broadcasting (Ostermeier 2012b; Overbey 2012). For example, in 1996, Clinton repeated a line from Senator John Glenn (D-OH): "You don't make America stronger by taking Big Bird away from 5-year-olds, school lunches away from 10-year-olds, summer jobs away from 15-year-olds, or student loans away from 20-year-olds." Romney no doubt was consciously invoking this earlier chapter of the culture wars, mimicking the old lines in order to indicate his allegiance with conservatives.

Fourth, in October 2012, the Obama campaign created an ad with Lena Dunham, the creator of the TV show *Girls*, using sexual innuendo to compare young women's first experience voting to "your first time," saying it should be with a "great guy" who understands and respects you (i.e., like Obama, not Romney). Some conservatives complained the ad was inappropriate, but as Maureen Dowd noted, "Ronald Reagan had a racier version 32 years ago" (Dowd 2012). In 1980, Reagan told a group of blue-color workers at a bar, "I know what it's like to pull the Republican lever for the first time, because I used to be a Democrat myself, and I can tell you it only hurts for a minute and then it feels just great" (Savan 2012).

The above four episodes were perhaps unusual in so closely replaying older spats in the culture wars, but they underscore the point that the culture wars are in many respects a constant and enduring fact of political life. Like classic pop songs, they are replayed over and over again and can be difficult if not impossible to escape.

Temporality

Even though the culture wars in 2012 often echoed, mimicked, or replayed the culture wars of previous decades, there is nevertheless something about them that is not timeless but rather time-bound. Specifically, the culture wars of 2012 were often couched—explicitly or implicitly—in terms of progress or regression, or how candidates' policies and worldviews are situated *vis à vis* the past, present, and future.

The temporal aspect of the culture wars can be seen in the campaign slogans of 2012. The Obama campaign's slogan was simply "Forward," as if the Republican alternative was necessarily backwards, with all that the word connotes. Not willing to concede the mantle of progress to Democrats, the main pro-Romney "super PAC" was called "Restore Our Future," perhaps an oblique reference to the popular 1985 film "Back to the Future," as if Obama were a present-day impediment to a prosperous future. Similarly, although Romney's official slogan "Believe in America" was less explicitly temporal, it arguably evoked a national greatness in both the past and the future, framing Obama's presidency as a temporary anomaly to be overcome. Of course, these temporal references are evocative of broader themes in American political culture, as politicians, pundits, and scholars have long debated what it is that progressives are progressing toward, or what it is that conservatives hope to conserve. This temporal language regularly crops up in debates about abortion, as pro-choice advocates say we must not "go back" to the days of back alleys

and coat hangers. Similarly, in terms of gay rights, Obama said his views were "evolving," as if acceptance were progressive and opposition were anachronistic and tied to a primitive past that has been adapted to and perhaps improved upon.

The above slogans and stereotypes figured in numerous attempts during the recent election cycle to use humor to political advantage by invoking unflattering caricatures of opponents' temporal status. For example, in his 2011 State of the Union speech, Obama used the phrase "winning the future" several times. He had appropriated the phrase from a 2005 book by Newt Gingrich, but other Republicans ridiculed the president's slogan. Governor Sarah Palin sarcastically used the colloquial shorthand expression "WTF" to ridicule Obama's catch-phrase (Jackson 2011).

In April 2012, David Axelrod derided Romney's allegedly retro policies: "I think he must watch *Mad Men* and think it's the evening news. He's just in a time warp.... Romney seems to look at the world through the rearview mirror. I mean, he wants to go back to the policies of the last decade on economics" (Dixon 2012). In October 2012, the comedian Dennis Miller joked about Romney's old-fashioned, "square" demeanor and 1950s-style diction, saying that after four years of having a postmodern "hipster president" in Obama, Americans might prefer a throwback "gosh president" like Romney (Barbaro and Parker 2012).

Even the candidates themselves engaged in these efforts, to score easy political points and to appear to have a sense of humor. Early in the third presidential debate, Obama invoked temporality to make the case for his campaign as follows: "We've now begun to make some real progress. What we can't do is go back to the same policies that got us into such difficulty in the first place. And that's why we have to move forward and not go back" (Federal News Service 2012). Romney responded, "I couldn't agree more about going forward, but I certainly don't want to go back to the policies of the last four years." At the end of the debate, Obama sarcastically told Romney, "The 1980s are now calling to ask for their foreign policy back.... You seem to want to import the foreign policies of the 1980s, just like the social policies of the 1950s and the economic policies of the 1920s" (Federal News Service 2012). In other words, Romney was a hapless and anachronistic retread of Reagan, Eisenhower, or even Coolidge, to say nothing of George W. Bush (Taranto 2012). Similarly, the weekend before the election, Vice President Joe Biden joked about the end of Daylight Savings time, saying, "It's Mitt Romney's favorite time of the year because he gets to turn the clock back" (Epstein 2012). And two days before the 2012 election, Romney belittled the Obama campaign's slogan and policies, telling a crowd in Iowa, "He calls them 'forward.' I call them 'forewarned'" (Epstein 2012).

After Obama's victory, commentators continued to press the theme of temporality via pop culture references. GOP strategist Chuck Warren said, "To be frank, we're a *Mad Men* party in a *Modern Family* world." Ross Douthat noted that liberals believed they had indeed won the future, as if "Republicans are now RadioShack to their Apple store, *The Waltons* to their *Modern Family*, a mediocre Norman Rockwell to their digital-age mosaic" (Douthat 2012c).

Beyond humor and pop culture, the questions of temporality also influenced the culture wars in terms of the perception of public opinion and demographics. In an op-ed in the *Washington Post* in October 2012, Harold Meyerson wrote, "The 2012 presidential election is fundamentally a contest between our future and our past. Barack Obama's America is the America that will be; Mitt Romney's is the America that was" (Meyerson 2012). For Meyerson, this distinction rested not just on Romney being fourteen years older than Obama, but on the related facts that younger voters disproportionately supported Obama while older voters disproportionately supported Romney and that younger voters held more liberal positions on social issues such as gay rights (Meyerson 2012). These points are related to another way of conceiving of the culture wars today, to which I now turn.

Prominence

While the culture wars in 2012 were certainly important, they were perhaps not quite as prominent as in some previous presidential elections, or at least they did not always rise to the same level of notoriety as in previous decades. There are several possible reasons for this. For example, it may be the case that today the culture wars are simply something that we have seen before, such that they are not new and hence not newsworthy. In other words, insofar as the culture wars in 2012 were just more of the same old thing, it is not surprising that they were not as prominent as they once were.

Second, cultural politics may now appear less prominent because it is arguably now a regular and enduring aspect of U.S. politics. Political culture has simply become a regular part of the broader American culture and a significant part of our lives. For example, Jon Stewart's faux news program *The Daily Show* attracts over 2.3 million viewers a night, including many young Americans who get much of their political information from the show (Jones 2010; Grondin 2012). Even pundits and pollsters are now part of the mainstream cultural discourse, "with *The New York Times's* Nate Silver now the talk of the sidelines at kids' soccer games" and the subject of interest in Hollywood (Hopkins 2012).

In addition to an increasingly politicized culture, more and more issues are in some sense cultural. And many issues have been captured by the culture wars to such an extent that they cannot be viewed without the lens of the culture wars. For example, as one professor lamented, "The public debate around climate change is no longer about science—it's about values, culture, and ideology" (Hoffman 2012).

Third, the actors in the culture wars may now be different and less visible. In particular, while in previous years organized interest groups were the primary actors, now it is arguably political parties. Specifically, on some accounts, the GOP has effectively subsumed or internalized parts of the old religious right. According to Clyde Wilcox, after the Christian Coalition collapsed, the Republican Party gradually stepped in to assume its functions: "Nearly all of the activities that the Christian Coalition conducted on behalf of George H. W. Bush in 1992 occurred again in 2004 on behalf of George W. Bush, but they were done by the party" (Wilcox 2009, 337–338). Developments since 2004 may have reinforced the institutionalization of culture war actors, and the lack of highly visible groups outside the political parties may render the struggles of the culture wars less visible.[4]

A fourth possible reason the culture wars seem less prominent is that they may be over, or rather one side has largely prevailed. By many post-election accounts, liberals have won the culture wars. For example, one week after the 2012 election, veteran cultural warrior Bill Bennett announced, "Republicans lost the culture war." Bennett said, "For decades liberals have succeeded in defining the national discourse," and that level of control translated into a Democratic victory in 2012. According to Bennett, as Republicans try to retool for the future, "we must address the problem at its source: the culture. Politics are downstream from the culture" (Bennett 2012). Similarly, a recent postelection article in a major British publication claimed that at least in terms of the issues of abortion, gay rights, and drug use, liberals "won the culture wars" (Enten 2012). In the *New York Times*, Thomas Edsall writes, "The right has lost the culture war.... To the dismay of the conservative movement, on virtually every burning issue that preoccupies the right, the country has moved steadily leftward." According to Edsall, "At the moment, in almost every region of the country except the South, the liberal stance is gaining adherents" (Edsall 2012). And Paul Waldman of *Salon.com* writes, "Liberals have won the culture war" (Waldman 2012). As one conservative Christian leader put it, "the entire moral landscape has changed.... An increasingly secularized America understands our positions, but has rejected them" (Goodstein 2012).

Beyond proclaiming liberal victory in the culture wars, some of the above journalistic accounts make the further point that liberals' successes with cultural issues now makes them the party more inclined to wage a culture war. Edsall says, "In many respects, the growing liberalization of America on social issues has made the culture war an attractive battleground for Democrats" (Edsall 2012). Similarly, Waldman writes, "when it comes to courting the American electorate, only one party wants to talk about traditional culture war issues, and it isn't the Republicans. It isn't that Republicans have changed their views about any of those issues. But they don't see any advantage in pushing them" (Waldman 2012). Thus, while Republicans used to happily run on "God, guns, and gays," they are now reticent to pursue cultural attacks. According to Phillip Gourevitch, "Today, solid majorities of Americans support gay rights, legal abortion, and women in combat. Yet the G.O.P. platform opposes them; the culture war that Buchanan trumpeted is no longer an insurgent cause but a permanent condition of the Republican Party, and, increasingly, it is being fought within the Party" (Gourevitch 2012).

Permanence
The culture wars have been declared dead, dormant, or decided many times before and yet have returned, and they are likely to do so again.

This is perhaps because the culture wars are permanent. As E. J. Dionne put it, "Is there a culture war in the United States? Of course. There always has been and always will be" (Dionne 2006). The question, then, is why the culture wars are so constant and enduring. Several answers suggest themselves. For example, perhaps the culture wars endure because culture is fundamental to politics, just as Bill Bennett suggested. Or as the popular website *electoral-vote.com* opined in September 2012, "the culture wars underlie everything in American politics" (Tanenbaum 2012).

Second, the culture wars may endure because parties and partisans have an interest in their continuation. Thus, the fight over cultural and social issues "energized core constituencies on both sides of the aisle who are accustomed to waging these fights on a biennial basis" (Stein and Terkel 2012). In other words, the culture wars persist because they excite parts of both parties' bases. As Douthat said, "in their heart of hearts, liberals love the culture wars, too" (Douthat 2010). This may be especially true now that liberals seem to be winning the culture wars.

Third, the culture wars may endure because there is something especially durable about the cultural aspects of American politics. Some of the episodes noted in this chapter may seem trivial, or more related to pop culture than to culture in a more constitutive sense, and no doubt some will quickly fade from memory. But others may well become a lasting part of the cultural iconography of American politics (Douthat 2012b). Indeed, the cultural aspects of politics may be longer-lived than the more substantive aspects of politics, perhaps because the former are more accessible or entertaining than the latter. As Ross Douthat wrote in early 2012:

> From election to election, politics is mostly about the economy and the state of the public purse—which is as it should be. But the arguments that we remember longest, that define what it means to be democratic and American, are often the debates over human life and human rights, public morals and religious freedom—culture war debates, that is, in all their many forms.... in the long run, no matter which side ultimately prevails, the debates that just re-erupted may do more to define how our era is remembered. (Douthat 2012a)

CONCLUSION

This chapter has surveyed the state of the culture wars in the 2012 presidential election by briefly situating the topic in a broader historical context, discussing four broad issue areas that factored into the culture wars during the election, and articulating four different ways of making sense of it all. The culture wars in 2012 were important, if somewhat less prominent, and echoed long-standing debates in American politics. As to whether America's culture war endures, evolves, or ends, only time will tell.

REFERENCES

Barbaro, M., and A. Parker. 2012. "Gosh, Who Talks Like That Now? Romney Does." *New York Times,* October 20.

Becker, J. 2012. "An Evangelical Back from Exile, Lifting Romney." *New York Times,* September 12.

Bennett, W. J. 2012. "Republicans Lost the Culture War." *CNN.com*, November 14.

Bjerga, A., and J. Oldham. 2012. "Gingrich Calling Obama 'Food-Stamp President' Draws Critics." *Bloomberg Businessweek,* January 25.

Boghani, P. 2012. "Democratic Platform Adds God, Jerusalem Amid Chaos." *Globalpost.com,* September 6.

Boorstein, M., and S. Clement. 2012. "Romney Won over White Evangelicals, Catholics, But They Weren't Enough to Win Race." *Washington Post,* November 7.

Bourgeois, J. 2012. "Presidential Debate: Morality, the Deficit, and Jim Lehrer." *Washington Post,* October 4.

Brooks, D. 2001. "One Nation, Slightly Divisible." *Atlantic Monthly,* December.

Brooks, D. 2004. "The Values-Vote Myth." *New York Times,* November 6.

Brooks, D. 2012. "Thurston Howell Romney." *New York Times,* September 17.

Brooks, D., and G. Collins. 2011. "Budget Wars or Culture Wars?" *New York Times,* February 23.

Buchanan, P. J. 1992. "Republican National Convention Speech." *Buchanan.org,* August 17.

Chait, Jonathan. 2012. "We Just Had a Class War." *New York,* November 11.

Chozick, A. 2012. "Beck Acts as a Bridge Between Romney and Evangelical Christians." *New York Times,* November 4.

Cooper, M. 2012. "Mourdock's Comments Pose Dilemma for Romney." *New York Times,* October 26.

Cotter, H. 2010. "As Ants Crawl Over Crucifix, Dead Artist Is Assailed Again." *New York Times,* December 10.

Dionne, E. J. 2006. "Why the Culture War Is the Wrong War." *Atlantic Magazine,* January/February.

Dixon, D. 2012. "David Axelrod: Mitt Romney's from 'Mad Men' Era." *Politico.com*, April 3.

Dodds, G. G. 2012. "Crusade or Charade? The Religious Right and the Culture Wars." *Canadian Review of American Studies* 42 (Fall).

Dombrink, J. 2012. "After the Culture War?" *Canadian Review of American Studies* 42 (Fall).

Douthat, R. 2009. "Faking Left." *New York Times*, May 12.

Douthat, R. 2010. "Why We Have a Culture War." *New York Times*, September 20.

Douthat, R. 2012a. "The Persistence of the Culture War." *New York Times*, February 7.

Douthat, R. 2012b. "President in Shining Armor." *New York Times*, October 28.

Douthat, R. 2012c. "The Liberal Gloat." *New York Times*, November 18.

Dowd, M. 2012. "Of Mad Men, Mad Women and Meat Loaf." *New York Times*, October 28.

Edsall, T. B. 2012. "The Culture War and the Jobs Crisis." *New York Times*, November 11.

Enten, H. J. 2012. "America's Roaring Twentysomethings: How Young Voters Won the Culture Wars." *Guardian*, November 13.

Epstein, J. 2012. "Biden: It's Romney's Favorite Time of Year ... He Gets to Turn the Clock Back." *Politico.com*, November.

Federal News Service. 2012. "Transcript of the Third Presidential Debate." *New York Times*, October 22.

Fiorina, M. P., et al. 2005. *Culture War?* New York: Longman.

Gagnon, F. 2012. "Ceasefire or New Battle? The Politics of Culture Wars in Obama's Time." *Canadian Review of American Studies* 42 (Fall).

Gigloff, D. 2007. *The Jesus Machine*. New York: St. Martin's Press.

Goodstein, L. 2012. "Christian Right Failed to Sway Voters on Issues." *New York Times*, November 9.

Gourevitch, P. 2012. "Republican vs. Republican." *New Yorker*, September 3.

Grondin, D. 2012. "Understanding Culture Wars Through Satire." *Canadian Review of American Studies* 42 (Fall).

Helderman, R. S. 2012. "Swing-State Suburban Voters Expected to Shape Election's Outcome." *Washington Post*, October 23.

Hoffman, A. J. 2012. "Climate Change as Culture War." *Stanford Social Science Review* (Fall).

Hopkins, D. 2012. "Election Reflections." *TheMonkeyCage.org*, October 29.

Hunter, J. D. 1991. *Culture Wars: The Struggle to Define America*. New York: Basic Books.

Hunter, J. D., and A. Wolfe. 2006. *Is There a Culture War?* Washington, DC: Brookings Institution.

Ivins, M. 1992. "Notes from Another Country: Republican Party Convention." *Nation*, September 14.

Jackson, D. 2011. "For Palin, Obama's 'Winning the Future' Phrase is WTF." *USA Today*, January 27.

Jones, J. 2012. "Gender Gap in 2012 Vote Is Largest in Gallup's History." *Gallup.com*, November 9.

Jones, J. P. 2010. "More Than 'Fart Noises and Funny Faces': *The Daily Show's* Coverage of the US Recession." *Popular Communication,* August 5.

Konczal, M. 2012."The Return of the Culture Wars!" Retrieved February 2, 2012 from https://us-intellectual-history.blogspot.ca.

Lindaman, K., and D. P. Haider-Markel. 2002. "Issue Evolution, Political Parties, and the Culture Wars." *Political Research Quarterly* 55 (1): 91–110.

Little, M. 2012. "Republicans Abandoning Romney over 'Gifts' Remark." *Los Angeles Times,* November 22.

Los Angeles Times. 1988. "Campaign '88: Dukakis Called 'Pagan' for Views, Jewish Wife." May 28.

Mak, T. 2012. "Santorum: JFK Speech 'Makes Me Want to Throw Up." *Politico.com,* February 26.

McConkey, D. 2001. "Whither Hunter's Culture War?" *Sociology of Religion* 52 (2): 149–174.

McMorris-Santoro, E. 2012. "Even as Culture War Dominates, Team Romney Insists Focus Is Still the Economy." *TalkingPointsMemo.com,* September 10.

Meyerson, H. 2012. "A Vote for the Future or for the Past?" *Washington Post,* October 30.

Oppel, R. A., Jr. 2012. "Santorum Questions Education System; Criticizes Obama." *New York Times,* February 18.

Ostermeier, E. 2012a. "Beyond Thurston Howell: Media Caricatures of Mitt Romney." Retrieved September 20, 2012 from http://blog.lib.umn.edu/cspg /smartpolitics/.

Ostermeier, E. 2012b. "Did Bill Clinton Launch the First 'Leave Big Bird Alone' Campaign?" Retrieved October 7, 2012 from http://blog.lib.umn.edu/cspg /smartpolitics/.

Overbey, E. 2012. "Mitt Romney, Big Bird, and the Million Muppet March." *The New Yorker,* November 23.

Perlstein, R. 2008. *Nixonland.* New York: Charles Scribner.

Redden, M. 2012. "Wingnut Theories on Rape and the Female Body: A Taxonomy." *New Republic,* October 24.

Rohter, L., and L. Robbins. 2008. "Joe in the Spotlight." *New York Times,* October 16.

Savan, L. 2012. "Lena Dunham's and Ronald Reagan's First Time." *Salon.com,* October 26.

Schulman, B. J. 2001. *The Seventies: The Great Shift in American Culture, Society, and Politics.* Free Press.

Silver, N. 2012. "When It Comes to Election-Year Gender Gaps, 2012 Ranks High." *New York Times,* October 21.

Stein, S., and A. Terkel2012. "Mitt Romney's Culture War Distraction: How a Job-Centric Campaign Got Sidetracked." *Huffington Post,* August 24.

Tanenbaum, A. S. 2012. "Romney: 47 Percent Dependent on Government." Retrieved September 18, 2012 from http://www.electoral-vote.com/evp2012/pres/maps/sep18.html.

Taranto, J. 2012. "Insane Anglo Warlord." *Wall Street Journal,* October 23.

Torregrosa, L. L. 2012. "U.S. Culture War with Women at Its Center." *New York Times,* April 3.

Waldman, P. 2012. "Have Republicans Lost the Culture War?" *Salon.com,* September 10.

Wilcox, C. 2009. "Of Movements and Metaphors: The Coevolution of the Christian Right and the GOP." In *Evangelicals and Democracy in America*, Vol. 2, edited by S. Brindt and J. R. Schroedel, 331–356. New York: Russell Sage Foundation.

Williams, R. 2012. "Immigration and National Identity in Obama's America: The Expansion of Culture Wars Politics." *Canadian Review of American Studies* 42 (Fall).

NOTES

1. The academic literature on the culture wars is vast, but my own scholarship has been informed especially by the following works: Hunter (1991), McConkey (2001), Lindaman and Haider-Markel (2002), Schulman (2001), Fiorina et al. (2005), Hunter and Wolfe (2006), Gigloff (2007), Perlstein (2008), Dodds (2012), Gagnon (2012), Dombrink (2012), Williams (2012), and Grondin (2012).

2. Re: school prayer, see *Engel v. Vitale* (1962) and *Abington School District v. Schempp* (1963). Re: racial discrimination in education, see *Green v. Connally* (1970), *Coit v. Green* (1971), and *Bob Jones University v. U.S.* (1983).

3. In April 2008, in the midst of his primary contest with Senator Hillary Clinton, Obama engaged in his own political-cultural stereotypes, as he confidentially explained his difficulty appealing to small-town working-class white voters as follows: "They get bitter, they cling to guns or religion or antipathy to people who aren't like them or anti-immigrant sentiment or antitrade sentiment as a way to explain their frustrations."

4. However, in 2009, Ralph Reed, who led the Christian coalition in the early 1990s, formed the Faith and Freedom Coalition in an effort to use high-tech data mining to identify and mobilize some two million new social conservative voters. Reed sought to appeal to a broad range of religious affiliations and to focus on economic issues, not just standard social issues (Becker 2012). After the election, Reed commented that his organization had done as about as much as it possibly could, as it circulated thirty million voter guides in 117,000 churches, sent out twenty-four million mailings, and made twenty-six million phone calls in battleground states (Goodstein 2012).

III. Rhetoric

Chapter 6

The Irrelevance of Truth
Postrhetorical Campaigning and the 2012 Conventions

Justin S. Vaughn, Boise State University

INTRODUCTION

In mid-October, as the 2012 election hurtled toward its culmination, a pair of political journalists issued observations in British periodicals of the state of the ongoing American presidential campaign that were remarkable not only for their prescience but also their accidental overlap. Separated by a week and included in separate media outlets, the two reports covered the lack of substance in first the Romney and later the Obama campaigns. On October 13, a piece published in *The Telegraph* and authored by American centrist/Republican writer John Avlon (2012) identified the ongoing struggle in the campaign as one between "narrative and facts" and lambasted the Romney/Ryan ticket for its tendency to saber-rattle without offering concrete specifics concerning its own foreign policy governing agenda.

A week later, Mark Mardell, North American editor for BBC News, acknowledged the criticism over Romney's lack of a manifesto before contending that Obama's campaign was even more guilty in this area and questioning whether this lack of substance was genuine or merely the function of campaign strategy. Mardell (2012), who has covered elections on both sides of the Atlantic for decades, wrote: "This is the first of the very many elections I have covered, in Britain and Europe, where the person in power doesn't make some firm promises about exciting new stuff they would do if they win again." He continued:

> It's not that President Obama hasn't said what he'd do, or that there's absolutely nothing new—it's just that what he is highlighting in speeches has the feeling of "keeping on, carrying on." It gives the campaign a quite different feel to that in 2008 when the suggestion was America was on the edge of a sparkling new future filled with possibility.

It would seem clear, then, that neither major party candidate did a commendable job of offering a clear and specific picture of what his administration would do after inauguration, though the verdict is out about *why* this was the case. Although Mardell does not really answer the question he poses about the motivation for the Obama campaign's agenda opacity, the overarching argument of this chapter seeks to provide one.

I argue that we have entered an era of what I and other scholars have termed "the postrhetorical presidency" (see Mercieca and Vaughn 2009; Hartnett and Mercieca 2007) and that campaigns for the presidency have increasingly taken a similarly postrhetorical turn in recent cycles. To demonstrate the presence and pervasiveness of the postrhetorical dimensions of the 2012 presidential campaign, I offer an analysis of what is perhaps the most postrhetorical component of any contemporary presidential election: the major party conventions. In doing so, I introduce three key characteristics of the postrhetorical campaign and identify their inclusion in the 2012 Democratic and Republican National Conventions. I conclude by offering observations on the normative consequences of this development and commentary on the direction future research should follow.

WHAT IS THE POSTRHETORICAL PRESIDENCY?

Scholarship concerning presidential leadership, particularly that which relates to linkages with the mass public, has long been shaped by the central ideas of Jeffrey Tulis's (1987) seminal work, *The Rhetorical Presidency*. In it, Tulis argued that early twentieth-century presidents—

namely Theodore Roosevelt and, especially, Woodrow Wilson—began to regularize the process of going around Congress and speaking about policy matters to the mass public directly, a fundamental departure from previous experience (Ellis 1998, 2). This led to a new model of presidential leadership, one best elaborated in Samuel Kernell's equally seminal *Going Public* (1986) and based on observations made by Richard Neustadt (1990), in which presidents strategically approached the public for support for their policy initiatives, support that would then lead to pressure—electoral and otherwise—on legislators to do the president's bidding.

For the next two decades, the "going public" and rhetorical presidency constructs became fundamental in the field of presidential studies. In recent years, however, both academic analysis and the activities of American presidents have caused many to reevaluate the explanatory power of these arguments. In particular, even as presidents do "go public," evidence that they are successful at doing so has proven to be rare, highly conditional, and fleeting (see Edwards 2003, but also Quirk 2007, Canes-Wrone 2006, and Rottinghaus 2010, forthcoming). Further, as Susan Herbst (2007) argues in a special double-issue of the influential journal *Critical Review* that was dedicated to the twentieth anniversary of the publication of *The Rhetorical Presidency*, the opportunities for significant presidential leadership via rhetoric are now likely limited to moments of extreme drama and national crisis, such as after the tragic events of 9/11. Indeed, because of a range of reasons—including, but not limited to, dynamics in presidential approach, audience, and the media filter between them—Herbst (2007, 337) goes so far as to pronounce presidential speech as "dying, and possibly even dead."

In this chapter, I stop short of such a declaration; I should, in fairness, also note that Herbst (2007, 342) later refers to her ominous phrasing as "somewhat exaggerated," too. Instead, I contend—building on the aforementioned previous work by Jennifer Mercieca, Stephen Hartnett, and myself—that the intersecting combination of declining effectiveness and a changing media/audience environment has driven our most recent presidents to adjust their rhetorical performance in such a significant manner that we are no longer in the age of the rhetorical presidency, but rather a postrhetorical one. This is a clear reference to and departure from Tulis's construct, which argued that presidents go around Congress and to the public in a Constitution-subverting attempt to lead the policy process. In the postrhetorical era, presidents no longer engage in this leadership model, both because of its futility and because they have different strategic aspirations. This (d)evolution of the going public model of leadership is driven by its increasing impossibility in an era of "white noise" and gaps between elite goals and mass preferences. Similarly, counter to Zarefsky's (2004, 611) claim, any previously possessed presidential power of reality definition has slipped away; instead, presidents occupy a political and cultural space defined less by what they can do than what they cannot, a list that includes not only the act of command (Neustadt 1990), but also the ability to persuade (Edwards 2003). Instead, the president today "does not define reality but fantasy . . . does not energize citizens but numbs them . . . does not attempt to inform and teach but instead dumb down and stupefy" (Hartnett and Mercieca 2007).

Previously, Jennifer Mercieca and I argued that the postrhetorical presidency was characterized by the use of presidential speech as a way "to distract and stymie the mass public" using techniques "designed to confuse public opinion, prevent citizen action, and frustrate citizen deliberation" (Mercieca and Vaughn 2009, 33–34). This utilization of rhetoric not for the purposes of policy leadership but rather as a strategic feint remains driven by presidential ambition. Indeed, this creation of "a pathology of vacuous rhetoric" (Lim 2008, 4), which is guided by a desire to seduce and obfuscate, simultaneously undermines public competence while enhancing the likelihood of presidential goal achievement. In sum, presidents operating in the postrhetorical era still utilize the communication tools of the modern institution, but no longer do so expressly in order to lead the policy process, but rather to *perform* presidential leadership while the business of governing is done elsewhere and generally out of the masses' field of vision.

CAMPAIGNING TO GOVERN IN THE POSTRHETORICAL ERA

The central argument in this chapter is that just as presidential public leadership efforts have (d)evolved from a going public model to a postrhetorical one, so too have the electoral campaigns waged to win control of the White House. If a rhetorical presidency based on appealing to public support for an agenda is preceded by a rhetorical campaign in which candidates make specific policy promises, the postrhetorical campaign features all of the talk with far less of the substance, akin to the postrhetorical in-term practices discussed above.

The idea that campaigns have become less substantive in recent years is not a new one, especially in recent cycles, nor is it a terribly controversial one (see, for example, Page 1978, Patterson 1980, Maisel, West, and Clifton 2007; though see also Geer 1996 and Claibourn 2011). Even those scholars who contend that the condemnation contemporary campaigns receive is overblown, or at least not fully deserved, must articulate fairly nuanced explanations in defense of their positions. For example, Michele Claibourn (2011), who contends that campaigns talk quite a bit about issues, also notes the *way* they talk about issues fails to engender meaningful issue debate. As Claibourn (2011, 41–42) notes: "Policy proposals are commonly released but not hyped by the candidates (or the media). The policy details and the campaign pledges are for coalition building, to appeal to segments within a party. They are not really intended for the voters at large except to signal seriousness about an issue." A campaign with "issue talk," as Claibourn (2011, 43) conceptualizes policy rhetoric without specific policy substance, fails to indicate priorities and commitments, a particular problem when most agenda items offered by either side of the aisle are rehashed boilerplate concerning the same revolving handful of salient and longstanding key issues. This emphasis on valence issues provides voters cues about whom to support, but does so without fully explicating the precise nature of the candidates' plans, something particularly problematic when campaigns today focus on a very small range of issues. The upshot is that today's presidential candidates talk about issues in a constrained and generic way that is geared toward manipulating emotional responses rather than justifying the nuances of concrete policy agenda items.

This observation dovetails with Lim's (2008) analysis of presidential speech, especially in what he refers to as "the substantive impoverishment of presidential rhetoric" (54). As Lim shows, "presidents have taken the rhetorical path of least resistance" and in doing so have offered "an easily digestible substantive menu devoid of argument and infused with inspirational platitudes, partisan punch lines, and emotional and human interest appeals" (54). As pathos has risen at the expense of logos in presidential speech in the months and years between elections, it also has done so in the campaign season leading up to every fourth November. This blurring of the lines has been noticed elsewhere, of course, and particularly in volumes concerning the permanent presidential campaign (Doherty 2012; Heith 2012; Ornstein and Mann 2000). If anything, this chapter flips the emphasis of these studies, noting that just as aspects of electoral politicking have crept into every nook and cranny of the institutional presidency, so too have behaviors associated with performing the presidency bled into the organized efforts to acquire the institution.

These behaviors are particularly evident when considering what Lempert and Silverstein (2012) have termed the "institutionalized calendrics" at work in electoral contests. Key events take place during election campaigns, generally in predictable intervals, some with considerable fanfare and, occasionally, considerable consequence. Such events include, in particular, candidate debates, key primaries and caucuses (i.e., Iowa, New Hampshire, more recently Nevada and South Carolina, the mammoth Super Tuesday), and the events that mark the end of the nomination season and the beginning of the final sprint to the Election Day finish line, the party conventions. The latter is the analytical focus of this chapter, the location where we search for evidence of a postrhetorical campaign.

WHY CONVENTIONS?

Once the site of the most important determinations (in terms of both candidate selection and platform content) in a presidential election year, for decades the major party conventions have strayed ever farther from their original purpose. Some of this is because of campaign reforms, while the advent of ever-sophisticated media coverage has also incentivized a turn away from the substantive. For these reasons and others, the major party conventions have not been deliberative institutions for more than forty years, and 2012 marked the sixtieth anniversary of the last time it took more than one ballot for a candidate to win nomination (Sizemore 2010, 1).

Instead, conventions today are rife with moments that are little more than "political stagecraft, carefully choreographed for television audiences and reporters, [that serve] only to validate results preordained months before" (Sizemore 2010, 1). They have evolved into "made-for-television political advertisements designed to market the parties' brands and their nominees for popular consumption. In the modern era, primary voters and caucus participants nominate presidents and conventions have become coronation ceremonies" (Sizemore 2010, 1).

As modern political conventions have become "marketing events aimed at the November electorate" (Sizemore 2010, 27), the functions they serve have accordingly changed. Today, conventions are designed to bolster personal candidate strengths, answer any lingering questions the voters might have about a candidate's character, and attack the strengths while exploiting the weaknesses of the opponent, all while emerging from the convention with greater levels of popular support than when the events began. Lacking, of course, from this set of objectives is any reference to elucidating or explaining key attributes of policy positions. Nevertheless, the elites in charge also verify these new objectives as the key to a successful convention. Take a recent example from the aforementioned Democratic convention in Denver: in a postelection interview, David Plouffe noted that the two goals going into the 2008 convention were "humanizing" then-candidate Obama and to "lay some wood" to McCain (Miller 2009, 156; see also Kenski, Hardy, and Jamieson 2010, 131; Mercieca and Vaughn 2009, 47). McCain's goals were similar, with the added necessity of introducing to the nation recently announced vice presidential candidate Sarah Palin, who at that point was a little-known governor from Alaska. In 2008, both the Obama and McCain campaigns generally accomplished these objectives, with vote preference increasing for each candidate following his respective convention (Kenski, Hardy, and Jamieson 2010, 148).

Bill Kennedy (2012), a Maryland-based writer, provides an optimal grassroots-level view of this new role for conventions in an article authored as the 2012 postconvention dust began to clear:

> The circuses have left town in Tampa and Charlotte and it's time for all of the clowns to go on the road to try to drum up interest in their particular favorite ringmaster. Of course, I refer to the Republican and Democratic Party conventions as the circuses. Both parties' get-togethers were about showing their chosen candidate in the best light without actually telling us voters what their plans were or how they intended to fulfill their promises.

Folksy vernacular aside, Kennedy's evaluation of the contemporary convention as a phenomenon primarily driven by the desire to sell a candidate without actually fleshing out the policy platform upon which that candidate stands is apt and an accurate rendering of what we could call the postrhetorical convention. Because of the characteristics of the contemporary convention, it marks the ideal location at which to search for evidence of postrhetorical campaigning. In the next section, I identify the characteristics of the postrhetorical campaign, and then assess the presence of these characteristics in each major party's 2012 convention.

ASSESSING THE POSTRHETORICAL CONVENTION

If we are to determine whether and how campaigns in general and conventions in specific have become postrhetorical, we must first have some idea of what a postrhetorical campaign/convention entails. Based on the previous discussion of the postrhetorical concept, what we should expect is not the absence of rhetoric, but rather rhetoric utilized for new and alternative purposes. If, as I (along with Jennifer Mercieca) have previously argued, presidential (and presidential candidate) rhetoric is now strategically designed not to lead but rather to stymie, confuse, and frustrate, we ought to be able to observe specific ways in which this occurs.

IDENTIFYING THE CHARACTERISTICS

I contend that this is the case, and I have identified three key characteristics that should be found in postrhetorical presidential and candidate rhetoric. These include the deployment of (often sensational) distractions, a lack of policy substance, and the manipulation of information that ranges from questionable to overt dishonesty. Audiences who are on the receiving end of postrhetorical messages that contain these characteristics will not only remain uninformed, but also find their attention directed away from the substantive dimensions that matter while they are fed information that leaves them less competent to be meaningfully involved in the business of governance. Stated simply, postrhetorical convention moments combine to direct audience attention toward the unimportant while avoiding policy substance and trading in misinformation.

Deployment of Distractions

The first of these characteristics, the utilization of distraction, is perhaps the most obvious and easiest to detect. In the postrhetorical era, presidential candidates compete for votes not primarily by emphasizing the details of their policy agendas, but by deflecting attention away from it. Such deflection is only possible, however, if there is something more interesting, or at least entertaining, to direct voters' attention toward. Occasionally, opportunities present themselves that can be subsequently exploited by enterprising campaigns; for example, recall the political hay George H. W. Bush's campaign made of Michael Dukakis riding in a tank, a stunt that itself was essentially a distraction. Other recent examples of exploited opportunities in this vein include George W. Bush's 2004 campaign's dissemination of photographs of John Kerry wind-surfing and the 2008 Obama campaign's push for prolonged discussion about former Democratic vice presidential nominee (and then–Hillary Clinton supporter) Geraldine Ferraro's potentially racially insensitive comments about its candidate. Another apt example of the latter is the 2008 McCain campaign's adoption of Samuel Wurzelbacher (aka "Joe the Plumber"), who rose to notoriety following a heated exchange with then-candidate Barack Obama as he was stumping in Ohio. Examples from 2012 abound, but most notably include the Obama team's focus on Mitt Romney's unfortunate practice of strapping his dog to the roof of his car and the Romney campaign's full court press on both Obama's (stripped from context) "you didn't build that" quote and the terrorist action at the nation's diplomatic compound in Benghazi, Libya, along with the Republican candidate's tacit consent (though not official embrace) of billionaire Donald Trump's antics, which ranged from stoking the fires of birtherism to a crusade for Obama to release his undergraduate transcripts.

More often, however, distractions are planned out and strategically deployed. These examples occur in a wide range of forms, from sensationalized advertisements (the most sensational of which are designed not even to be aired on television, but simply to be covered by a hungry media looking for ratings and desperate to fill news holes) to the recruitment and support of particular surrogates whose purpose is less to foster citizen deliberation than to incite confusion and angst. The most noteworthy and attention-grabbing of these distractions frequently involve popular culture celebrities, who are positioned both to give candidates a certain cachet that has nothing to do with their policy agendas and also to carry negative messages forward in a way that allows candidates to appear, at least superficially, as if their hands are clean. The role of celebrity surrogates in presidential elections is not a new phenomenon, of course, but the proliferation of them and the focal roles they have begun to play illustrate a shift from the rhetorical to the postrhetorical era.

Lack of Policy Substance

To suggest that the 2012 campaign was utterly bereft of substance would be as inaccurate as would be a claim that all campaigns prior to the postrhetorical era were replete with policy minutia and little else. It is a matter of course that campaign rhetoric blends substance with style; after all, every platform needs a narrative and every policy initiative demands to be cloaked with a digestible trope to ensure public consumption. The difference regarding substance between the rhetorical and postrhetorical eras is in balance and proportion. Rather than use narrative to explain and advance understanding of policy proposals, the postrhetorical candidate emphasizes style almost exclusively. Such is the difference between, say, "the New Deal" as a frame that organized a range of disparate policies beneath a central narrative umbrella and "hope and change" (Obama's slogan in 2008) or "restore our future" (a key Romney campaign phrase in 2012). These recent examples from both sides of the aisle communicate nothing about the platforms of the candidates beyond a vague notion of being distinct from the incumbent party.

The absence of substance—and, conversely, the overwhelming focus on the immaterial—was impossible to miss in 2012. Indeed, seasoned observers Maggie Haberman and Alexander Burns noted that despite the 2012 campaign being perhaps the most important in a generation, it was also the "smallest." According to Haberman and Burns (2012):

> The Obama and Romney campaigns spend all day strafing each other on Twitter, all while decrying the campaign's lack of serious ideas for a serious time. Yet at most junctures when they've had the opportunity to go big, they've chosen to go small. Obama has spoken in broad strokes about his accomplishments but has not yet outlined a detailed agenda

for a second term. Romney has openly declared that he will not detail his policy proposals—slashing the size of government, for example—so as to avoid giving his opponents ammunition. Instead, they have embraced a campaign that has been defined almost entirely by tactics and daily trench warfare, whether that's the chair of the Democratic Party labeling Romney a "job cremator" or the Romney campaign driving its campaign bus in circles around an Obama event honking the horn, in a stunt right out of a third-tier frat house. Some antics satisfy their partisans but don't focus the national dialogue.

Haberman and Burns identified the linkage between the lack of policy substance and the rise of the politics of distraction, as discussed previously. Their analysis remained focused on the broader contours of campaign politics, but concentrating on the individual events that make up a campaign can also reveal example after example of instances when presidential candidates and their campaign elites forewent the opportunity to embrace substance and instead chose to pursue the nebulous and symbolic. Nowhere is this more discernible than in the actual words of the candidates themselves.

Overt Dishonesty and Questionable Manipulation of Information

When presidential candidates and their campaigns are not attempting to distract convention audiences or avoid substantive matters, the information they do provide is often woefully inaccurate. The proliferation of high-profile fact-checking services indicates the growing awareness in at least the mainstream media of presidential campaign duplicity, or at the very least, a tendency for campaigns to play fast and loose with the facts. By the end of the 2012 campaign, one was hard-pressed to find a single major campaign event, from convention addresses to debate responses, where either candidate offered statements that were unquestionably true and accurate. Instead, the bulk of their messages were fraught with "facts" that ranged from somewhat off-the-mark to flagrantly and knowingly dishonest.

In recent years, scholars have become increasingly attuned to presidential deception, with analyses ranging from the empirical (Pfiffner 2004; Alterman 2004) to the theoretical (Mearsheimer 2011). In previously referenced earlier work on the postrhetorical presidency, Jennifer

Mercieca and I (2009, 35–38) discussed the role of intentional lies in the postrhetorical era. We acknowledge there that although it is typically impossible to know conclusively whether a president is lying (only the alleged deceiver can ever know that fact), we can rest reasonably well upon the consensus of fair-minded observers. In that essay, we also reference Wayne Booth's (2004) concept of "rhetrickery," which he defines as the art of *producing* misunderstanding. Although there is a clear conceptual (and possibly moral) difference between issuing falsehoods and manipulating information to produce misunderstanding, both are consistent with this dimension of the postrhetorical era. This is particularly so because providing an audience with false or manipulated information in order to sell people on an idea or candidate is the antithesis of sincere rhetorical practice, where information is provided in order to persuade the audience of a position's righteousness. Much as one cannot truly win a debate with lies, one cannot truly persuade without factual rigor. In this sense, the postrhetorical candidate, like the postrhetorical president he seeks to remain/become, is uninterested in persuasion and deliberation, but instead only in seeking control, a fundamentally antidemocratic difference.

Having identified the three key postrhetorical characteristics, I now turn to examining the two campaigns' rhetorical performance in the 2012 major party conventions. I proceed in the order the conventions occurred, beginning with Mitt Romney and the Republicans and concluding with Barack Obama and the Democrats.

ANALYZING THE REPUBLICANS

There was considerable evidence of a postrhetorical campaign throughout the Republican National Convention (RNC), which was held August 27–30, 2012, in Tampa, Florida. Indeed, the convention was sensationalized from the outset, both by natural events beyond the RNC's control (e.g., forced delays because of Tropical Storm Isaac) and by staged political acts, such as party chairman Reince Priebus's calling the convention to order on Monday, August 27, in order to start a "debt clock," only to gavel the convention into recess (until the next day) ten minutes later. Further, the convention's daily themes—"We Can Do Better," "We Built It," "We Can Change It," and "We Believe In America"—reveal the generic focus of the party's messaging. As would be expected in a postrhetorical convention, the content was long on filler and short on substance; indeed, the platform itself was hammered out prior to the convention and merely approved at the convention itself.

The Romney campaign maintained strict control over content, as well, including demanding right of review of nominee runner-up Ron Paul's address and the Texas congressman's full endorsement in exchange for a speaking slot (Paul refused). The speeches that were approved alternated between tossing red meat to the conservative audience (i.e., key addresses by Republicans such as governors John Kasich of Ohio, Chris Christie of New Jersey, and Nikki Haley of South Carolina) and attempting to humanize candidate Romney (Harris and Burns 2012); the latter was the primary objective of the speech delivered by Romney's wife, Ann, the objective of which, according to journalist Lois Romano (2012), was "to try to accomplish what the sharpest minds in Republican politics have failed to do: present her stiff and awkward husband as a likeable guy."

Also among the roster of speakers at the convention were the expected gaggle of candidates for state and federal office, party functionaries, and business leaders. There were a few relatively unexpected additions to that list of usual suspects, however, including Filipino boxing champion Manny Pacquiao (a successful politician in his own right), Neal Boyd (the 2008 champion of NBC's *America's Got Talent* competition program), actress Janine Turner (best known for her role as Maggie O'Connell on the CBS series *Northern Exposure*), and Clint Eastwood, the famous actor/filmmaker/one-time mayor, whose surprise role was unveiled after days of the party touting a "mystery guest." These nontraditional, and in some cases obscure, appearances were consistent with the postrhetorical practice of distraction. Their presence was not arranged to foster the audience's understanding of Romney's policy agenda nor was it designed to further citizen deliberation; these individuals were there to entertain even if officially under the auspices of leadership.

This was especially true for Eastwood's performance, which was not only secretly teased for days in the run-up to his actual appearance, but also elicited such a bewildered response from viewers that its dada-esque nature not only received immediate satirical attention but also overshadowed Romney's own acceptance address later that same evening. Ironically, Eastwood's off-the-cuff interrogation of an empty chair, which was to represent President Obama, was one of the only moments not carefully controlled by the Romney team. In this case, the campaign's strategic deployment of celebrity-driven distraction backfired, drowning out the candidate's own message and providing multiple cycles of unfavorable media coverage.

Although the set of RNC speeches as a whole received criticism for being heavy on bluster and light on meaningful content (see Rothkopf 2012), it was Mitt Romney's own speech, delivered on the closing night of the convention, that most exemplified the second characteristic of the postrhetorical campaign: lack of policy substance. The speech began with a focus on humanizing his candidacy, something consistent with the previous days of the convention, and did so quite well. What the speech did not do well, or much at all, was talk in detail about what a Romney presidency would offer the American people (see Corn 2012). As Jonathan Cohn (2012b) wrote in *The New Republic*:

> The first two-thirds of the speech played on emotion: Romney talked about America, his own life, and his (professed) disappointment that Obama didn't succeed. Then he turned to policy—and devoted all of 200 words to his economic plan, at least by my count. I don't think the passage lasted more than three minutes. It certainly didn't contain a lot of detail. It was, instead, a recitation of Romney's five-point plan—a mix of nonsense proposals, like making North America energy independent, plus sweeping but unspecific promises to reduce the deficit, reduce taxes and reduce regulations.

Cohn continued: "Convention acceptance speeches don't have to be wonky. Nominees use these speeches primarily to introduce themselves to the voters and to lay out the broad themes of what they hope will be their presidencies. But, in this case, the lack of specificity is of a piece with Romney's whole campaign." Other observers lambasted not only Romney's lack of specificity about those policies he did mention, but his avoidance entirely of other major issues facing the nation, most notably the absence of any reference to the ongoing military conflict in Afghanistan. This de-emphasis on substance was not accidental or mere oversight, but apparently rather strategic, having become an aspect of Romney's campaign well before the conventions started (Klein 2012). As Anthony Resnick (2012) noted, "The strategy heading into the Republican Convention seemed to be threefold: highlight the failures of the Obama administration, make Romney look more human, and say as few substantive things as possible." In short, it was in keeping with the previously discussed dictates of the postrhetorical campaign.

If the Republican convention lacked substance, it certainly did not lack prevarication, the third pillar of the postrhetorical presidential campaign. Beyond the broad disingenuousness of having a key campaign theme based on a purposeful misquote of the president (i.e., the infamous "you didn't build that" quote; see Chandler 2012), many of the specific addresses made during the Republican convention fared poorly when assessed by the ubiquitous fact-checkers of the 2012 campaign.[1] It was vice presidential candidate and member of the U.S. House of Representatives Paul Ryan, however, whose speech proved to be the most glaringly inaccurate and dishonest.

Critiques of Ryan's speech ranged from mentioning the vice presidential nominee's use of "factual shortcuts" (AP) to deeming it "breathtakingly dishonest" (*Washington Post*) and full of "brazen lies" (*Salon*) to questioning whether it was the most dishonest convention speech ever (*The New Republic*) and hailing it as an examplar of the "post-truth convention speech" (*The Atlantic*). *The New York Times* published a 1,200-word fact-checking essay by Michael Cooper (2012) that detailed numerous misstatements and untruths on Ryan's part, from condemning Obama for the shuttering of an automotive plant in his Wisconsin hometown that occurred during the George W. Bush administration to a series of factually dubious claims about Obama's debt commission and auto bailout, the reasoning behind the downgrade of the nation's Standard & Poor's credit rating, and future plans for Medicare solvency, among other statements.

Ryan's willingness to traffic in half-truths and falsehoods marked a new frontier in the expansion of campaign dishonesty, previously primarily limited to negative advertising. As Cohn (2012a) observes, "At least five times, Ryan misrepresented the facts. And while none of the statements were new, the context was. It's one thing to hear them on a thirty-second television spot or even in a stump speech before a small crowd. It's something else entirely to hear them in a prime time address, as a vice presidential nominee is accepting his party's nomination and speaking to the entire country." That these factual evasions and manipulations of information took place on one of the biggest stages of the election year marks how far postrhetorical campaigning had advanced in the Republican effort to win back the White House. As the next section of this chapter shows, however, Republicans were not the only party engaging in postrhetorical politics.

ANALYZING THE DEMOCRATS

Similar to the Republican National Convention, the three identified characteristics of the postrhetorical campaign were on display throughout the Democratic Party's 2012 gathering, which was held September 4–6 in Charlotte, North Carolina. Possessing the power of incumbency and not having to deal with a major tropical storm, the Democrats were able to approach their convention on a more even keel. This is not to say, however, that the convention was without its momentary shake-ups and scrambling. With comparatively little notice, the Obama campaign scrapped its plan to have the president deliver his acceptance address outdoors at Bank of America Stadium and instead held it indoors, despite little real threat of stormy weather, in a venue with less than one-third the capacity, a move some observers attributed not to meteorological motivation but rather concern over being unable to fill the seventy-two-thousand-seat outdoor stadium. Moreover, this would not be the only problem football stadiums posed for the Democrats: the National Football League had to reschedule the season's kickoff game to accommodate the president's speech and, in turn, the campaign had to move Vice President Joe Biden's address up earlier in the convention to avoid interfering with that rescheduled match between the New York Giants and the Dallas Cowboys.

Beyond these adaptations, the Obama campaign matched the Romney team in its effort to control the convention agenda. Among the dozens of vetted speakers on the convention's multiday roster were the kinds of speakers routinely featured at the DNC, a mix generally filled with Democratic candidates for offices around the nation, party and business elites, union leaders, and liberal activists. Sprinkled among these typical participants were numerous otherwise undistinguished speakers, identified as "teachers," "mothers," "students," "grandmothers," "veterans," and so on, "regular" citizens who could testify in an unsophisticated way about the merits of Obama's leadership, a parade of everymen and -women strategically deployed to communicate moral authority. Chief among this group were speakers like Maria Ciano, a "stay-at-home mother and former Republican voter" and Benita Veliz, the first person to address a major party convention while illegally residing in the United States; these and others were given access to the podium not to communicate the details of what might be a second Obama administration's policy agenda, but instead to communicate visually and symbolically to key voter groups—in this case, so-called "soccer moms" and Latinos—the righteousness of a vote for the incumbent. These speakers were complemented by former "employees" of Romney's Bain Capital firm—at least one of which never actually worked at Bain, but was in fact employed at the time by the United Steelworkers of America as a regional director charged with representing steelworkers employed by GST Steel, a Kansas City plant then controlled by Bain (Karl 2012).

Nevertheless, at least with these "regular" speakers there was some policy linkage with the Obama campaign's vague platform. However, another group of individuals were featured for the same reason their names appear in bold in tabloid news coverage: celebrity. In this case, the DNC meeting outdid the RNC; not only were there more Hollywood stars on the roster, but one was even a campaign co-chair (Eva Longoria, best known for her star turn on ABC's *Desperate Housewives*). Featured celebrities included award-winning actress Scarlett Johansson (*Lost in Translation, The Avengers*), whose address received a prime speaking slot on the evening of Obama's nomination between Representative James Clyburn and Democratic scion Caroline Kennedy; actress Kerry Washington (*The Last King of Scotland, Django Unchained*); and well-known Latina journalist and Spanish-language talk show host Cristina Saralegui. Despite Longoria's role as co-chair and Johansson's high-profile assignment, the most influential celebrity of the convention was arguably actor Kal Penn, who is best known for his role in the Harold & Kumar stoner comedy films, and who also has worked in spurts between films in the Obama White House's Office of Public Engagement. In addition to delivering his own speech at the convention, Penn was tasked with hosting coverage of the convention and leading a Web-only convention program emphasizing celebrity support for Obama (Bendery 2012). In the run-up to the convention, Penn and Obama also produced a campaign video that featured the president soliciting by phone a strong convention performance from Penn, who, it hinted, was high on drugs at the time and watching cartoons with actor John Cho, Penn's partner on the Harold & Kumar films.[2]

There was also considerable evidence of the second postrhetorical campaign characteristic (lack of substance) on display during the Democratic National Convention. Just as observers assailed Romney's speech for lack of substance, so too were many campaign-watchers disappointed by the relative emptiness of Obama's nomination acceptance address in Charlotte. Conservative commentator Charles Krauthammer, admittedly no supporter of Obama's quest for a second term, declared that he was stunned by the absence of policy detail: "There was nothing in it...there was nothing in there that tells us how he's going to go from today to tomorrow" (FOX News Insider 2012). Such critique may be expected— and even dismissed—coming from an avowed conservative and clear opponent of the president. However, observers with far less of a stake in the partisan game—not to mention the president's own allies—also expressed similar observations. For example, *Business Insider* referenced the speech as "mediocre and largely void of substance" while *National Journal* featured a piece by award-winning journalist Ron Fournier (2012) that declared the speech fell short due to its lack of specificity. Even liberal journalist Kevin Drum (2012) wrote in progressive outlet *Mother Jones* that Obama's speech was too full of disconnected riffs, "short collections of platitudes with no real meat behind them and no promise of what a second term might bring."

If the lack of substance was on par with the RNC and the utilization of celebrity distractions exceeded it, the DNC probably featured somewhat less informational manipulation and dishonesty. This is not to say that the Democratic convention resembled a choir of angels, but only that none of the speeches in Charlotte demonstrated the level of disingenuous that characterized Paul Ryan's speech in Tampa. Even so, fact-checkers found much to be desired in the Democrats' performance. For example, throughout the convention numerous speakers repeatedly referenced inaccurate numbers concerning how a Romney presidency would financially burden senior citizens with increased Medicare costs, while other misinformation referenced false Massachusetts job creation statistics during Romney's time in the governor's office there and inaccurate statements about Romney's personal tax records (Memmott 2012; see also Wemple 2012).

The convention's keynote speaker, San Antonio mayor Julian Castro, received the most criticism for his flexibility with the facts. Although the frequency and degree of his misstatements may not have equaled Ryan's, objective observers pointed out multiple "factual shortcuts," including a claim that Romney would raise taxes on middle-class Americans. Although one might be able to argue either side of that hypothetical, another statement made by Castro was clearly false: he stated that 4.5 million new jobs had been created under Obama's leadership; in actuality, the economy had only regained 4 million of the 4.3 million jobs that had been lost since Obama's inauguration (Memmott 2012). In sum, the three characteristics of the postrhetorical campaign were present, if at varying degrees from the RNC, at the Democratic Party's convention, as well.

CONCLUSION

The preceding analysis shows that both major party conventions were filled with postrhetorical moments, moments that combined to avoid meaningful policy discussion while (and by) distracting the audience, both in the convention halls and watching in their living rooms at home, with celebrity-driven distractions and by misinforming viewers, often deliberately, about the positions of the presidential and vice presidential candidates as well as those of their opponents. This has an unfortunate and deleterious effect on the quality of American democracy, as voter competence is undermined and linkages between promises and performance become muddled and disjointed. As political scientist Jamie Chandler (2012) notes:

> Herein lies the rub of a modern election campaign. Campaigners default so quickly to what they perceive as easy ways to win votes, they forget that the truth of the message is one of the most crucial determinants of

victory. Our political elite has placed such a focus on propaganda this season that we simply lack the requisite information to cast an informed vote in November.

Clearly, as the contemporary convention has transitioned from a traditional emphasis on deliberation to one exclusively centered on spectacle (Sizemore 2010, 19), it represents ground zero for the postrhetorical campaign. This also, however, presents a potential critique to the very notion of the postrhetorical campaign. Conventions are particularly well suited to postrhetorical practices, so the possibility remains that the postrhetorical practices that manifest there may be less present in other electoral arenas. The extent to which postrhetorical characteristics are present in other aspects of the contemporary presidential campaign remains an open question and one that should be the subject of future research. This is particularly true not only for campaign advertisements, which scholars have studied, but also debate rhetoric and candidate stump speeches. Future scholarship should also go beyond descriptive analysis of key sources of rhetoric; it should also examine the factors that drive the postrhetorical phenomenon and investigate both its point of departure and dynamics over time. Until scholars are able to more fully analyze the causes and consequences of postrhetorical campaigning, we must be vigilant in assessing precisely what campaigns are saying to voters—and what they are not saying—and stay attuned to the implications this holds for American democracy and republican governance.

REFERENCES

Alterman, E. 2004. *When Presidents Lie: A History of Official Deception and Its Consequences.* New York: Penguin.

Avlon, J. 2012. "U.S. Election 2012: Why Mitt Romney Is All Talk and No Substance on Foreign Affairs." *Telegraph,* October 13. Retrieved from http://www .telegraph.co.uk/news/worldnews/us-election/9606617/US-election-2012 -why-Mitt-Romney-is-all-talk-and-no-substance-on-foreign-affairs.html.

Bendery, J. 2012. "Obama Teams Up with Kal Penn in New Campaign Video." *Huffington Post,* September 4. Retrieved from http://www.huffingtonpost. com/2012/09/03/kal-penn-obama-video_n_1852809.html.

Booth, W. C. 2004. *The Rhetoric of Rhetoric: The Quest for Effective Communication.* New York: Blackwell.

Canes-Wrone, B. 2006. *Who Leads Whom? Presidents, Policy, and the Public.* Chicago: University of Chicago Press.

Chandler, J. 2012. "Though Convention Humanized Romney, It Lacked Substance." *U.S. News & World Report*, August 31. Retrieved from http://www.usnews.com /debate-club/was-the-republican-national-convention-a-success-for-mitt -romney/though-convention-humanized-romney-it-lacked-substance.

Claibourn, M. P. 2011. *Presidential Campaigns and Presidential Accountability*. Urbana, IL: University of Illinois Press.

Cohn, J. 2012a. "The Most Dishonest Convention Speech…Ever?" *New Republic*, August 29. Retrieved from http://www.newrepublic.com/blog/plank/106730 /ryan-most-dishonest-convention-speech-five-lies-gm-medicare-deficit -medicaid.

Cohn, J. 2012b. "Romney's Closing, Obama's Opening." *New Republic*, August 31. Retrieved from http://www.newrepublic.com/blog/plank/106750/romney -convention-speech-economic-no-policy-details-jobs#.

Cooper, M. 2012. "Fact-Checking Ryan's Convention Speech." *New York Times*, August 30. Retrieved from http://thecaucus.blogs.nytimes.com/2012/08/30 /in-ryan-critique-of-obama-omissions-help-make-the-case/.

Corn, D. 2012. "Will Obama Take Advantage of Romney's Big Convention Mistake?" *Mother Jones*, September 5. Retrieved from http://www .motherjones.com/politics/2012/09/obama-dnc-speech-charlotte.

Doherty, B. 2012. *The Rise of the President's Permanent Campaign*. Lawrence, KS: University Press of Kansas.

Drum, K. 2012. "Did Obama Phone It In?" *Mother Jones*, September 6. Retrieved from http://www.motherjones.com/kevin-drum/2012/09/obama-phones-it -dnc-finale.

Edwards, G. C. III. 2003. *On Deaf Ears: The Limits of the Bully Pulpit*. New Haven, CT: Yale University Press.

Ellis, R. 1998. *Speaking to the People: The Rhetorical Presidency in Historical Perspective*. Amherst, MA: University of Massachusetts Press.

Fournier, R. 2012. "Why Obama's Great Speech Fell Short." *National Journal*, September 13. Retrieved from http://www.nationaljournal.com/2012 -conventions/why-obama-s-great-speech-fell-short-20120906.

FOX News Insider. 2012. "Analysis: Charles Krauthammer Calls Obama's DNC Speech "One of the Emptiest I've Ever Heard on a National Stage."" *FOX News Insider*, September 6. Retrieved from http://foxnewsinsider.com/2012/09/06 /analysis-krauthammer-calls-obamas-dnc-speech-one-of-the-emptiest-ive -ever-heard-on-a-national-stage/.

Geer, J. G. 1996. *From Tea Leaves to Opinion Polls*. New York: Columbia University Press.

Haberman, M., and A. Burns. 2012. "The 2012 Campaign Is the Smallest Ever." *Politico*, June 20. Retrieved from http://www.politico.com/news/stories /0612/77620.html.

Harris, J. F., and A. Burns. 2012. "Mitt Romney RNC: GOP Still Frets about Candidate's Image." *Politico*, August 28. Retrieved from http://www.politico .com/news/stories/0812/80230.html.

Hartnett, S. J., and J. R. Mercieca. 2007. "A Discovered Dissembler Can Achieve Nothing Great; or, Four Theses on the Death of Presidential Rhetoric in an Age of Empire." *Presidential Studies Quarterly* 37: 599–619.

Heith, D. J. 2012. *The Presidential Road Show: Public Leadership in an Era of Party Polarization and Media Fragmentation.* Boulder, CO: Paradigm.

Herbst, S. 2007. "The Rhetorical Presidency and the Contemporary Media Environment." *Critical Review* 19 (2–3): 335–343.

Karl, J. 2012. "Steelworker Featured at DNC Didn't Work for Bain." *ABC News,* September 6. Retrieved from http://abcnews.go.com/blogs/politics/2012/09 /steelworker-featured-at-dnc-didnt-work-for-bain/.

Kennedy, B. 2012. "Conventions Lack Substance." *Carroll County Times,* September 17. Retrieved from http://www.carrollcountytimes.com/columnists/opinion /bill_kennedy/bill-kennedy-conventions-lack-substance/article_d6967334 -9849-5f18-9830-772ac83fbe25.html.

Kenski, K., B. W. Hardy, and K. H. Jamieson. 2010. *The Obama Victory: How Media, Money, and Message Shaped the 2008 Election.* Oxford: Oxford University Press.

Kernell, S. 1986. *Going Public: New Strategies in Presidential Leadership.* Washington, D.C.: CQ Press.

Klein, E. 2012. "The Massive Policy Gap between Obama and Romney." *Washington Post,* August 6. Retrieved from http://www.washingtonpost.com/blogs /wonkblog/wp/2012/08/06/the-massive-policy-gap-between-obama-and -romney/.

Lempert, M., and M. Silverstein. 2012. *Creatures of Politics: Media, Message, and the American Presidency.* Bloomington, IN: Indiana University Press.

Lim, E. 2008. *The Anti-Intellectual Presidency: The Decline of Presidential Rhetoric from George Washington to George W. Bush.* Oxford: Oxford University Press.

Maisel, L. S., D. M. West, and B. M. Clifton. 2007. *Evaluating Campaign Quality: Can the Electoral Process Be Improved?* New York: Cambridge University Press.

Mardell, M. 2012. "Barack Obama Makes Few Promises in 2012 Campaign." *BBC News,* October 20. Retrieved from http://www.bbc.co.uk/news/world-us -canada-20017136.

Memmott, M. 2012. "Democrats Unleashed Some 'Dubious or Misleading Claims,' Fact Checkers Say." *NPR,* September 5. Retrieved from http://www.npr.org /blogs/itsallpolitics/2012/09/05/160591872/democrats-unleashed-some -dubious-or-misleading-claims-fact-checkers-say.

Mercieca, J. R., and Justin S. Vaughn. 2009. "The Post-Rhetorical Legacy of George W. Bush." In *Perspectives on the Legacy of George W. Bush*, edited by Michael Orlov Grossman and Ronald Eric Matthews, Jr., 31–52. Newcastle upon Tyne: Cambridge Scholars Publishing.

Mearsheimer, J. J. 2011. *Why Leaders Lie: The Truth about Lying in International Politics.* Oxford: Oxford University Press.

Miller, A. F., ed. 2009. *Campaign for President: The Manager's Look at 2008.* Lanham, MD: Rowman & Littlefield.

Neustadt, R. E. 1990. *Presidential Power and the Modern Presidents.* New York: Free Press.

Ornstein, N., and T. Mann, eds. 2000. *The Permanent Campaign and Its Future.* Washington, DC: AEI Press / Brookings.

Page, B. I. 1978. *Choices and Echoes in Presidential Elections: Rational Man and Electoral Democracy.* Chicago: University of Chicago Press.

Patterson, T. E. 1980. *The Mass Media Election: How Americans Choose Their President.* New York: Praeger.

Pfiffner, J. P. 2004. "Did President Bush Mislead the Country in His Arguments for War with Iraq?" *Presidential Studies Quarterly* 34: 25–46.

Quirk, P. J. 2007. "When the President Speaks, How Do the People Respond?" *Critical Review* 19 (2–3): 427–446.

Resnick, A. 2012. :Judging the Party Conventions." *Construction,* September 12. Retrieved from http://www.constructionlitmag.com/politics/election-2012 /judging-party-conventions/.

Romano, L. 2012. "Ann Romney's Task: Humanize Mitt." *Politico,* August 28. Retrieved from http://www.politico.com/news/stories/0812/80221.html.

Rothkopf, D. 2012. "GOP Speeches Bluster, Not Substance." *CNN,* August 29. Retrieved from http://www.cnn.com/2012/08/29/opinion/rothkopf-gop -convention/index.html.

Rottinghaus, B. 2010. *The Provisional Pulpit: Modern Presidential Leadership of Public Opinion.* College Station, TX: Texas A&M University Press.

Rottinghaus, B. Forthcoming. "Overcoming Institutional Burdens: President Obama's Rhetorical Leadership in His First Year." In *The Rhetoric of Heroic Expectations: Establishing the Obama Presidency,* edited by J. S. Vaughn and J. R. Mercieca. College Station, TX: Texas A&M University Press.

Sizemore, J. 2010. "Conventions: The Contemporary Significance of a Great American Institution." In *The Year of Obama: How Barack Obama Won the White House,* edited by L. J. Sabato, 1–30. New York: Longman.

Tulis, J. K. 1987. *The Rhetorical Presidency.* Princeton, NJ: Princeton University Press.

Wemple, E. 2012. "Obama and Biden Speeches: Fact-Checking Yields Substance." *Washington Post,* September 7. Retrieved from http://www.washingtonpost. com/blogs/erik-wemple/post/obama-and-biden-speeches-fact-checking -yields-substance/2012/09/07/7889562a-f897-11e1-8398-0327ab83ab91_blog .html.

Zarefsky, D. 2004. "Presidential Rhetoric and the Power of Definition." *Presidential Studies Quarterly* 34 (3): 607–619.

NOTES

1. The full RNC coverage of the Annenberg Public Policy Center's Factcheck.org project can be found online at http://www.factcheck.org/tag/republican-national-convention/. Similarly, all posts related to the DNC meeting can be found online at http://www.factcheck.org/tag/democratic-national-convention/.

2. The video can be viewed online via the official BarackObama.com YouTube channel at http://youtu.be/h7O_ADbgQ8k.

Chapter 7

The Politics of Inequality
How Team Obama Appealed to the Base in the 2012 Presidential Election

Matthew R. Miles, Brigham Young University–Idaho

INTRODUCTION

Two approaches dominate efforts to mobilize voters in support of presidential candidates. One approach focuses on appealing to the center to persuade "swing" voters to support a candidate. Since the party base is likely to support the party candidate regardless and the same is true of the opposing party's base, resources are best used to convert the undecided, ideologically moderate voters to support one side's candidate (Stimson 2004; Mayer 2007; Calmes and Harwood 2004). Downs (1957) theorized that this is the ideal election-winning strategy. The "base-mobilization" strategy is another approach, used more recently, which ignores the broader electorate and focuses on mobilizing a candidate's core supporters to win the election (Dowd 2012). In 2004, the Bush team spent almost half of its budget on efforts to mobilize the base, which was three times the 2000 budget for similar efforts (Morton 2006). The Democratic Party's strategy for winning Ohio in 2004 also involved considerable effort to mobilize partisans in densely populated urban areas and Democratic suburbs at the expense of trying to convert undecided voters in other areas (Bai 2004). Contrary to Downs, recent campaigns seem to be using targeted efforts to mobilize key elements of the parties' bases (Issenberg 2012). Indeed, some reports suggested that in the final weeks of the 2012 election Team Obama spent nine out of ten dollars on mobilizing the base (Horsley 2012).

To some extent, the competition between the two approaches is moot. As a Democratic strategist recently reminded me, campaigns are interested in both mobilizing the base and converting undecided moderates to support their policy positions. However, successful campaigns strategically choose to emphasize some issues at the expense of others in attempts to accomplish one of these two goals. Given a bell-shaped distribution of voter preferences, no one strategy will successfully accomplish both goals of mobilizing the base *and* appealing to "swing" voters simultaneously. As such, the positions candidates take and the emphasis they place on particular issues during a political campaign provide important information about which strategy a candidate is employing to secure electoral victory.

In December 2011, President Obama traveled to Osawatomie, Kansas, to commemorate a speech given a century earlier by Teddy Roosevelt and to lay out his vision for the coming election. President Obama argued that, in essence, this was a make-or-break moment for the middle class. His speech emphasized that the high level of income inequality in the United States was hurting current middle-class families and creating an atmosphere that would prevent future generations from climbing out of poverty and into the middle class, regardless of how hard they might work. In addition, he proposed changing the country's tax code to eliminate loopholes and shelters that allow the wealthiest 1 percent to avoid paying their fair share in taxes. Finally, he argued that enacting laws aimed at making sure everybody plays by the same rules, investing in education, and shaping a tax code that makes everybody pay their fair share were the keys to rebuilding the economy (Obama 2011). These themes were so central to the Obama reelection campaign that each of them was mentioned in the president's closing statement in the third and final presidential debate of 2012 (Obama and Romney 2012).

President Obama may have chosen to highlight economic inequality in the United States in order to rally his base and increase the probability that these voters would turn out to vote for him on Election Day. If so, this would provide support for the proposition that the focus of Obama's 2012 campaign was on his base. Another possibility is that President Obama decided to highlight economic inequality in America in order to persuade "swing" voters to vote for him. If this is true, it would support the position that the focus of Obama's 2012 reelection campaign was on the political center. This distinction is significant. The focus of a presidential election campaign has considerable influence on the policies presidents pursue *after* the election (Halperin and Harris 2006; Levendusky 2010).

Since campaign managers are reluctant to reveal their actual strategies, aims, and approaches, for they regard such information as trade secrets (Issenberg 2012), I employ a deductive approach of inferring the strategy employed based on the outcomes produced by the strategy. Though it is possible that Team Obama miscalculated or failed to accomplish its purpose with a particular strategy, I will assume that the campaign team collected sufficient data throughout the 2012 campaign that some change of message would have occurred between December 2011 and the concluding remarks of the final televised presidential debate had the strategy been identified as being off-target.

In the remainder of this chapter, I explore the effect that the rhetoric of inequality had on public opinion. Using data gathered in a survey experiment in the summer of 2012, I find that source cues (the person delivering the message) was a more influential determinant of policy support than the content of the message. Although the message of inequality resonated with those from every part of the political spectrum, partisans seemed to attend more to the messenger than the message.

INEQUALITY RHETORIC AS AN APPEAL TO THE CENTER

There is good reason to presume that Team Obama's inequality rhetoric was designed to appeal to swing voters and persuade moderates to support President Obama. While some argue that the voting public has become more polarized over the last decade (Abramowitz 2010; Abramowitz and Saunders 1998), others argue that the public is no less extreme in their ideological positions, but the dominant parties seem to offer a polarized set of electoral options from which to choose (Fiorina and Abrams 2009). To some extent this debate hinges on how one treats survey respondents that identify as political independents, but indicate in a subsequent question that they lean closer to the Democrat or Republican parties. Rather than viewing independent leaners as "hidden" partisans, Dalton (2013) argues that partisan leaning is a reflection of short-term partisan preferences. He estimates the number of truly independent voters to be roughly 20 percent of the electorate. This group of voters (termed "Apartisan") is much more likely to choose a candidate based on candidate qualities and policy positions than are the partisans (those that identify with either the Republican or Democratic Party in the initial question). These voters are politically knowledgeable, aware, and make their political decisions based on other criteria than partisans (Dalton 2013). In a race that was decided—in key states—by less than 1 percent of the popular vote, the potential to persuade some portion of 20 percent of the electorate to support one's candidate cannot be ignored.

Income inequality could be the ideal issue to convert Apartisans to support President Obama. Over the last several decades, concern about the rising level of income inequality in America increased substantially (Bartels 2008). Moreover, concern about income inequality does not seem to be a concern chiefly among Democrats (Page and Jacobs 2009). Polls taken in November 2011 showed that two-thirds of Democrats and independents perceived the gap between the wealthy and the poor to be much larger than it has been historically, and 58 percent of self-identified independents thought that the federal government should pursue policies that reduce the wealth gap between the rich and the poor ("November Monthly—Obama/Economy/2012 Presidential Election" 2011). In addition, the poll found that 30 percent of Republicans were supportive of federal government intervention to reduce the level of income inequality in America.

Though Republican support for policies that reduce the wealth distribution gap in America may seem surprising given the traditional lack of Republican support for such policies, this assumption may be misguided. Analyses of the 1984 presidential election showed that support for Reagan was in large part driven by perceptions that he would govern more fairly than Mondale. Citizens voted not merely based on the personal benefits they hoped to receive from the candidate, but Reagan supporters in particular judged the candidates based on their perceived records of procedural fairness (Rasinski and Tyler 1988). Though Republicans in America may be supportive of policies that *increase* income inequality because they lack sufficient political sophistication to understand the implications of their issue positions (Bartels 2008, 186), an alternative view is that they nonetheless support such policies because of their concern about fairness. Indeed, Page and Jacobs (2009) show that a majority of Republicans and the wealthy are supportive of more evenly distributing money and wealth. Thus a priori there is no reason to presume that Team Obama chose to place significant emphasis on economic inequality in the 2012 presidential election to do anything other than appeal to the center and persuade "swing" voters to support their candidate on Election Day, congruent with Downs (1957).

INEQUALITY RHETORIC AS AN APPEAL TO THE BASE

Two weeks before Election Day 2012, Matthew Dowd (the chief architect of the base-mobilization strategy for the Bush 2004 campaign) argued that the 2012 presidential race more closely resembled that of the 2004 race than the 1984 race. He saw changes in demographics that indicated that the 2012 election would be determined by the degree to which each campaign successfully mobilized its base (Dowd 2012). Microtargeting is a voter mobilization technique, first used by Romney in his gubernatorial campaign in 2002, which uses statistical analyses of consumer, demographic, and political information on each individual within a household to identify the messages and techniques that will encourage specific individuals to turn out on Election Day. The Bush 2004 reelection team invested considerable resources into microtargeting specific voters in key swing states, Team Obama used it in 2008, and both Romney and Obama utilized these tactics in their 2012 campaigns (Issenberg 2012). Microtargeting is typically used to encourage those who would vote for a candidate, but are not likely to vote, to make the decision to come to the polls and vote on Election Day.

However, rallying the base can also generate broad support among likely voters. Levendusky (2010) argues that individuals with ideological or issue positions that are out of line with that of their political party are sensitive to the positions taken on issues by party elites. For example, a conservative Democrat might be concerned about the level of economic inequality in the United States, but be unwilling to support redistributive tax policies because they are not congruent with his or her ideological leanings. Similarly, a liberal Republican might share the concerns about economic inequality in America, but be unwilling to support redistributive tax policies because they are not congruent with the platform of the Republican Party. When party elites take a position on an issue heretofore ignored by the party, constituents notice these positions and adjust their own positions accordingly. In rare circumstances, individuals will adjust their party identification to match that of their ideological or issue position (as when a liberal Republican becomes a Democrat). Most often, though, people change their ideological or issue positions to conform to their partisan identity (as when a conservative Democrat becomes more liberal). As this process is replicated over a series of elections, the voting public gradually sorts themselves such that their ideology more closely matches the ideological position of their chosen political party (Levendusky 2010).

The most relevant finding is that once a person is sorted he becomes a stronger partisan than he was previously. The process of sorting predicts that instead of being the Apartisan ideal envisioned by Dalton (2013), independent leaners gradually become stronger partisans as they adjust their independent views to conform more closely to that of the political party. Thus, instead of a growing group of politically active, sophisticated voters who change their support for candidates between elections depending on the quality of the candidates or the campaign, sorting predicts fewer partisan leaners and smaller overlap between the issue positions of the political parties. Since the number of independent voters depends on how one defines the term, the existing evidence could support either theoretical approach to an election. Sorting implies that this growth in independent leaners provides an opportunity for a campaign to convert Democrat-leaners into strong Democrats by taking a position on an issue heretofore ignored, causing these individuals to shift their own ideological and issue positions to that of their party leader.

VALUES VS. PARTISANSHIP

Democrats and Republicans may have different values. The differential support for wealth redistribution policies between the parties could be a function of the differing values rather than a partisan-related calculus. If partisans differ in value orientations, perceptions of system fairness are a likely mechanism that explains the difference. Rasinski and Tyler (1988) showed that support for President Reagan in the 1984 election was motivated by perceptions that he would govern more fairly than Walter Mondale. The concept of procedural fairness is distinct from distributive fairness, in part because outcomes do not influence evaluations of procedural fairness. Republicans tend to support unequal political outcomes if they perceive the process leading to the outcome to be fair (Lind and Tyler 1988).

The degree to which institutions operate in a manner perceived to be procedurally fair influences public trust in and support of the institutions. Similarly, procedural fairness influences public support for a variety of policy proposals. Evaluations of the fairness of an economic system may influence individual support for redistributive policies in that system. However, Republicans might be more responsive than Democrats to the fairness of the process leading to the inequality. Stated more formally, partisan attachment might mediate the relationship between evaluations of fairness and support for redistributive tax policies. Procedural fairness might influence Democrats' and Republicans' support for policies differently (H1).

METHODS AND ANALYSIS

It is now common practice to use experimental manipulation to explore causal mechanisms behind relationships of interest (Druckman 2011). Thought experiments are particularly effective at examining the role of values and beliefs without the biasing influences of self-interest and group membership (Fishkin 1996; Mitchell et al. 2003). In the summer of 2012, I conducted a nationally representative survey experiment to explore the attitudes and values of Americans regarding income inequality. One portion of the experiment asked respondents to make assessments about income inequality in a hypothetical system and report on the preferred course of action to correct the inequality. Individuals were randomly assigned to one of the conditions described in Table 7.1. The first condition represents inequality caused by market forces, the second condition represents inequality caused by differences in training opportunities, and the final condition represents inequality caused by differences in political participation.

Table 7.1 Text Used in the Experimental Manipulations

Market Forces	Lack of Training	Political Participation
There is a high level of economic inequality in Society Beige. *The reason for the gap is the market economy. Everyone has the same opportunity for economic advancement, but some work harder than others.*	There is a high level of economic inequality in Society Beige. *The reason for the gap is that some sections of the labor force are not adapting to changes in the economy. They were trained for jobs that no longer exist and they do not have the opportunity to be trained for better, higher paying jobs.*	There is a high level of economic inequality in Society Beige. *The reason for the gap is a difference in political participation. Those with more money have more time and opportunity to contact their elected officials. The wealthy are more likely to vote, have opinions on the issues, and let their elected officials know their stance on the issues.*

We would expect that partisanship would not influence support for raising taxes on the wealthy in these hypothetical systems, but rather that support for raising taxes would be influenced by the degree to which the system operates fairly, however partisanship might mediate that relationship (H1). Market forces are perceived by most to be a fair process of allocating goods and services. Certainly more conservative individuals would be more likely to favor this as a fair process of allocating goods and services. Inadequate training could be perceived as an unfair process by some, but it could also be viewed as a result of poor individual choices. The political participation condition is the only condition that clearly represents unfair procedures of governance. When those who are wealthy are benefiting disproportionally because they are able to exert unequal influence over the political process, people would be expected to express lower ratings of the fairness of the system.

Respondents were told that this hypothetical system was considering "a tax proposal that will significantly increase the amount of taxes paid by the wealthiest 1 percent and help reduce the gap between the rich and poor." Respondents indicated how much they agreed with the proposal on a scale from one to ten with higher values indicating stronger agreement with the proposal. Figure 7.1 plots the mean scores by treatment

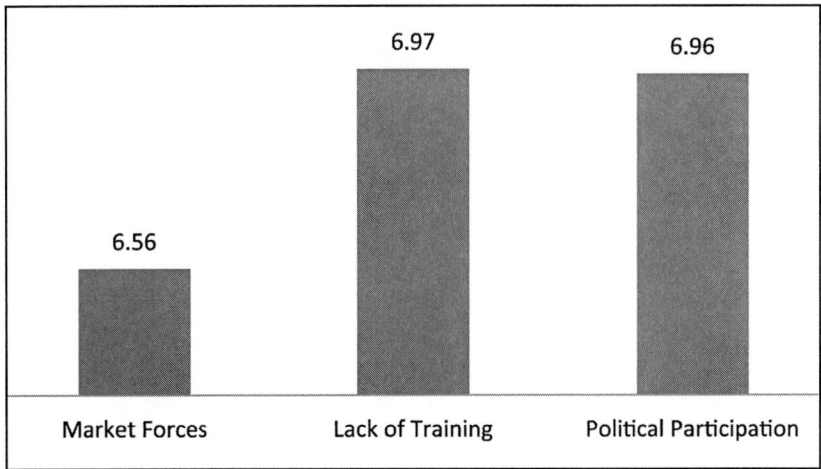

Figure 7.1 Support for Raising Taxes on the Wealthy in a Hypothetical System

Note: Entries represent mean scores on a scale where 1 represents complete disagreement and 10 represents complete agreement with the statement. The difference between market forces and the other two conditions is statistically significant at the p < 0.05 level.

condition. On average, those in the political participation treatment condition and the lack of training treatment condition were significantly more supportive of raising taxes on the wealthy than those in the market forces treatment condition. Subsequent analysis suggests that stems from individual perceptions of fairness. Those in the lack of training and the political participation conditions evaluated the hypothetical system of government to be much *less* fair than those in the market forces treatment condition (Figure 7.2). This suggests that when people think that the process leading to income inequality in a system is unfair, they are *more* supportive of higher taxes on the wealthy.

Do partisans respond differently to the treatments? Figure 7.2 illustrates the findings from a pooled regression analysis that included interaction terms for perceptions of fairness and party identification. In the full sample (all treatment conditions), Democrat support for raising taxes on the wealthy is not related to perceptions of system fairness; something else is causing them to support raising taxes on the wealthy. However, Republicans and Independents are significantly *less* likely to support raising taxes on the wealthy when they perceive the process leading to

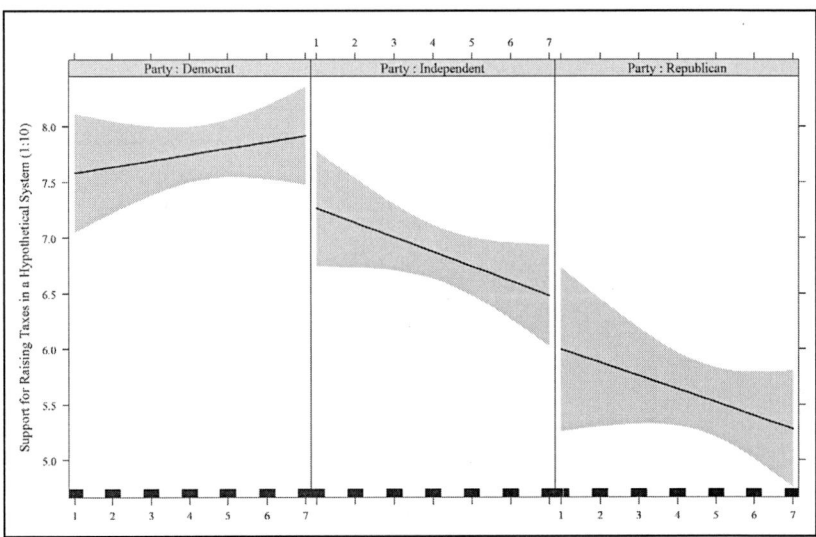

Figure 7.2 Partisanship as a Mediator of the Relationship between Concern about Income Inequality and Support for Raising Taxes on the Wealthy in a Hypothetical System

Note: Simple slopes plotted using the effects package in R 2.14. Gray bars represent the 95% confidence interval of the estimate.

the income inequality gap to be fair than they are when they perceive it to be unfair (H1). This suggests that procedural fairness matters more to independents and Republicans than it does to Democrats. When independents and Republicans perceive the process leading to wealth inequality to be unfair, they are more supportive of redistributive tax policies, at least in a hypothetical system. In addition, all subgroups are more supportive of raising taxes on the wealthy in order to reduce income inequality when they perceive the process leading to the gap to be unfair.

The broad opposition expressed by Republicans for raising taxes on the wealthy does not result from a difference in values. Given the proper motivation, Republicans could be expected to support raising taxes on the wealthy. The next section thus explores whether those conditions are present in the United States. Figure 7.3 displays the results of a simple t-test between treatment groups in the hypothetical system and evaluations of the United States.

The growth of wealth inequality over the last two decades is well documented. Do Americans perceive the process leading to the inequality in

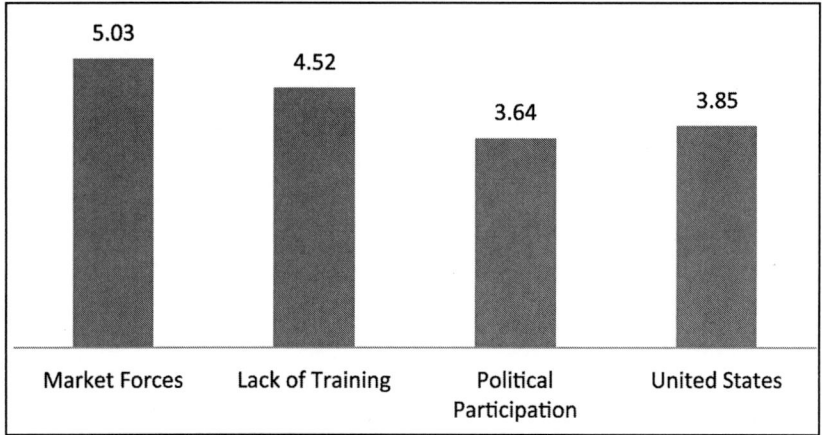

Figure 7.3 Public Evaluations of the Fairness of Hypothetical Systems and the United States

Note: Entries represent mean scores on a scale where 1 represents complete disagreement and 7 represents complete agreement with the statement. All differences are statistically significant at the p < 0.05 level.

the United States to be fair? Those in the market forces condition evaluated the hypothetical system to be significantly more fair than the process in the United States (t = 13.97, p = 0.00). The size of this effect is large and substantively significant. Nearly three-fourths (Cohen's D = 0.73) of those in the market forces condition thought that the process of government was more fair than the process of government in the United States. Those in the lack of training condition also evaluated the hypothetical system to be significantly more fair than the process in the United States (t = 7.54, p = 0.00). Two-thirds (Cohen's D = 0.39) of those in the lack of training condition thought that the process of government in the hypothetical system was more fair than the process of government in the United States. Those in the political participation condition evaluated the hypothetical system to be significantly less fair than that of the United States (t = -2.213, p = 0.02), but the effect size is negligible. Only 54 percent rated the United States to be more fair than the political participation condition (Cohen's D = -0.11). Broadly speaking, Americans think that the process leading to income inequality in the United States is unfair.

All things being equal, Americans *should* be supportive of a proposal to raise taxes on the wealthy in order to reduce income inequality in America. Democrats should be supportive, because they typically support such proposals. Independents should be supportive, because they also were more supportive than Republicans of raising taxes on the wealthy in a hypothetical system to correct high levels of income inequality. Republicans should be supportive of the proposal, because the process leading to the wealth gap in the United States is perceived to be very unfair—nearly as unfair as the political participation condition. Therefore, we should expect the same relationship in the United States that we saw in the hypothetical system.

THE UNITED STATES

What was Team Obama hoping to accomplish by making wealth inequality a central theme of the president's 2012 reelection campaign? The preceding analyses demonstrate that an appeal to the center *and* an appeal to the base are plausible motivations behind this emphasis. However, the Apartisan American and sorting hypotheses yield very different predictions about how the American public will respond to presidential rhetoric on this issue. The Apartisan American hypothesis expects that politically interested individuals will carefully weigh various considerations and choose the policy that most closely matches their own views. In this context, that means that independents should be more likely to support raising taxes on the wealthy in the United States when they perceive the process to be unfair, and less likely to support the proposal if they perceive the process to be fair (H2). The same would be true of Republicans (H3). Evidence that cognitively mobilized independents are supportive of raising taxes on the wealthy in the United States would suggest that Team Obama emphasized income inequality in the president's 2012 reelection campaign in an attempt to appeal to the center and convert independent voters.

The sorting hypothesis yields different predictions. According to this view, elite cues provide information to independents and independent-leaners about the position they should take on a particular issue. In the U.S. context, the sorting hypothesis predicts that independents will discard their values (willingness to raise taxes on the wealthy) when the process of government is unfair, and thus respond directly to the cues given by party elites (H4). The same would be true of Republicans and Democrats (H5). Evidence that cognitively mobilized independents' support of the proposal to raise taxes on the wealthy was dependent on the source cue would suggest that Team Obama emphasized income inequality in order to appeal to and mobilize Democratic core supporters.

Table 7.2 Text Used in the Experimental Manipulations

Some	Some Republicans	President Obama
Some have proposed reforming the tax code in the United States to eliminate loopholes and shelters that allow the wealthiest Americans (the multimillionaires and billionaires) to pay a lower tax rate than the middle class.	*Some Republicans* have proposed reforming the tax code in the United States to eliminate loopholes and shelters that allow the wealthiest Americans (the multimillionaires and billionaires) to pay a lower tax rate than the middle class.	*President Obama* has proposed reforming the tax code in the United States to eliminate loopholes and shelters that allow the wealthiest Americans (the multimillionaires and billionaires) to pay a lower tax rate than the middle class.

These hypotheses are tested in the same national survey. To avoid contamination effects, the questions about the United States were asked at the very beginning of the survey, and the experiment discussed in the previous section was the final portion of the survey. The intervening survey asked questions on a wide variety of topics from obesity to evaluations of democracy. Table 7.2 shows the experimental conditions to which respondents were randomly assigned. The text for the dependent variable in this experiment is identical to the text in the preceding experiment and was taken from a speech given by President Obama in late 2011. The only variation is in the source cue.

To assess the support of various groups for the proposal to raise taxes on the wealthy in the United States, I used pooled regression analysis with interaction terms to explore the conditional relationships of interest. I expect that Republicans will be *less* supportive of raising taxes on the wealthy in the United States if they perceive the process leading to the gap to be fair than they are if the process is unfair (H3). Figure 7.4 shows that this clearly is *not* the case. Republicans are more supportive of raising taxes in the United States when they perceive the process to be fair. Indeed, Republican-leaners (t = 1.87, p = 0.06) and strong Republicans (t = 1.98, p = 0.048) are significantly *more* likely to support raising taxes on the wealthy when they perceive the process to be fair. The fairness of the process has no effect on independents or Democratic-leaners (H2).

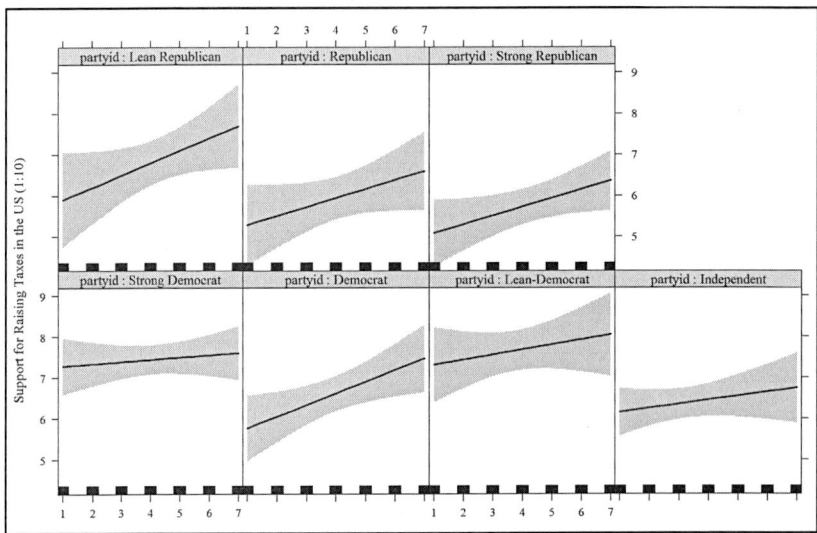

Figure 7.4 The Relationship between Perceptions of Fairness and Support for Raising Taxes on the Wealthy in the United States Mediated by Party Identification

Note: Simple slopes plotted using the effects package in R 2.14. Gray bars represent the 95% confidence interval of the estimate.

Consistent with the Apartisan American hypothesis, cognitively mobilized independents should be more supportive of raising taxes on the wealthy than those low in cognitive mobilization (regardless of partisan affiliation). This is tested using an interaction term for partisanship and cognitive mobilization. The Sobel test for this term fails to achieve statistical significance, which indicates that cognitive mobilization does not moderate support for raising taxes on the wealthy among partisan subgroups. Figure 7.5 displays the relationship. Cognitive mobilization did not influence one group differently than another. There is no evidence that a group of cognitively mobilized independents are rising above the partisan fray to express support consistent with their own values. There is little support for the Apartisan American hypothesis in these results.

In addition, Figure 7.6 suggests that the cognitively mobilized may also be responding to source cues. Independents high in cognitive mobilization are expected to rise above the partisan noise and make decisions based on the relevant information. Source cues should have no influence

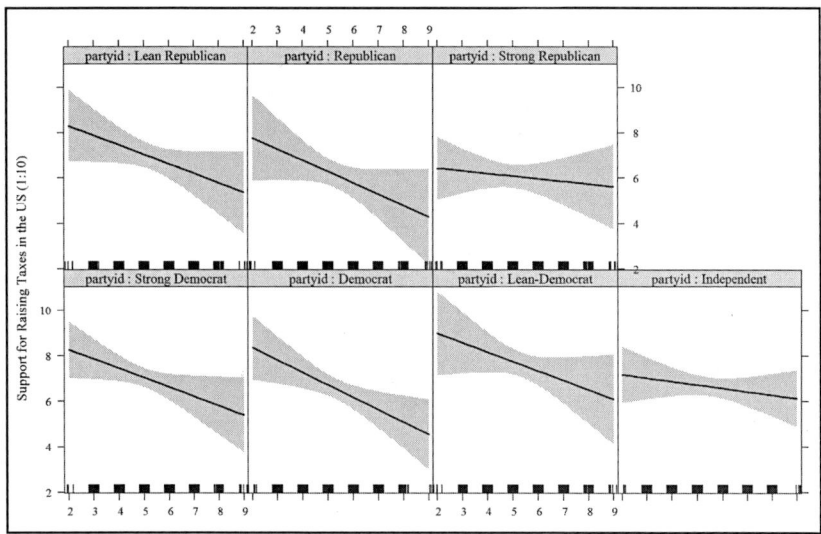

Figure 7.5 The Relationship between Cognitive Mobilization and Support for Raising Taxes on the Wealthy Mediated by Party Identification

Note: Simple slopes plotted using the effects package in R 2.14. Gray bars represent the 95% confidence interval of the estimate.

on their support for a policy proposal. Yet, these individuals are *less* likely to support a proposal for raising taxes on the wealthy in the United States when it is attributed to either Obama or Some Republicans. While it is possible that the lack of support in the Republican condition could be driven by a lack of Republican credibility on the issue, this cannot explain the diminished support in the President Obama condition. Indeed, independents high in cognitive mobilization may simply have a bias *against* partisan proposals; however, that is beyond the scope of this chapter. The results presented in this section are sufficient to conclude that cognitively mobilized, independent-minded individuals may be able to rise above the noise of the political environment and make reasoned choices based on the facts before them, but in the case of income inequality they did not do so (H2, H3).

The unexpected prevalence of partisan affiliation over individual values when considering a policy proposal in the United States may provide evidence for the sorting hypothesis. Republicans that otherwise would have been less supportive of raising taxes on the wealthy because

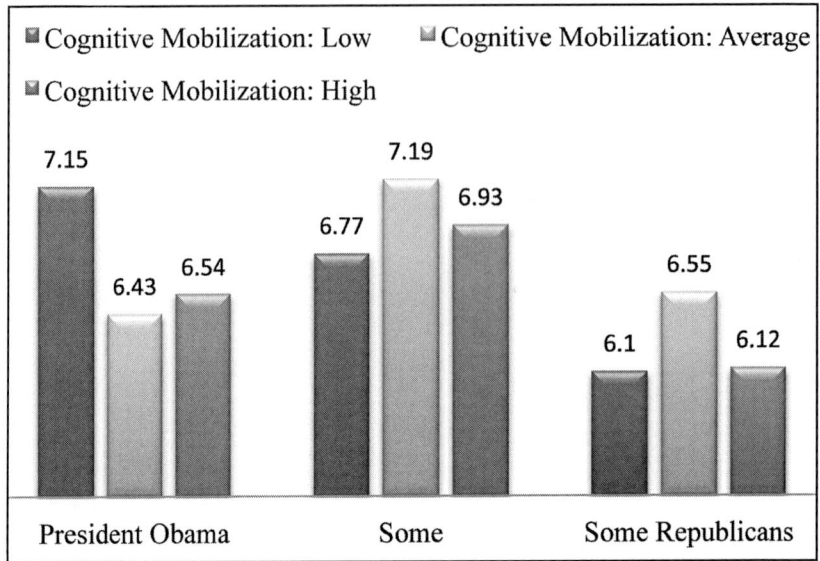

Figure 7.6 The Relationship between Cognitive Mobilization and Support for Raising Taxes on the Wealthy Mediated by Source Cue

Note: Entries are predicted levels of support for raising taxes on the wealthy by category calculated using the Effects package in R 2.14.

they perceived the process leading to the gap to be fair may have expressed support based on the messenger, rather than the message. The sorting hypothesis predicts that the public will determine their position on a particular issue in response to source cues. If this is true, we would expect partisans and partisan leaners to shift their policy preference based on the source of the proposal. Republicans would be more supportive of policies proposed by Republicans and independent leaners would behave likewise (H4, H5).

Each experimental condition differed only in the group to whom the proposal is attributed. Using pooled regression analysis with a dummy for source attribution and an interaction between that dummy and party identification allows us to test the influence of source cues relative to other hypothesized relationships. Evidence that the source of a proposal is more important in the individual calculation of support for a proposal to raise taxes on the wealthy than their own fairness values would support the sorting hypothesis. In addition, evidence of sorting in the electorate would suggest that Team Obama emphasized inequality in America in order to mobilize their core constituents. Emphasizing redistributive solutions to economic inequality would be a strategy designed to mobilize the base rather than convert the opposition.

Table 7.3 Predictors of Support for Raising Taxes in the United States

(Intercept)	6.672***
	(-1.218)
U.S. Process Fair	0.109
	(-0.092)
Party: 1 = Strong Democrat	-0.487*
	(-0.23)
Ideology: 1 = Very Conservative	0.231*
	(-0.107)
Attribution: Some Republicans	-2.289***
	(-0.425)
Attribution: President Obama	0.708
	(-0.42)
Cognitive Mobilization	-0.460**
	(-0.177)
Income: 40k–100k/Less than 40k	0.039
	(-0.19)
Income: More than 100k/Less than 40k	-0.18
	(-0.283)
Race	0.116
	(-0.07)
Gender: Female/Male	-0.305
	(-0.174)
Educ: High School/Less than High School	0.996
	(-0.739)
Educ: Some College/Less than High School	1.741*
	(-0.74)
Educ: Bachelor's Degree/Less than High School	1.934*
	(-0.778)
Educ: Graduate Degree/Less than High School	2.683**
	(-0.841)
Party x U.S. Process Fair	0.01
	(-0.021)

Party x Ideology	0.025
	(-0.026)
Party x Attribution: Some Republicans	0.447***
	(-0.1)
Party x Attribution: President Obama	-0.307**
	(-0.1)
Party x Cognitive Mobilization	0.038
	(-0.037)
R-squared	0.111
N	1377

Note: Main entries are regression coefficients obtained using OLS regression in R 2.14. Standard errors in parentheses. $p < 0.10 = *$, $p < 0.05 = **$, $p < 0.01 = ***$.

The source of the proposal to raise taxes on the wealthy in the United States is significant. Table 7.3 displays the results of the statistical model from which the graphs of predicted probabilities are derived. All things being equal, the source of the proposal is the only statistically significant moderator of the relationship between party identification and support for the proposal. Figure 7.7 illustrates this relationship. Regardless of political ideology, attitudes about fairness of the process in the United States, or cognitive mobilization, partisans respond to source cues. When Republicans propose raising taxes on the wealthy, Republicans support the proposal and if President Obama proposes *exactly* the same thing, Republicans are opposed. A strong Republican in the "Some Republicans" condition is nearly twice as supportive of the proposal as a strong Republican in the "President Obama" treatment condition. Likewise, when Republicans propose raising taxes on the wealthy, Democrats are opposed and if President Obama proposes *exactly* the same thing, Democrats will support it. A strong Democrat in the "Some Republicans" treatment condition is 18 percent *less* likely to support the proposal as a strong Democrat in the "President Obama" treatment conditions. In the experimental treatment condition in which the messenger is unclear (attribution "some"), the pattern is very similar to the condition where the proposal is attributed to President Obama. In all, this pattern of findings suggests that support (opposition) for redistributive tax policies in the United States is strongly influenced by the messenger, rather than the content of the message.

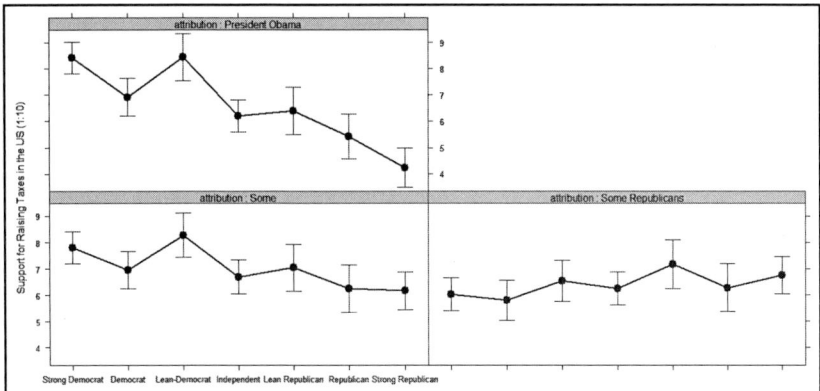

Figure 7.7 The Relationship between Party Identification and Support for Raising Taxes on the Wealthy Mediated by Source Cue

Note: Dots are the mean predicted probabilities calculated using the effects package in R 2.14. The horizontal lines represent the 95% confidence interval of the estimate.

Allow me to emphasize the significance of these findings. When individuals are randomly assigned to experimental conditions, the results suggest more than an associative relationship. Approximating laboratory conditions yields findings of a causal nature. Controlling for the primary competing explanations, these analyses demonstrate that the source of a proposal *causes* partisans to respond differently. This suggests that neither ideological preferences, nor individual values, nor cognitive mobilization is sufficient to overcome the influence of source cues on individual policy preferences.

CONCLUSION

This chapter began with a discussion about the reelection strategy used by Team Obama in the 2012 presidential election. Some argue that when the distribution of voter preferences resembles that of a bell-curve and the majority of the electorate has moderate ideological positions, the most effective strategy to gain the support of a majority of the electorate is to propose an agenda that appeals to moderate voters (Downs 1957). In this view, effectively persuading moderate voters that your candidate will deliver moderate policies after an election motivates the largest number of voters to support your candidate in the election. Indeed, Dalton (2013) argues that nearly one-third of the U.S. electorate holds moderate political views and tends to choose moderate candidates for office. Though many hold strong ideological positions and rely on partisan cues to determine their vote choice, cognitively mobilized independent voters rise above the partisan noise and make voting decisions consistent with their individual values.

Others argue that as the two political parties have become polarized in their policy platforms, elections can be won by appealing to mobilizing a party's core constituents. In this view, presidential elections are less about persuasion and more about mobilization. Since a majority of those with moderate views will not actually cast their vote and it is difficult to persuade those who identify with the other political party to support an opposing candidate, this strategy focuses effort on getting sufficient numbers of partisan supporters to the polls to overwhelm the opposition (Dowd 2012; Issenberg 2012). One of the tools of this strategy is to take a position on a new issue in order to persuade individuals to become stronger partisans. When liberal Republicans change to liberal Democrats because an elite takes position that resonates with the voter, they become stronger partisans than they otherwise would have been (Levendusky 2010). Thus, a candidate can choose to emphasize issues in a campaign that appeal to his or her own core constituents, emphasize mobilizing the base, and expect to persuade some nominally independent ideologues to switch their partisan affiliation and join with their own base in strongly supporting the candidate.

This chapter tested the two competing theories using a national survey experiment that explored the major theme of Obama's 2012 reelection campaign to identify the relative success of the competing strategies. I used a deductive approach of inferring the strategy employed based on the outcomes produced. There is no evidence to support the cognitive mobilization hypothesis. President Obama's solution to wealth inequality did not persuade independent voters to support his position. In addition, cognitive mobilization did not moderate support for the policy proposal in the United States among all partisan groups; independent leaners did not respond differently from strong partisans. If the purpose of Team Obama's emphasis on redistributive solutions to income inequality in the United States was to persuade independents or independent-leaners, this strategy failed.

However, the partisan mobilization theory finds considerable support. Partisans that were supportive of redistributive policies in a hypothetical system—depending on the level of fairness in that system—only expressed similar support in the United States if the partisan cues suggested that it was the appropriate course of action. Though respondents evaluated the United States to be nearly as unfair as the worst hypothetical system, partisans were not supportive of redistributive policies to correct the inequality *unless* someone from their own party proposed the policy. When party elites take a position on an issue heretofore ignored by the party, constituents notice these positions and adjust their own positions accordingly—and once a person is sorted, he or she becomes a stronger partisan.

The findings presented in this chapter suggest that Team Obama used the rhetoric of income inequality and redistributive solutions to the problem as a means to help individuals sort themselves into the Democratic Party and become stronger partisans. Though significant numbers of independents voted for President Obama, that was not his primary purpose in using this particular appeal. The rhetoric of income inequality was not an appeal to the median, moderate voter; rather, it was an appeal to those that already supported President Obama.

REFERENCES

Abramowitz, A. I. 2010. *The Disappearing Center: Engaged Citizens, Polarization, and American Democracy.* Yale University Press.

Abramowitz, A. I., and Saunders, K. A. 1998. "Ideological Realignment in the US Electorate." *Journal of Politics* 60 (3): 634–652.

Bai, Matt. 2004. "The Multilevel Marketing of the President." *New York Times Magazine,* April 25.

Bartels, L. M. 2008. *Unequal Democracy: The Political Economy of the New Gilded Age.* New York, Princeton: Russell Sage Foundation, Princeton University Press.

Calmes, J., and J. Harwood. 2004. "Bush's Big Priority: Energize Conservative Base." *Wall Street Journal,* August 30.

Dalton, R. J. 2013. *The Apartisan American: Dealignment and Changing Electoral Politics.* Thousand Oaks, CA: CQ Press.

Dowd, M. 2012. "This Week with George Stephanopoulos." *ABC News.*

Downs, A. 1957. *An Economic Theory of Democracy.* New York.

Druckman, J. N. 2011. *Cambridge Handbook of Experimental Political Science.* Cambridge, New York: Cambridge University Press.

Fiorina, M. P., and S. J. Abrams. 2009. *Disconnect: The Breakdown of Representation in American Politics*. Julian J. Rothbaum Distinguished Lecture Series. Norman: University of Oklahoma Press.

Fishkin, J. S. 1996. *The Dialogue of Justice: Toward a Self-Reflective Society*. Yale University Press.

Halperin, M., and J. F. Harris. 2006. *The Way to Win: Taking the White House in 2008*. New York: Random House.

Horsley, S. 2012. "Obama Pushes Early Voting on Swing State Tour." *National Public Radio*, October 24. Retrieved from http://www.npr.org/2012/10/24/163572770 /obama-pushes-early-voting-on-swing-state-tour.

Issenberg, S. 2012. *The Victory Lab: The Secret Science of Winning Campaigns*. New York: Crown.

Levendusky, M. 2010. *The Partisan Sort: How Liberals Became Democrats and Conservatives Became Republicans*. Chicago: University of Chicago Press.

Lind, E. A., and T. R. Tyler. 1988. *The Social Psychology of Procedural Justice*. Springer U.S.

Mayer, W. G. (2007). "The Swing Voter in American Presidential Elections." *American Politics Research* 35 (3), 358–388.

Mitchell, G., P. E. Tetlock, D. G. Newman, and J. S. Lerner. 2003. "Experiments behind the Veil: Structural Influences on Judgments of Social Justice." *Political Psychology* 24 (3): 519–547.

Morton, R. B. 2006. *Analyzing Elections*. The New Institutionalism in American Politics Series. New York: W. W. Norton.

November Monthly—Obama/Economy/2012 Presidential Election. 2011. *ABC News/Washington Post*, Roper Center.

Obama, B. 2011. "Remarks by the President on the on the Economy in Osawatomie, Kansas." The White House, December 6. Retrieved from http://www .whitehouse.gov/the-press-office/2011/12/06/remarks-president-economy -osawatomie-kansas.

Obama, B., and M. Romney. 2012. "Third Presidential Debate: Full Transcript." *ABC News,* October 22. Retrieved from http://abcnews.go.com/Politics /OTUS/presidential-debate-full-transcript/story?id=17538888.

Page, B. I., and L. R. Jacobs. 2009. *Class War?: What Americans Really Think about Economic Inequality*. University of Chicago Press.

Rasinski, K. A., and T. R. Tyler. 1988. "Fairness and Vote Choice in the 1984 Presidential Election." *American Politics Research* 16 (1): 5.

Stimson, J. A. (2004). *Tides of Consent: How Public Opinion Shapes American Politics*. Cambridge, New York: Cambridge University Press.

Chapter 8

No Soviet Domination
Presidential Debates, the Media, and Public Reaction
Douglas Mock, Boston University

INTRODUCTION

The presidential debate has been a staple of presidential campaigns since 1976, having taken a respite during the presidential campaigns of 1964, 1968, and 1972, after John Kennedy and Richard Nixon first debated in the fall of 1960. Although no law could require the major parties' nominees to debate, the process is now an institution, with the Commission on Presidential Debates (hereafter, "the Commission"), a quasi-governmental body, having taken over production since 1992. As usual, in 2012, the Commission sponsored three debates between the presidential candidates, Democratic president Barack Obama (hereafter, "Obama") and the Republican candidate, former Massachusetts governor Mitt Romney (hereafter, "Romney"). These debates consisted of a single moderator, with one event devoted to domestic policy, a second (the third, chronologically) to foreign and defense issues, while the third used the "town-hall" style format that was first introduced during the 1992 campaign.

The 2012 debates were perhaps the most anticipated in campaign history, with the probable exception of the initial encounters between Kennedy and Nixon in 1960. Most pundits and pollsters suggested that this election would be particularly close. Obama, in addition to the advantages his incumbency afforded, was viewed as a particularly adept debater; after the 2008 Democratic nominating process, he certainly was an experienced one. The challenge was daunting for Romney: he needed to "hit it out of the park" or "deliver a knockout punch" (more about these sporting metaphors below).

But is the conventional wisdom regarding the importance of debates correct? As a threshold question, do they make—or have the potential to make—a difference in the outcome of an election? The answer to that question is problematic enough, as only twice since 1976 (a cliffhanger election) has the outcome on election night been dramatically close, and both times the candidate who was widely perceived as the *loser* in the debates (George W. Bush, in both instances) won the election. But the more crucial question is whether the debates matter in a meaningful sense. This chapter will suggest that the answer to that question is "no." Ultimately to blame is the format of the debates, a format that emphasizes trivialities, platitudes, and the "horse race" aspect of the campaign at the expense of serious discussion about public issues. The result is a media spectacle that panders to the least common denominator. Perhaps this state of affairs would be tolerable were it merely a matter of no net effect. It is not. The debates, as currently (and it appears, permanently) constructed, have a deleterious effect on the serious discussion of issues a president addresses.

This chapter will proceed as follows: First, a brief literature review will examine previous research on the effects of presidential debates. Second, that research will be reexamined in light of the 2012 election. Finally, a proposal to replace the current regime with something more meaningful will be advanced.

LITERATURE REVIEW

Surprisingly, the literature regarding presidential debates is sparse, and at times, the findings are (somewhat) contradictory or at odds with current understandings in the field of political science. An example is demonstrate. Juxtaposed with the slight informational gain that studies show, there are larger effects that highlight the negative aspects of debates as currently structured.

For example, the media are wont to treat presidential debates as akin to sporting events, complete with an analysis of where the "horse-race" stands and what expectations exist for the combatants. It is a commonplace that each presidential campaign spends plenty of time and effort downplaying its own candidate's abilities and emphasizing the other candidate's strengths. Media handicapping worked against Obama in 2012, as he was portrayed as an outstanding and experienced debater, perceptions that exacerbated the fallout from his poor performance in his first encounter with Romney. Blankenship and Kang (1991) have demonstrated that predebate analysis by media outlets emphasizes that one candidate—normally the one who trails in the polls—must "hit it out of the park" or deliver a "knockout punch" in order for the debate to matter. This media analysis might become self-fulfilling prophecy. Immediately after the debate, analysts spend an inordinate amount of time discussing whether one candidate did knock another to the canvas or whether one made a devastating gaffe.

Self-fulfilling prophecy or not, it appears that the candidate trailing in the polls must deliver an emphatic "win" to change many voters' perceptions. Even when that happened, as it did in the first Reagan-Mondale debate in 1984, the predebate preference for Reagan did not come close to being eliminated, despite the predictions of many pundits that "the tide had turned" in favor of Mondale (Schrott and Lanoue 2008). Moreover, even where a candidate can be said to have "won," his or her chances for election may not improve, and sometimes specific issues turn favorably in the other candidate's direction. Lanoue and Schrott (1989) find that viewers were impressed with Mondale's clarity and specific answers regarding his support for a tax increase; still, the authors' subjects moved slightly in the direction of opposing tax increases after watching the debate.

More troubling is that the media and viewers' decisions as to a debate winner usually seem to have little to do with substance. Wall, Golden, and James (1988) find that speech experts considered Carter the winner of his single debate against Reagan in 1980, but viewers awarded the decision to Reagan. Most instructive is a study conducted by Fein, Goethals,

Miller and MacKuen's (1979) conclusion, bound by the period during which it was written, that partisan preference in presidential elections was becoming less important, a conclusion few would accept today. Still, some broad findings can be accepted.

There is some indication in the literature that debates do inform the public, although with certain limitations. Unfortunately, the effect seems ephemeral. There is little or no evidence that debates make a *dispositive* difference, that is, that voters tend in significant numbers to make up or change their minds as a result of listening. As Wall, Golden, and James (1988) point out, the single most important factor in determining a viewer's opinion on the winner of a debate is predebate disposition.

Still, debates perform an important public service. Studies show that viewers are more informed than they otherwise would be, and this matters even if it does not affect the outcome of presidential elections. Miller and MacKuen (1979) have found that although the public's evaluation of candidates changed only slightly as a result of debates, the viewers showed a greater awareness of issues than they had previously. Holbrook (1999) finds a similar effect, but suggests that it is very inconsistent, showing up markedly in some years, but only very slightly in others.

Miller and MacKuen (1979) and Holbrook (1999) also conclude that the effect is greater on viewers that are already generally well informed prior to the debate. In other words, the "rich get richer" and the gap in knowledge between the most-informed and least-informed voters grows.

Finally, Holbrook finds that debates have a greater informational effect when they occur earlier in the election season—in the primaries, for example—rather than late in the general election season. Consistent with that analysis, Holbrook also finds that the first debate has by far the greatest information influence. Subsequent debates have minimal or even nonexistent effects. Although it is generally conceded now that the first debate is the most important, this had to be established empirically rather than intuitively. According to Richard Nixon, who along with John Kennedy was the first to engage in presidential debates, his advisors argued that audiences would build while the debates progressed, and that the last debate would be the most important (Self 2005).

It is clear from the literature that debates matter in some sense. But that effect is not primarily informational, as viewer and media reaction and Kugler (2007) after the 1984 debates. Reagan's performance in his debates with Mondale raised questions about his age and mental acuity. Viewers thought he performed much better in the second debate, but the analysis of Fein et al. raises questions as to why. Reagan unleashed two clever one-liners in that second debate. First, he deflected questions about his age and stamina by saying that he would not make an issue of his opponent's "youth and inexperience" (Commission on Presidential Debates, "1984 Debates," 2012). Second, in response to a question about national defense, he ridiculed a Mondale ad showing Mondale standing on the deck of the *U.S.S. Nimitz*, noting that Mondale had voted against funding for the ship, and that if Mondale had had his way, he would have been standing in the middle of the ocean rather than on the deck of the ship (Commission on Presidential Debates, "1984 Debates," 2012). Both lines got hearty laughter and applause.

Interested in assessing the effect that crowd reaction would have on viewers' assessments of the candidates' performance, Fein, Goethels, and Kugler (2007) randomly assigned a group of college students to three groups. One group watched the debate exactly as the original viewers did. A second group watched the debate with the sound bites deleted. A third group viewed it with the sound bites left in, but with the vigorous audience response deleted. Not surprisingly, the students who watched the debate as it actually aired viewed Reagan as the winner. The group watching with the sound bites deleted judged Mondale to be the winner. Most tellingly, the third group who watched the encounter with Reagan's sound bites left in, but with the audience reaction deleted, overwhelmingly selected Mondale as the winner, indicating that viewers were responding not so much to the sound bites themselves, as they were reacting to the audience's reaction.

Media performance and analysis doesn't do much better than that of the public at large. Rarely does that analysis focus on which candidate was better at sustained argument, partly because such argument is virtually absent given the debates' formats. Instead, reporters are often on the lookout for gaffes and factual errors. While there are numerous examples, the most famous remains Gerald Ford's odd claim in 1976 that there was no Soviet domination of Eastern Europe (Commission on Presidential Debates, "1976 Debates," 2012). Ford was attempting to make a rhetorical point about the spirit of Eastern European citizens, but ended up sounding as if he was unfamiliar with basic geopolitical realities. Still, the point appeared unimportant to the public at first; it was only after media sources emphasized the "gaffe" for a prolonged period of time (to the exclusion of every other feature of the debate) that Americans viewed Carter as the winner.

Or, more to the point, Americans viewed Ford as the loser. Schrott and Lanoue (2005) have persuasively shown that debates are much more commonly perceived as having been lost—usually when a candidate underperforms, that is, falls short of expectations—than as being won. Their research highlights again the tendency for analysts to search for a gaffe that makes good copy, as in the 1976 foreign policy debate between Ford and Carter. As the incumbent president, and as a former congressman of nearly a quarter-century's standing, Ford was supposed to have a decided advantage over the former one-term governor of Georgia. But it was Ford who came off badly, because of a single poorly worded claim that overwhelmed the reporting process.

Finally, there is the issue of the role of the moderator or moderators in the debates. Jackson-Beeck and Meadow (1979) have concluded that there are three agendas in debates: that of the candidates, that of the voters, and that of the journalists charged with moderating. There is very little overlap among the three agendas; with limited exceptions, candidates have not been responsive to specific questions, but have instead used them as sounding boards for delivering prerehearsed mini-speeches. And the questions journalists select are not the questions that members of the public would ask.

MEMORABLE MOMENTS FROM DEBATE HISTORY

If one were called on to select a top-ten list of the most memorable moments in debate history, it is doubtful whether *any* of them would involve a substantive discussion of policy or the candidates' qualifications, except very tangentially. Possible contenders for such a list follow.

Perhaps the most famous moment in debate history was not in a presidential encounter, but in the 1988 face-off between vice presidential contenders Dan Quayle (R) and Lloyd Bentsen (D). After George H. W. Bush selected the forty-three-year-old Indiana senator Quayle as his running mate, the choice was widely derided, even by some prominent Republicans. Quayle seemed uncomfortable in the spotlight and often appeared unable to grapple with basic questions of governance and policy. By contrast, the Democratic presidential nominee, Massachusetts governor Michael Dukakis, chose one of the elder statesmen of the Democratic Party, sixty-seven-year-old Texas senator Bentsen. Although polls pointed to an electoral victory by the Bush/Quayle ticket, many analysts saw Quayle as an albatross around the ticket's neck, a possible exception to the rule that vice presidential candidates do not make a difference in presidential elections.

Living up (or down) to low expectations, Quayle's performance in the debate was awkward and stumbling. Several times, he would not answer a question regarding the first action he would take if he were to become president (or take the other obvious alternative, to suggest that the question was a silly one). Instead, he referred repeatedly to the number of years he had served in Congress, and at one time said, accurately, that he had been in Congress as long as John Kennedy had been when Kennedy was elected president. Responding to the last iteration of the question, Quayle noted that "I have far more experience than many others that sought the office of vice president. I have as much experience in the Congress as Jack Kennedy did when he sought the presidency." To great applause and laughter, and to Quayle's visible consternation, Bentsen responded, "Senator, I served with Jack Kennedy. I knew Jack Kennedy. Jack Kennedy was a friend of mine," concluding with the now legendary line, "Senator, you're no Jack Kennedy." The exchange helped seal Quayle's reputation as a lightweight. Quayle managed only a feeble "that was really uncalled for" in response (Commission on Presidential Debates, "1988 Debates," 2012).

Ronald Reagan is typically credited with two of the most effective zingers. In his single 1980 debate with Jimmy Carter, Carter pounded Reagan's positions relentlessly, part of a strategy to make Reagan appear extreme and dangerous. The difficulty for Carter was that Reagan did not appear extreme, but rather genial, reasonable, and articulate. At one point, near the end of the debate, Carter accused Reagan of having begun his political career by "going around the country opposing Medicare" (Commission on Presidential Debates, "1980 Debates," 2012). Carter's charge was accurate, but it was Reagan's response—"there you go again"

(Commission on Presidential Debates, "1980 Debates," 2012)—that has stuck. The response highlighted that Carter's attempt to make Reagan appear scary to the American public did not succeed. If Carter had hoped to provoke Reagan into anger, and possibly into defending statements that the majority of Americans would have viewed as extreme, he failed. Reagan's response affected sorrow and a sort of humorous weariness, thus turning the tables on Carter, who ending up looking mean and petty. Factual accuracy was not even relevant, let alone important, to the exchange.

Four years later, Reagan's halting performance in his first debate with Walter Mondale led many analysts to question the seventy-three-year-old president's competence. The second Reagan-Mondale encounter took on added drama, if not significance, as Reagan continued to enjoy a commanding lead in the polls, despite the perception that Mondale had roundly defeated him previously. Viewers waited to see if Mondale or one of the questioners would raise the issue of Reagan's age and mental competence. In fact, Henry Trewhitt tackled the question head-on, remarking that President Kennedy had to go for several days with very little sleep during the Cuban Missile Crisis, and asking Reagan if he would be up to such a challenge. Reagan's humor won the day, as he proclaimed that he would "not make an issue of my opponent's youth and inexperience" (Commission on Presidential Debates, "1984 Debates," 2012). The camera even captured Mondale, on a split screen, laughing heartily. Again, the exchange did not turn on a telling debate point, or logical analysis. Reagan, after making an obviously rehearsed joke, was not called on again to answer questions about his age and stamina, although a single one-liner could hardly have been said to put to rest those concerns.

Several debate "moments" have been tied, not to a candidate's words, but to his actions and appearances. For example, George H. W. Bush repeatedly looked at his watch during his 1992 town-hall debate with Bill Clinton and Ross Perot, giving the impression that he wanted to be someplace else. Bush later explained that he was concerned that Clinton was getting more time. Richard Nixon, who had been hospitalized in the weeks prior to his first of three debates with John Kennedy in 1960, appeared emaciated and tired. Most television viewers considered

Kennedy the winner of that debate, while most radio listeners awarded the decision to Nixon. In 2000, Al Gore's facial gestures and audible sighs in the first of three debates served to make George W. Bush appear sympathetic and the debate winner. Gore, perhaps unaware that he was being seen by a national audience on a split screen, repeatedly looked exasperated and rolled his eyes as Bush was responding to questions.

In contrast to these and other famous moments in debate history, any but the keenest observer of presidential debates would be hard-pressed to recall specific examples of a candidate actually out-debating his opponent. Recalling a moment when a candidate managed to persuasively expose the flaws in his opponent's policy proposals, or when one candidate revealed himself to be obviously unprepared for the presidency is difficult (one exception is Quayle's poor performance in his vice presidential debate, discussed above). Nonetheless, such reasoned analysis is typically the hoped-for end result of most debates in other contexts. It is not clear why political "debates" in general, and presidential-level debates in particular, should be the exception to that rule.

The First Debate

The first debate in 2012 was among the most anticipated in history. The television viewing audience approached seventy million, the biggest for any debate in twenty years (the 2008 debate between vice presidential candidates Joe Biden and Sarah Palin attracted a bigger audience, probably because of Palin's status as a media phenomenon, flawed vice presidential pick, and darling of conservative Republicans) (CBS News 2012). The debate's moderator was Jim Lehrer of the Public Broadcasting System, and the debate was focused on the economy and domestic policy.

Postdebate analysis focused on two major themes. First, Obama seemed (according to the commentators) unengaged to the point of being listless. His answers were too "discursive" and he seemed "nervous," "unprepared," and in need of caffeine, according to typical comments (Journalism Foundation 2012). Respected ABC news commentator Jeff Greenfield wrote that the debate was as "one-sided as any I have ever seen" (Greenfield 2012). By contrast, the challenger, Romney, was seen as having taken advantage of his opportunities, avoided stumbles, and exceeded low expectations (Blake 2012). Media analysis of the two candidates' performance emphasized Obama's perceived poor showing much more than any successes by Romney, consistent with Schrott and Lanoue's (2008) analysis that debates tend to be lost rather than won.

Moderator Jim Lehrer was subjected to withering criticism for his role in the debate. Specifically, analysts complained that he permitted the candidates, especially Romney, to ignore time limitations, interrupt each other repeatedly, and to "roll right over him repeatedly" (Journalism Foundation 2012). In no previous presidential debate had the moderator become the story to the extent that Lehrer did here (in the second debate the moderator became the center of attention to an even greater degree).

Media reaction was unusual in declaring a clear winner in the absence of any particular, outstanding gaffe by the "losing" candidate, or another noteworthy, memorable "moment." Obama did not make any major mistakes, and Romney did not have any "there you go again"- type rejoinders. Still, the consensus was that Romney had won, due in part to Obama's mannerisms and his failure to be aggressive and to correct perceived misstatements of fact by Romney.

One major theme of Obama's attack on Romney was that Romney proposed a $5 trillion tax cut favoring the rich. Obama made this charge at least five times during the course of the evening, and Romney continued to respond that he had no such proposal. Viewers might have been left very confused as to where the truth lay. In fact, Romney had proposed continuing the Bush-era tax cuts that were set to expire. Although as a percentage, those tax cuts affected taxpayers equally across the board, taxpayers who pay a higher rate (the "rich") naturally would receive more in total dollar amounts. Whether Romney's proposed cuts added up to $5 trillion depends on whose numbers one believes. Obama noted that Romney, while saying that his economic plans were revenue-neutral regarding upper-income taxpayers, did not specify which tax deductions he proposed eliminating to reach that goal (Fox News, "Transcript of First Debate," 2012).

Despite a lack of specifics, Romney had a much clearer message than Obama, centering on a five-point plan he introduced in his response to Lehrer's first question. This five-point plan, centering mostly on domestic and economic policy, was one of Romney's main themes throughout the debate cycle, even in the debate that was supposed to center on foreign and defense policy.

Despite the clear and overwhelming perception of a Romney win, the polls moved only slightly in Romney's favor. The first postdebate poll, conducted by Reuters, showed that Romney cut Obama's lead from seven to five points (Sullivan, "Romney Gains Ground," 2012). Gallup showed a slightly bigger bounce for Romney; the final predebate poll showed the challenger behind by five points, whereas the first postdebate poll showed that the race was even (Fox News, "Poll Gives Romney National Edge," 2012). The final vote tally from Election Day ended up being much closer to the 5-point predebate gap.

The Second Debate

Perhaps boosted by Romney's surprisingly strong performance in the first debate, the second debate's television audience was nearly as large as that for the first (Hayward 2012). The postdebate analysis, however, was far different.

The second debate was a "town-hall" style encounter, the type that the Commission introduced in 1992. Noncelebrity, nonjournalist Americans submitted and asked the questions, and debate moderator Candy Crowley of CNN News selected which were to be used.

Obama made a concerted effort to be much more engaged and aggressive than he had been in the first debate; repeatedly, he interrupted Romney's comments with some version of the statement "that's just not true." The president accused Romney of saying something that was not true no fewer than seven times, on issues ranging from whether there were fewer public lands open to oil exploration, to whether Obama sought a bipartisan solution to immigration issues, to whether Romney had advocated permitting big automakers to go bankrupt. Obama's answers focused largely on Romney's plans and statements (Fox News, "Transcript of Second Debate," 2012). In contrast to the first debate, Obama's manner was animated and engaged.

Romney's strategy appeared similar to what he had employed in the first debate. Romney, too, was aggressive and often critical of his opponent, but this time he was met with an opponent who performed similarly. Obama forced Romney to be much more defensive and specific regarding his proposals and record, at one point ridiculing Romney's "five-point plan" as being really a "one-point plan" favoring the wealthy (Commission on Presidential Debates, "2012 Debates," 2012).

The second debate was also the occasion for the historic "moment" that future generations and historians will recall. Going into the debate, much of the news cycle focused on the events in Benghazi, Libya, where four American diplomats had recently been killed by a group of militants. The Obama administration maintained that the attacks were spontaneous and in response to an anti-Islamic video. Critics of the administration argued that the attacks were the result of a planned terrorist attack (Shane 2012). A common argument was that the Obama administration wanted to give the impression that success in the "War on Terror" was proceeding apace, and thus deliberately misled the public regarding the actual events in Libya. Whether or not the administration had referred to the attacks as "terror" became fodder for media comment and Republican criticism.

The issue famously came to a head in this debate. Responding to a question on the Benghazi attack, Romney claimed that Obama had not referred to the incident as a "terrorist attack" until two weeks after it occurred, in the meantime pressing the story line that it had instead been a spontaneous demonstration. After some back and forth between the two candidates, moderator Candy Crowley interjected that "he did call it an act of terror" on September 12, 2012, the day after the attack (Commission on Presidential Debates, "2012 debates," 2012). At that point, some in the audience broke the rule against applauding; Obama had his "moment," and it had come courtesy of the moderator. While "fact-checkers" (particularly on Crowley's own network of CNN) generally reported that Crowley was correct, the truth was a bit more shaded. In the main part of the September 12 remarks, Obama referred to the attack as "outrageous" and "shocking." At the conclusion of his remarks, he said that "no act of terror will ever shake the resolve of this great nation" (Fox News, "Transcript of President Obama's Remarks," 2012). In short, the specific comments that Obama directed toward this incident did *not* include the word "terror"; the generic comments made toward the end of his statement did, but were not applied (one suspects deliberately not applied) to this particular situation, leaving open the possibility that terror may or may not have been involved. Whether Obama did use the word "terror" in referring to the Benghazi attacks was certainly open to interpretation. Nevertheless, Crowley had stated definitively that Obama was correct and that Romney was incorrect, giving Obama a clear boost. Given the research by Fein et al. cited above, the applause may have been crucial. Obama probably "won" the debate at that moment, especially given that nothing Romney said evoked a similar reaction.

Crowley was not the first moderator to interject herself into a debate, although she was perhaps unique in coming down so firmly on the side of one candidate when the two candidates disagreed. Max Frankel spoke with barely disguised contempt when Gerald Ford gave his infamous reply about Soviet domination of Eastern Europe to Frankel's question about the Helsinki Agreements. In fact, Ford's time to respond to the question had expired, and the debate moderator (not Frankel) had already called on Jimmy Carter to respond when a visibly stunned Frankel interrupted and demanded to know whether he had understood Ford's response correctly (Commission on Presidential Debates, "1976 Debate," 2012). As a result of Frankel's reaction, Ford's statement became the focus of postdebate commentary continuing for a full day (1976 was before the era of the twenty-four-hour news cycle). This encounter between Ford and Carter became the clearest example of media reaction determining the "winner." Polls immediately following the debate showed that the public initially viewed Ford as having gotten the better of it, whereas polls taken after extensive media commentary showed Carter the decisive winner.

During the vice presidential debate of 1988, featuring Dan Quayle and Lloyd Bentsen, questioner Brit Hume did little to disguise his contempt for Quayle. Quayle was asked four times (twice by Hume) about the first action he would take if he suddenly became president, and he responded by emphasizing his years in the House and Senate. The second time he asked the question, Hume was plainly sarcastic, eliciting laughter from the crowd when he noted "you said you would say a prayer and you said something about a meeting. What would you do next?" (Commission on Presidential Debates, "1988 Vice-Presidential Debate," 2012).

Going into the second Obama-Romney debate, the "expectations game" was dramatically different than before the first clash. This time, it was Obama who successfully downplayed his abilities as a debater and Romney from whom a great deal was expected. Combined with Crowley's intervention and Obama's much more aggressive manner, it was not surprising that Obama was credited with being the winner. Postdebate polls showed viewers giving Obama a decisive fifteen-point advantage (Politico 2012).

Heading into the debate, Gallup had showed Romney with a 4-point advantage in the national polling (Fox News, "Poll Gives Romney National Edge," 2012). Most national polls that were completed after the second debate showed the matchup almost exactly tied at 47 or 48 percent. Thus, the polls moved slightly in Obama's favor, although whether this was attributable to his performance in the second debate is uncertain.

The Third Debate

The third debate was held only six days after the second, on October 22. CBS News correspondent Bob Schieffer moderated. Schieffer managed to be the only moderator of the 2012 presidential-level debates who himself was not the subject of extensive postdebate commentary.

In keeping with the usual pattern in the three-debate cycle, both candidates appeared to pull their punches in the final encounter, resulting in no clear winner according to many analysts, although polls gave Obama the edge. Some predicted that Romney would revisit the Benghazi issue during this debate, devoted as it was to foreign policy, but he did not. Instead, Romney frequently indicated his agreement with Obama's foreign policies, often stating his support for those policies (CNN, "Transcript of Third Presidential Debate," 2012). For the first time, Obama was clearly the more aggressive of the two.

Romney's performance contrasted sharply with his approach in the first two debates. Those few criticisms of Obama's foreign policy record Romney did make were couched in the mildest terms. Romney did not go on the attack against Obama at all in his first several responses, and when he did so it was to express disappointment at the "unfortunate" choice to "pul[l] our missile defense program out of Poland" (Commission on Presidential Debates, "2012 Debates" 2012). Obama, although not as aggressive as he was in the second debate, was less gentle than Romney. The president took several jabs at Romney that appeared effective, including one that got the most postdebate coverage: his ridiculing of Romney's claim that the U.S. Navy had its lowest number of ships since 1917. Obama argued that the military had fewer bayonets and horses than it did in 1917 as well (Commission on Presidential Debates, "2012 Debates," 2012) Obama's response may have been witty, but its factual accuracy was questionable, and it was plainly illogical: Romney was not claiming that the Navy had fewer ships than it did in 1917, but fewer than at any time since 1917 (including, for instance, the year 2009), nor was he arguing (as Obama's response suggested) that the Navy *should* be similar to what it was in 1917, but rather that it *is* similar to what it was in 1917 and should not be. No matter. History has shown that debate witticisms need not be grounded in fact or logic to be effective.

Some general conclusions may be offered about the debates of 2012. First, and with the notable exception of Romney in the third debate, the candidates were more negative than in any other debate cycle. In the second debate particularly, the presidential candidates responded to virtually every question by spending as much time attacking each other as they did making and defending affirmative proposals. Each frequently made claims that the other candidate's statements were untrue.

Second, the candidates and the media were both focused, to a greater extent than before, on "fact-checking." The candidates made so many conflicting statements of fact that it became difficult to sort them out. Did Romney propose a $5 trillion dollar tax cut? Obama said he did; Romney denied it. Did Obama refer to the attack in Benghazi as "terrorism"? Romney said he did not; Obama said he did. Did the Obama administration cut permits to drill for oil on federal land? Romney said it did; Obama said it did not. And so on. The format of the debates left the viewer with little opportunity to reach conclusions on these matters. Commentators attempted to fill that role. Most notably, there was the question of the Benghazi attacks, as a result of Crowley's defense of Obama in the town-hall debate. Predictably, CNN analysts (Crowley reports for CNN) came to her defense, insisting that Obama (and, by extension, Crowley) was correct that he had labeled the attacks "terrorism" on the day following their occurrence. Some other networks demurred, and as noted elsewhere, the issue was much more clouded than either of the candidates or Crowley would have had us believe.

Third, the candidates resisted any attempt to be specific with respect to proposals, speaking instead in the vaguest generalities. Romney, who had made the elimination of tax credits central to his economic program, refused to specify which ones he would propose eliminating. Obama and others pressed him to do so, to no avail. Obama, a talented and experienced orator, used his rhetorical skills to obscure his unwillingness to be much more detailed. His answer to a question regarding his plans for Social Security was instructive:

> You know, my grandmother, some of you know, helped to raise me. My grandparents did. My grandfather died awhile back. My grandmother died three days before I was elected president. And she was fiercely independent. She worked her way up, only had a high school education, started as a secretary, ended up being the vice president of a local bank. And she ended up living alone by choice. And the reason she could be independent was because of Social Security and Medicare. She had worked all her life, put in this money and understood that there was a basic guarantee, a floor under which she could not go. And that's the perspective I bring when I think about what's called entitlements. You know, the name itself implies some sense of dependency on the part of these folks. These are folks who've worked hard, like my grandmother. And there are millions of people out there who are counting on this. (Fox News, "Transcript of First Debate," 2012)

Although Obama did provide a few specifics later in this answer, the bulk of both candidates' time was spent in vague generalities such as these. Obama's rhetoric, above, was of a kind with most of the answers both candidates delivered throughout the debate cycle. This was consistent with the literature finding that most candidates merely use the journalists' questions to segue into their speeches of choice.

Ultimately, the debates in 2012 appear to have been a wash with the public. Although commentators and polls showed Romney as the decisive winner of the first debate, traditionally thought to be the most important, polls showed Obama winning both the second and the third contests. When asked which candidate did the better job overall, the result was a statistical tie, with 46 percent choosing Romney and 44 percent choosing Obama (Reuters 2012). Not surprisingly, and in keeping with prior research, the overwhelming majority of each candidate's supporters declared that their candidate had gotten the better of the encounters. The idea that the first debate is the most important may have been called into question in 2012 (as it also was in 1984), as Romney was seen as having decisively won that debate, while his percentage of votes received on Election Day ended up being much closer to his predebate poll numbers rather than his postdebate poll numbers. Gelman and King

(1993) famously concluded that a presidential candidate's share of the popular vote could be predicted with uncanny accuracy *months* before the election—and thus, before any debating takes place. If their conclusion is correct, debates probably do not matter electorally, at least not so far, and that appears to be confirmed by the 2012 election.

A modest proposal that does not involve cooking children (apologies to Jonathan Swift): Change the structure of one or two debates so as to get a meaningful exchange. We need not accept a state of affairs that trivializes debates in particular and campaigns in general. Historically, it is difficult to think of a *single example* of a presidential or vice presidential debate that turned on substance, and this holds true for the 2012 encounters. In future years, 2012 will be remembered as the year of Candy Crowley's intervention on the "did he call it terrorism?" issue. Whether one applauds Crowley's comment or not, such semantic hair-splitting is not what America should be taking away from the debate process. As illustrated above, similar examples from prior encounters abound.

Almost as famous as the one-liners are gestures or physical appearances that are now legendary. Even those who can't remember a word Nixon or Kennedy said in 1960 will recall Nixon's five-o'clock shadow and emaciated appearance. George H. W. Bush's glance at his watch became metaphorical for his supposed lack of caring, especially when juxtaposed with Bill Clinton's warmer and more obviously empathetic approach. Bush's explanation that he was concerned the moderator was awarding Clinton more time was unavailing. And Al Gore's invading of George W. Bush's space in 2000, to say nothing of his audible sighs and eye-rolling, highlighted Gore's unlikeability.

The 2012 debates took much of the silliness to new heights (or depths). Instead of a serious discussion throwing light on issues, Americans were treated to persistent squabbling over whose turn it was to speak, which candidate had been awarded more time, whether one more rebuttal or counter-rebuttal would be permitted, and the parsing of words as part of a misleading "fact-checking" process.

The debate format the Commission now proscribes is largely to blame. The Commission appears to have inherited the format's essentials from earlier debates sponsored by the League of Women Voters. There have been slight modifications, including the reliance on a single moderator, and the addition of the "town-hall" style of debate, but we've kept the short opening and closing statements, the alternating of questions between the two (or three) candidates, the limited amount of time (typically two minutes) for response, and the even more limited amount of time (typically a minute and a half) for rebuttal. Devoting one debate to domestic and economic policy and a second to foreign and defense policy is a further relic. Finally, although there were four debates between Kennedy and Nixon in 1960 and only a single debate (due to a dispute over whether to include independent candidate John Anderson) in 1980, three debates have become the norm.

None of these debate characteristics need be written in stone, and all have flaws. The opening and closing statements have become prepackaged, standard stump-type speeches that add little or nothing to the candidates' dialogue. The shortcomings of having a single moderator were vividly illustrated in 2012, when one moderator, Jim Lehrer, appeared to completely lose control, and a second, Candy Crowley, became the story herself.

The Commission's major innovation was the introduction of the town-hall style format beginning with the 1992 elections. Studies showing that the questions journalists posed were not those that would be asked by the public may have prompted this change. But the town-hall style format suffers from some of the same defects that other single-moderator debates have, with the additional problem that the questions and answers are surpassingly silly. The worst type of political pandering results, from the false and fawning familiarity the candidates assume with the "regular Americans" ("That's a great question, Bertha") who submit the questions, to the implausible guarantees that candidates often offer respecting a questioner's individual circumstances. From the 2012 town-hall debate: Questioner: "What can you say to reassure me, but more importantly, my parents, that after I graduate, I will be able to get a job?" Romney: "I'm going to make sure you get a job. Thanks, Jeremy. Yeah, you bet" (Fox News, "Transcript of Second Presidential Debate," 2012).

In the 1992 town-hall debate, one questioner asked the candidates to "cross our hearts… and meet our needs… and not yours" (Commission on Presidential Debates, "First-Half Debate Transcript," 1992). While the candidates' responses to questions such as these may demonstrate their empathy, they do not elicit much other than boilerplate regarding policy proposals. And the desire to appear empathetic can drive candidates to patent absurdities as in Romney's promise that he was going to make sure that his questioner got a job.

It is time to do away with the town-hall format. It adds nothing to the existing formats except the minimal consolation of giving the impression that the public is participating. That participation is ephemeral, and the pandering that the format encourages outweighs any marginal benefit that might accrue.

Any proposal to do away with the traditional format will be met with resistance. One objection will be the fact that the current format *has* become traditional; it is a format that has been approved by a bipartisan commission and the respective parties, and gained acceptance from the viewing public. A further objection will focus on the attention span of the American audience. Most viewers, it will be argued, will have little patience with and little capacity for understanding extended policy discussions. Third, media representatives have a vested interest in the status quo. Reporters have vast powers in setting the parameters of debates (and in influencing public perceptions of the outcome).

The vested interests notwithstanding, the current debate formats do not serve the public interest. And there are members of the public and press who would applaud a move toward a more substantive debate. At least one debate in the three-debate cycle, or perhaps two debates in a four-debate cycle, ought to be structured differently. A proposal that would bring real "debates" to the presidential campaign:

- Increase the period of the debate to three hours
- Eliminate the moderator(s), replacing him or her instead with a time-keeper
- Have the questions selected by the Commission on Presidential Debates
- Give the first candidate ten minutes to answer an initial question
- Give the second candidate fifteen minutes to respond to his or her opponent's answer
- Give the first candidate five minutes to offer a rebuttal to the response
- Reverse the order of speakers for the next question

- Eliminate the meaningless opening and closing statements
- Eliminate the studio audience

This proposal, if adopted, would give candidates the opportunity to offer in-depth analysis of issues, not only for the sake of the analysis itself, but also to give viewers the opportunity to view each candidate's ability to participate in a sustained exchange, as opposed to delivering prepackaged and memorized mini-speeches, an ability that has little correlation with the characteristics needed to be an effective president.

A further benefit of such a format is that candidates would have the opportunity to explore nuances. Televised campaign commercials are notoriously poor conveyors of information because they routinely make another candidate's policy positions (past or present) sound ridiculous by not including important facts or leaving out relevant context. Debates should not replicate that, but they do. The result is the sort of "he said, he said" confrontations that were so typical in 2012. Unfortunately, the analysis rarely goes beyond that. If a candidate attempts to explain such issues in depth, he or she is usually met with an exasperated moderator who complains that "we're out of time" and must "move on," sometimes together with promises that "you'll have plenty of time" or "we'll get back to that." The candidate's "plenty of time" must then be given to other issues and the debaters either do not "get back to that" or have, at a later time, forgotten, along with the audience, the particular point at issue.

Finally, a word on doing away with the studio audience. Although routinely advised that they are not to react with approval or disapproval, audience members frequently do. Research has demonstrated that audience reaction can be vital in molding perceptions of which candidate won a debate, just as television producers of situation comedies know that viewers will laugh at things that are not funny with strategically placed laugh tracks. The situation highlights, unfortunately, the entertainment aspects of the debates.

CONCLUSION

Some years ago, a couple of prescient scholars offered caution about the presidential debate process. "[I]t is clear that debates ought not to be considered a panacea for problems in democratic government," they wrote. "[T]hey are exciting, glittering events reinforcing the value of elec-

tions and campaigns. But... 'all that glitters is not gold.' Perhaps advocates of debates will take this suggestion to heart before supporting unrevised televised presidential debates formats in the future" (Jackson-Beeck and Meadow 1979, 179). That suggestion was not adopted. A pity. Debates can be improved upon, and they can make a meaningful contribution to presidential elections. But now they do a disservice to American democracy, and a law of inertia seems to prevent any corrective action. It is time to take another look.

REFERENCES

Blake, A. 2012. "Six Reasons Romney Won the First Debate." *Washington Post,* October 4. Retrieved from http://www.washingtonpost.com/blogs/the-fix /wp/2012/10/04/six-reasons-mitt-romney-won-the-first-debate/.

Blankenship, J., and J. G. Kang. 1991. "The 1984 Presidential and Vice Presidential Debates: The Printed Press and 'Construction' Metaphor." *Presidential Studies Quarterly* 21 (2): 307–318.

CBS News. "Nielsen: 67M Viewers for 1st Presidential Debate." October 4. Retrieved from http://www.cbsnews.com/8301-207_162-57526519/nielsen -67m-viewers-for-1st-presidential-debate/.

CBS News. 2012. "Poll: Sizeable Win for Obama in Third Debate." October 22. Retrieved from http://www.cbsnews.com/video/watch/?id=50133681n.

CNN Politics. 2012. "Transcript of Third Presidential Debate." October 22. Retrieved from http://politicalticker.blogs.cnn.com/2012/10/22/transcript -third-presidential-debate/.

Commission on Presidential Debates. 2012. "Debate History." Retrieved from http://www.debates.org/index.php?page=debate-history.

Fein, S., G. Goethals, and M. Kugler. 2007. "Social Influence on Political Judgments: The Case of Presidential Debates." *Political Psychology* 28 (2). 165–192.

Fox News. 2012. "Poll Gives Romney National Edge, Underscoring Stakes for Obama at Second Debate." October 16. Retrieved from http://www.foxnews. com/politics/2012/10/16/pressure-on-obama-to-halt-romney-surge-at-ny -debate/.

Fox News. 2012. "Transcript of First Presidential Debate." October 3. Retrieved from http://www.foxnews.com/politics/2012/10/03/transcript-first -presidential-debate/.

Fox News. 2012. "Transcript of President Obama's Remarks Following Deadly Attacks at US Consulate in Libya." September 12. Retrieved from http://www .foxnews.com/politics/2012/09/12/transcript-president-obama-remarks -following-deadly-attacks-at-us-consulate-in/.

Fox News. 2012. "Transcript of Second Presidential Debate." October 16. Retrieved from http://www.foxnews.com/politics/2012/10/16/transcript-second -presidential-debate/.

Gelman, A., and G. King. 1993. "Why Are American Presidential Campaign Polls So Variable When Votes Are So Predictable?" *British Journal of Political Science* 23 (1): 409–451.

Greenfield, J. 2012. "After the Debate, We'll Find Out If We Have a Race." October 4. Retrieved from http://news.yahoo.com/after-the-debate-debacle-for-obama --we%E2%80%99ll-find-out-if-we-have-a-race.html.

Hayward, J. 2012. "TV Audience Remains Huge for Second Debate." *Human Events,* October 17. Retrieved from http://www.humanevents.com/2012/10/17 /tv-audience-remains-huge-for-second-presidential-debate/.

Holbrook, T. 1999. "Political Learning from Presidential Debates." *Political Behavior* 21 (1): 67–89.

Jackson-Beeck, M., and R. G. Meadow. 1979. "The Triple Agenda of Presidential Debates." *Public Opinion Quarterly* 43 (2): 173–180.

Journalism Foundation. 2012. "Media Reaction: Presidential Debate 2012." October 2. Retrieved from http://www.thejournalismfoundation.com/2012/10 /media-reaction-presidential-debate-2012/.

Lanoue, D., and P. Schrott. 1989. "Voters' Reactions to Televised Presidential Debates: Measurement of the Source and Magnitude of Opinion Change." *Political Psychology* 10 (2): 275–292.

Miller, A., and M. MacKuen. 1979. "Learning About the Candidates: The 1976 Presidential Debates." *Public Opinion Quarterly* 43 (3): 326–346.

Politico. 2012. "National '12 Presidential General Election." Retrieved from http:// www.politico.com/p/2012-election/polls/president/national/national-12 -president-general-election-2016/.

Reuters. 2012. "Who Won the Third Presidential Debate? Gallup Says Obama Won Third Debate, But Romney Wins Overall." *Latin Times*, October 26. Retrieved from http://www.latintimes.com/who-won-third-presidential-debate-gallup -says-obama-won-third-debate-romney-wins-overall-124239.

Schrott, P., and D. Lanoue. 2008. "Debates Are for Losers." *Political Science and Politics* 41 (2): 513–518.

Self, J. 2005. "The First Debate over the Debates: How Kennedy and Nixon Negotiated the 1960 Presidential Debates." *Presidential Studies Quarterly* 35 (2): 361–375.

Shane, S. 2012. "Clearing the Record about Benghazi." *New York Times,* October 17. Retrieved from http://www.nytimes.com/2012/10/18/us/politics/questions -and-answers-on-the-benghazi-attack.html?ref=libya.

Sullivan, A. 2012. "Romney Gains Ground on Obama after Strong Debate." *Reuters News,* October 4. Retrieved from http://www.reuters.com/article/2012/10/04 /us-usa-campaign-poll-idUSBRE8931E420121004.

Wall, V., J. Golden, and H. James. 1988. "Perceptions of the 1984 Presidential Debates and a Select 1988 Presidential Primary Debate." *Presidential Studies Quarterly* 18 (3): 541–563.

Chapter 9

Barack Obama's Evolutionary Rhetoric as a Strategy for Supporting Same-Sex Marriage

Casey Malone Maugh, University of Southern Mississippi–Gulf Coast

INTRODUCTION

Same-sex marriage in the United States has been routinely avoided, rejected, and carefully tiptoed around by politicians in the past decade. Discourse surrounding the 1996 Defense of Marriage Act (DOMA) and the 1994 institution of "Don't Ask, Don't Tell" (DADT) served to contain gay rights within particular legal frameworks, allowing politicians to hide behind Supreme Court decisions. In the case of same-sex marriage, DOMA, supported by former president Bill Clinton, defines marriage as a union between a man and a woman, restricting same-sex marriages. Rhetorical strategies used to codify the legal ruling in support of DOMA relied on religious doctrine and Christian ethics to define marriage as restricted to one man and one woman. Since the institution of DOMA, this religious support for DOMA was used by countless politicians, as expected by those on the right, and as a way to hide behind religion on the left. President Barack Obama, since before his candidacy for president, maintained opposition to same-sex marriage, justifying this support through his Christian religious beliefs.

In 2004, during Obama's race for an Illinois Senate seat, candidate Obama began a long, winding, rhetorical evolution toward his decision to support same-sex marriage in 2012. By the time of his election in 2008, Obama's opposition to same-sex marriage, couched in his religious affiliation as a Christian, allowed him to distance himself from engaging on the subject. Jakobsen and Pellegrini (2009), in a provocative essay on Obama's Neo-New Deal rhetoric, argue that during his candidacy and first year in office, the president couched his discourse within a narrative of personal responsibility, in which sexuality is tied to economic decision making. Jakobsen and Pellegrini assert that Obama could support gay rights only if he was pushed from the left on this issue because, "Obama will certainly support a vision of marriage as a stabilizing force that continues to regulate race and class for the nation" (2147). Furthermore, the authors conclude their work by stating that "if Christian secular responsibility remains the mantra of the Obama administration, to be ritually invoked wherever the legacy of neoliberalism needs to be incorporated into Obama's new deal, then this presumption is also part of the framing for a new social formation" (2149). In 2009, this certainly seemed the case. Obama's rhetorical distancing created space for then candidate Obama to remain free from obligations to engage in conversations about the repeal of DOMA. However, candidate and later president Obama remained faithful to his pledge to repeal "Don't Ask, Don't Tell" legislation and worked to strengthen civil union laws. In accordance with his rhetoric of personal responsibility, Obama could oversee the repeal of DADT to satisfy the left because the repeal was not in conflict with his Christian ethic. However, to move toward the dissolution of DOMA and support of same-sex marriage would call for a rejection of his Christian-based rhetoric of responsibility.

This chapter will create a rhetorical roadmap of Barack Obama's discourse on same-sex marriage from 2004 through his 2012 announcement that he no longer opposed it. This roadmap reveals a carefully planned rhetorical strategy in which Obama began to distance himself from the rhetoric of Christian secularism and move toward an Enlightenment rhetoric of change. Obama used the notion of "evolution" as his rhetorical token to advance his continuous shift on the issue of same-sex marriage. This chapter argues that Obama's rhetoric of evolution allowed for a gradual, thoughtful, rhetorical response that eventuated into a drastically different outcome from his position on same-sex marriage in 2004. Finally, the chapter concludes with a discussion of the political implications of this gradual, rhetorical shift toward supporting same-sex marriage in 2012, which minimized the negative backlash typically felt when such major rhetorical shifts occur in politics. Obama's rhetoric of evolution proved successful.

RHETORICAL ROADMAP

Mapping a speaker's significant rhetorical moments within a defined narrative provides a rhetorical roadmap of, in this case, same-sex marriage discourse. In the mainstream media, Barack Obama's first recorded statement on the issue of same-sex marriage came during his response to the moderator in a 2004 local Chicago televised debate. In the broadcast of WWTW Chicago Public Television, Obama said, "What I believe is that marriage is between a man and a woman" (Klein 2012). During this time he couched his decision in his religion and practice of faith within a Chicago church community; in the 2004 debate, when asked by the moderator, "What in your religious faith calls you to be against gay marriage?" Obama responded:

> What I believe, in my faith, is that a man and a woman when they get married, are performing something before God, and it is not simply the two persons who are meeting. But that doesn't mean that that necessarily translates into a position on public policy or with respect to civil unions. What it does mean is that we have a set of traditions in place that I think need to be preserved. But I also think we have to make sure that gays and lesbians have the same set of basic rights that are in place. And, I was glad to see that the president today apparently stated that he was in favor of civil unions. This may be a reversal of his position, but I think it's a healthy one. (WWTW Chicago)

From 2004 until after his election to the presidency, then Senate candidate Obama and presidential candidate Obama remained firm on advocating civil unions while maintaining opposition to same-sex marriage. Couching his stance on the issue within the context of his religious beliefs allowed Obama to quickly evade conversations about same-sex marriage while still allowing for discussion of the secondary issue of civil unions. Not much was publicly recorded during Obama's brief tenure as a U.S. senator; however, the issue resurfaced during the 2008 election cycle, and this time, Obama's rhetoric began to move away from religious justification and toward incremental support for same-sex marriage.

During the 2007 primary race, Obama concentrated his responses on stronger civil unions and remained opposed to the legalization of same sex-marriage; however, he began to eliminate the religious support for his decision. In March 2007, during the primary race against Hillary Clinton, Obama, pressed on his beliefs about homosexuality, submitted a written statement in which he declared, "I do not agree...that homosexuality is immoral" (Davis 2007). The issue of morality and homosexuality, while not directly in opposition to his previously held religious justifications against same-sex marriage, began to open a door toward a softening on his opposition to same-sex marriage. During the CNN/YouTube debates in July 2007, Obama responded to Anderson Cooper's question about the constitutionality of same-sex marriage by stating, "We've got to make sure that everybody is equal under the law," and then arguing that individual religious groups were responsible for determining how they wished to handle the issue of same-sex marriage. He said, "With respect to marriage, it's my belief that it's up to the individual denominations to make a decision as to whether they want to recognize marriage or not. But in terms of, you know, the rights of people to transfer property, to have hospital visitation, all those critical civil rights that are conferred by our government, those should be equal" (Part I: CNN/YouTube 2007). The indirect use of religious denominations reflected a careful rhetorical move away from Obama's personal religious beliefs and left space for those denominations that were already performing same-sex marriage in states where laws allowed for its practice. In the 2008 election cycle, both during the primaries and in the race against John McCain, Obama continually redirected questions pertaining to same-sex marriage toward strengthening civil unions. In April 2008, he went on *Hardball* with Chris Matthews and reaffirmed this, stating, "I'm not in favor of gay marriage, but I'm in favor of a very strong civil union" (MSNBC 2008). He concluded his remarks on civil unions by making an important rhetorical shift, which showed the emergence of an evolution toward support for same-sex marriage, by saying, "I think young people are way ahead of the curve on this issue, and I think it's important for the rest of the country to catch up and make sure that everybody is treated the same, regardless of sexual orientation." Obama began to make a significant rhetorical turn in the ever-evolving narrative of same-sex marriage. By beginning to reference youth as the most progressive voice on this issue, although his personal position still involved distancing, he used the voice of the youth as a way to gesture toward future movement on this issue.

After his election, attention turned toward ending DADT as it had been a campaign promise. Reportedly, in his first meeting with the Joint Chiefs of Staff during 2010, Obama presented the repeal of DADT as a top priority (Bumiller 2010). In his State of the Union address in 2010, the president advocated for repeal, stating, "This year, I will work with Congress and our military to finally repeal the law that denies gay Americans the right to serve the country they love because of who they are" (Obama 2010). Obama's rhetoric related to DADT consistently included the inevitable conversations about same-sex marriage. By the end of 2010 and before the repeal of DADT, the president's evolutionary rhetoric emerged as an active component of what would eventually lead to his support for same-sex marriage.

During the work to repeal DADT in 2010, the president was asked about his stance on gay marriage, given his strong opposition to the military policy. Simultaneously, President Obama was fighting governmental administrative statements limiting marriage to that between a man and a woman. Throughout 2010 and 2011, the president softened his position, fully retreating from rhetoric reliant on faith or religion, moving toward a humanizing rhetoric. He spoke of the bonds he had with friends and colleagues who desired marriage as gay couples. In October 2010 as the repeal of "Don't Ask, Don't Tell" neared its end, he stated:

> I have been to this point unwilling to sign on to same-sex marriage primarily because of my understandings of the traditional definition of marriage, but I also think...that attitudes evolve, including mine. And I think that it is an issue that I wrestle with and think about because I have a whole host of friends who are in gay partnerships. I have staff

members who are in committed, monogamous relationships, who are raising children, who are wonderful parents. And I care about them deeply. And so while I'm not prepared to reverse myself here, sitting in the Roosevelt Room at 3:30 in the afternoon, I think it's fair to say that it's something that I think a lot about. That's probably the best you'll do out of me today. (Sudbay 2010)

The DADT debate created a space for the president's narrative to gradually evolve away from religious arguments against marriage, and by the end of 2010, prior to the congressional mandate to move toward formal repeal of DADT, to open himself up to the possibility of a rhetorical shift in support of same-sex marriage. By the time he announced his support of same-sex marriage in 2012, he revealed that "he had decided to support gay marriage some time ago, but had been deciding the most appropriate time to publicly announce it" ("Will Obama," 2012). It seems likely that the president used an evolutionary narrative to gradually shift toward full support without abruptly changing course and seeming disingenuous or setting himself up for the accusation of flip-flopping to gain political cachet.

Further revealing Obama's shift toward supporting same-sex marriage, Attorney General Eric Holder sent a letter to John Boehner, Speaker of the House, stating, "the President and I have concluded that classifications based on sexual orientation warrant heightened scrutiny and that, as applied to same-sex couples legally married under state law, Section 3 of DOMA is unconstitutional" (Holder 2011). The repeal of DADT officially came in July 2011 and was instituted on September 20 of that same year. The letter sent by Attorney General Holder, the repeal of DADT, and Obama's continually evolving rhetoric all led to speculation that the president was leaning toward an announcement in support of same-sex marriage.

The president showed his hand during an interview with George Stephanopoulos (Transcript 2011), who asked about his shift from civil unions to supporting same-sex marriage. Obama stated, "I probably won't make the news right now, George. But I think that there's no doubt that as I see friends, families, children of gay couples who are thriving, you know, that has an impact on how I think about these issues." Stephanopoulos and other media commentators used the term "evolving" during interviews and in media coverage of Obama's rhetorical choices. The emergent theme of evolving ideals helped Obama to frame same-sex marriage as an issue on which the nation was changing its opinion. Over the three years between his election and his official support of same-sex marriage, Obama's shifting rhetoric aligned with the shifting public attitudes on same-sex marriage approval. Ratings for the repeal of DADT rose from just 44 percent in 1993 to nearly 75 percent in 2010 (O'Keefe & Agiesta 2010). Even more strikingly, 51 percent of Americans polled favored same-sex marriage (Gates 2012). Most significantly, 73 percent of eighteen to twenty-nine-year-olds, a voting bloc Obama hoped to win once again, favored same-sex marriage (Connelly 2012).

The rhetorical roadmap above outlines the shifts in Obama's same-sex marriage discourse, highlighting the specific language used by the president to align with a growing population of same-sex marriage supporters. Obama utilized an evolutionary rhetoric that moved away from religious justifications against the issue and flowed toward humanizing discourses that placed real people at the center of his decision. The movement away from a religious reprisal occurred as Obama couched his rhetoric in a conversation about equal rights over religious freedoms, allowing for a smoother transition to same-sex marriage support.

NARRATIVE OF EVOLUTION

On the eve of President Obama's announcement that he now supports same-sex marriage, Vice President Joe Biden created an exigence for rhetorical response. Biden, on the Sunday morning talk show *Meet the Press*, overzealously noted that the president was "absolutely comfortable" with letting gays and lesbians marry (Yellin 2012). As a result of Biden's rhetorical slip-up, Obama's advisers decided to make a public announcement a full week earlier than planned. Obama came out in support of same-sex marriage in the most public and least traditionally presidential way imaginable. He announced, in an interview with ABC News' Robin Roberts (Transcript 2012), that "for me personally it is important for me to go ahead and affirm that I think same-sex couples should be able to get married." Announcing his change of heart—not in a public speech, at a private fundraising event, or at a political rally, but rather on national television—created the perfect setting for his final rhetorical turn on this issue. Keith V. Erickson (2000) suggests that "Presidents stage photo-opportunities to influence, manipulate, entreat, entice, amaze, or otherwise assume power over witnesses" (139). Presidents use visual fragments to capture an audience and construct a moment in time. Biden's accidental leak and the staged interview leaks both the evening before and the morning of its airing created a heightened sense of intrigue among the public, imagining what the president would reveal in this prime-time interview. Although Biden forced a change to the original plan, the administration still staged the announcement so as to carefully control the messaging.

An analysis of his interview with Robin Roberts reveals carefully crafted language to complement the existing rhetoric of evolution constructed in the media. The language of the interview also employs the humanizing rhetoric of previous statements about gay right issues. Second, the interview discourse relied on future and changing perspectives on the issue, such as the perspective of the president's children. Third, Obama maintained his announcement was part of his own evolving beliefs and should remain a local issue rather than a federal issue. Fourth, the religious elements of marriage were mentioned as a way to maintain alliances with faith-based groups. Finally, the president relied on the precedent of "Don't Ask, Don't Tell" as an extension of the decision to support same-sex marriage.

Humanizing Rhetoric

Most forcefully, the president utilized humanizing discourse as part of his evolutionary rhetoric on same-sex marriage. In statements leading up to his May 9 interview, the president withdrew his reliance on religious arguments against gay marriage and increasingly turned toward his human relationships with gay couples. Obama stated, "When I hear from them the pain they feel that somehow they are still considered less than full citizens when it comes to their legal rights then for me, I think it, it just has tipped the scales in that direction." One consistent shift in Obama's discourse leading up to the public announcement of full support was a reliance on rhetoric that identified human struggle as the important turning point. By couching his change of heart within a discourse of human connection, the president was able to add a sense of human emotion and connection as justification for the change. Obama further placed his decision within a narrative of human relationships by speaking about family values and reinforcing a preexisting definition of "family" by stating, "If you look at the underlying values that we care so deeply about when we describe family, commitment, responsibility, looking after one another, you know, teaching our kids to, to be responsible citizens and caring for one another, I actually think that, you know, it's consistent with our best and in some cases our most conservative values, sort of the foundation of what made this country great." In a full abandonment of any religious-based denial of same-sex marriage for moral reasons, the president used the notion of values and family to ground his support. Invoking the ideals of conservative values, namely the family, allowed for rhetoric of institutionalized respect for "commitment" and "responsibility" (Transcript: Robin Roberts 2012).

Carefully crafted rhetorical turns, such as those utilized by President Obama during his announcement to support same-sex marriage, rarely occur just in a single address. As noted above, in addresses and public announcements leading up the May 9 interview, Obama thoughtfully plotted out a rhetorical strategy to get him to the point where he could co-opt conservative values as a justification for supporting same-sex marriage. Values-based rhetoric was not the only strategy employed in the announcement, but future generations were used to highlight the progressive generational change on the issue of same-sex marriage.

Children Are Our Future

A consistent argument used in pro-gay rights discourse relies on ideals projected on future generations and how the youth of America view these important social issues. In his announcement in support of same-sex marriage, President Obama invoked this rhetorical strategy as an effective means of bolstering a potential voting bloc as well as placing future concerns squarely on the shoulders of youth not yet able to vote. He also strategically inserted progressive social values as a place of agreement among younger voters. Obama stated, "Some of this is also generational. You know, when I go to college campuses, sometimes I talk to college Republicans who think that I have terrible policies on the, the economy or on foreign policy but are very clear that when it comes to same-sex equality or, you know, sexual orientation that they believe in equality. They're much more comfortable with it." Obama's reliance on the more liberal politics of youth voters provides a point of convergence for youth who may not be fiscally or geostrategically aligned with Obama's issue positions but can find agreement on the issue of same-sex marriage. By speaking directly to this group of voters, he may have found an issue on which he, and the Democratic Party over the longer term, can gain votes.

Another rhetorical strategy that Obama employed in past speeches on same-sex marriage relied on his two daughters' desire to see their friends' same-sex partnered parents legally allowed to marry. Obama spoke of this in the May 9 interview as well:

> Malia and Sasha, they've got friends whose parents are same-sex couples. And I—you know, there have been times where Michelle and I have been sittin' around the dinner table. And we've been talkin' and—about their friends and their parents. And Malia and Sasha would—it wouldn't dawn on them that somehow their friends' parents would be treated differently. It doesn't make sense to them. And—and frankly—that's the kind of thing that prompts—a change of perspective. You know, not wanting to somehow explain to your child why somebody should be treated—differently, when it comes to—the eyes of the law.

The invocation of his own children and their relationship with the issue of same-sex marriage presented an opportunity for the president to both remind audiences of his own family values in action and to present an alternative view of the issue. Relying on a scenario that a parent could imagine, having to explain to a child why some people have rights and access to social goods while others do not, would present a challenge to a parent. Common rhetorical tropes in the debate over same-sex marriage focus on what the nation will look like if same-sex marriage were to be legalized, and Obama's reliance on family values carefully broke apart these clichés. Capitalizing on values claimed by the political right, the president's opposition provided a rhetorical space for change, including the relationship between states' rights and the role of the federal government. Obama deferred to states' rights on issues of marriage, aligning himself with a strong position held by the conservative base in opposition to his perceived progressive political views. In this case, Obama's reliance on state legislation worked to remove his opinions from the issue and give hope to members of the conservative base who believe they have power to lobby individual states more successfully than the federal government.

States' Rights vs. Federal Government

As his announcement came the day after the state of North Carolina passed a constitutional amendment banning same-sex marriage (Karimi 2012), President Obama had to carefully navigate the discourse surrounding states' rights and the intervention of the federal government. Maintaining the position that marriage has always been an issue for individual states to legislate, Obama could position himself as "personally" in favor of same-sex marriage while at the same time asserting the right of states to debate the topic, which had the effect of preventing Obama from being seen as an interventionist on the subject. Had he taken a stronger position or encouraged a federal mandate, he would have risked further scrutiny and potential backlash. In his announcement, he argued, "What you're seeing is, I think, states working through this issue in fits and starts, all across the country. Different communities are arriving at different conclusions, at different times. And I think that's a healthy process and a healthy debate. And I continue to believe that this is an issue that is going to be worked out at the local level, because historically, this has not been a federal issue." Obama's talking points in the interview with Robin Roberts included this direct response to the fear that he would attempt to exploit same-sex marriage as a federal issue because of his work in the prior months to both end DADT and to have the Supreme Court overturn the Defense of Marriage Act. At the same time that the president had to solidify his position on where he stood with respect to intervening on states' rights, the president also relied upon the successful ending of DADT to further justify his support of same-sex marriage.

Reliance on the Precedent of Don't Ask, Don't Tell

During the height of the debates over DADT, political pundits dramatized the fears of the oppositionists to create a sense of fear that undoing the law would affect unit cohesion and create ineffective soldiers (Hollar 2010, 5). The president's position, along with that of the Joint

Chiefs of Staff, held that the law was discriminatory. After the DADT policy was repealed, the controversy died down and to date no negative repercussions of the repeal have been felt. Obama, relying on the success related to the repeal of DADT, needed to insert a reminder that he had initiated the repeal and that the issue of same-sex marriage affects that same group. He said, "When I think about those soldiers or airmen or marines or sailors who are out there fighting on my behalf and yet, feel constrained, even now that Don't Ask, Don't Tell is gone, because they're not able to commit themselves in a marriage." In order to craft a strong, pointed argument in support of same-sex marriage, Obama had to include the soldiers affected by DADT, pointing out that they had been doubly discriminated.

Religion

Religion was the most challenging rhetorical roadblock that President Obama needed to surmount in this announcement address. He stated, "That they're respectful of religious liberty, that you know, churches and other faith institutions are still going to be able to make determinations about what their sacraments are, what they recognize" (Transcript: Robin Roberts 2012). Obama's relationship with the church and with organized religion, particularly within African American churches and communities, relies on a delicate balance between supporting the morals of the church and supporting religious freedoms broadly. Many African American churches are opposed to same-sex marriage and this issue was one that had the potential to lose voters with strong ties to churches. He tried to combat this by stating, "We're both—practicing Christians. And—and obviously—this position may be considered to put us at odds with—the views of—of others. But—you know, when we think about our faith, the—the thing—you know, at—at root that we think about is not only—Christ sacrificing himself on our behalf—but it's also the Golden Rule, you know? Treat others the way you'd want to be treated" (Transcript: Robin Roberts 2012). Shifting the argument from one of religion and the Christian doctrine opposed to same-sex marriage to a rhetoric based in Christ's teaching of the Golden Rule allowed Obama to excise himself from the confines of a religious ethic through its most used doctrinal teaching. Without the mention of his Christian faith, after years of using it as his defense against same-sex marriage, Obama was compelled to speak to his faith to find a way to support the choice he announced. To ignore his evolutionary shift away from a religious justification against same-sex marriage would have opened him up to far more scrutiny from the church.

President Obama's announcement in support of same-sex marriage on May 9, 2012, though accelerated due to Vice President Biden's overzealous response on a Sunday morning talk show, utilized thoughtfully constructed rhetorical strategies addressing the constituencies most affected by the announcement. Obama addressed the conservative base by appealing to the values of marriage, the youth voters on both the left and right, the religious community (especially those African American churches inclined to disagree on moral grounds), and strengthened his messaging to the gay community, in particular the military personnel affected by Don't Ask, Don't Tell. So, what of the outcomes? Barack Obama was reelected president in November 2012. How did his evolution toward supporting same-sex marriage impact his reelection?

OUTCOMES OF CHANGE AND CHALLENGES TO CHANGE

As a result of his decision to publicly support same-sex marriage, President Obama faced several challenges and a potential loss of support during the 2012 election cycle. Andrew Sullivan (2012) asserts that although Obama planned to make his support of same-sex marriage known for personal reasons and even when political gain might have been compromised, the president needed the support of the gay community. More than support, the president needed the money that came with the support of the gay community. Sullivan argues that, along with the youth vote, "One in six of Obama's fundraising bundlers is gay, and he needs their money." In addition, by speaking out on the issue of same-sex marriage, Obama was able to reintroduce a topic that his opponent wanted to avoid. In 1994, Mitt Romney said "he would do more for gay rights than his opponent [late Senator Edward Kennedy]" ("Will Obama," 2012). Romney tried to keep the discussion turned toward the economy and away from his past position in support of gay marriage. Ultimately, Romney found himself avoiding the topic altogether while Obama successfully negotiated a shift from opposition to support of same-sex marriage through his reliance on evolutionary rhetoric. This meant that rather than Obama being in the spotlight for his changing position, he was praised for political risk-taking and Romney was left without a clear rhetorical strategy, only aversion.

Although Obama's decision to publicly support same-sex marriage just months before the election was popular with youth voters and gay rights backers, Obama faced his harshest critics within the religious community. Both the Catholic Church and African American churches opposed Obama's support of same-sex marriage. Fortunately for Obama, many of his supporters in each of the religious communities were not going to withhold their votes over this one issue. Representative Emanuel Cleaver (Goff 2012), in an interview with *The Root*, stated, "Will there be some black voter drop because of the same-sex marriage issue? The answer is, unquestionably, yes. Will it be significant? No. . . . They are sophisticated enough to know that it is not a smart move to reject an individual for public office on one issue, because they would be opposed to Mitt Romney on 313 issues." Obama's position was met with rebukes from behind some pulpits on the Sunday following the announcement, but ultimately, the black vote was strong.

As for the Catholic Church, Obama did lose white Catholic votes by seven percentage points according to a Pew Research Exit Poll ("How the Faithful Voted," 2012). The Catholic Church publicly denounced same-sex marriage in the Vatican newspaper, writing, "The church is called to present itself as the lone critic of modernity, the only check . . . to the breakup of the anthropological structures on which human society was founded" ("Vatican Says" 2012). The disaffection of white Catholic voters was not entirely due to Obama's support of same-sex marriage, but it may have had an impact along with the debate over Catholic services health care providers being required to pay for birth control and also the ongoing debate over abortion. The Obama administration faced these major social issues that drew opposition by the Catholic Church. However, among Hispanic Catholics, polling data revealed an increase in support for Obama over the 2008 election ("How the Faithful Voted," 2012).

President Obama found some resistance to his announcement in support of same-sex marriage; however, overall, the president gained political capital with his announcement. As Jacob Weisberg (2012) argued, "Even some on the right praised the president for acting on principle when the politics seemed against him." Although the announcement seemed rushed at the time, in retrospect, the announcement, just as the Republican primaries were winding down and Mitt Romney emerged as the Republican candidate, was a way to inspire the disillusioned voters of 2008. Weisberg further argued that "the politics of that issue may actually be on Obama's side. Taking a moral stance on an issue of civil rights reanimated liberal voters who had drifted into disaffection, especially young voters who were crucial to his 2008 victory." Obama's rhetorical strategy likely quelled much of the potential for backlash against his decision. Polling data just after his announcement showed that "More than half of Americans say they approve of President Obama's stance that same-sex couples should be allowed to marry legally, but 60% say that his shift in position will have no bearing on how they vote in the November election" (Madhani and Norman 2012). Polling data revealed that Obama's announcement would not have a significant impact on voting decisions in either direction. Indeed, this chapter has argued that due to Obama's use of evolutionary rhetoric over time, as a strategy toward revealing a progressive decision, as detailed in the rhetorical roadmap above, created the space for the president to make such an announcement without significant backlash from voters in the 2012 election.

MODELING A RHETORICAL STRATEGY

Obama's rhetorical strategy of evolutionary change, which entailed gradually shifting his position on same-sex marriage over time, resulted in a successful model for future political rhetoric. Obama began his presidential campaign in 2007 in opposition to same-sex marriage for religious reasons. His rhetoric evolved on the issue leading up to his election and through his first term as president. From the beginning, it would have been hard to imagine such a dramatic shift happening during such a relatively short timeframe. In order to successfully traverse the large space between complete denial of same-sex marriage in favor of stronger civil unions to a public announcement supporting gay marriage on national television, Obama had to make some careful rhetorical moves. These shifts began slowly with the removal of religious rhetoric, evolving his language away from his faith and toward his human relationships with gay friends and staff members. Another significant rhetorical move included his focus on his own family, including his wife's public support for same-sex marriage as well as his daughters' relationships with children of same-sex couples. Obama's discourse eased away from civil unions entirely as he began to speak about human rights and equality. Andrew Sullivan (2012) critiqued the president for supporting civil unions in 2007, claiming it was effectively a "separate but equal" policy for gays. Taking a stand in favor of human rights for all through equality in marriage allowed Obama to navigate this complex political issue in a personal way.

The savvy rhetorical choices leading up to Obama's announcement of his support of same-sex marriage ultimately minimized backlash from his opposition and created a strengthened political position at the time of the election. Timing is everything in politics, and politics is perception. If both are true, then making his announcement months before the election allowed for financial support as well as a healthy distancing from the issue in the five months leading up to Election Day. In the weeks and months after coming out in support of same-sex marriage, Obama rarely spoke about same-sex marriage. He mentioned it briefly in his nomination acceptance at the Democratic National Convention. Evolutionary rhetoric created the perfect space for the president's shifting position to be heard, anticipated, absorbed, and critiqued quickly and with minimal impact to his overall reelection campaign. The brilliant ground game employed by the Democratic Party to reelect Obama served him well, allowing constituencies in support of same-sex marriage to feel supported while those in opposition only on this single issue could find ways to support him elsewhere.

Rather than shying away from an important political announcement because of political uncertainty, President Obama utilized an evolutionary rhetorical strategy to successfully support same-sex marriage after having strongly opposed it. Whether this was the product of strategic political foresight, a series of coincidences, or a mixture of both, the president positioned himself well for the change. In his second inaugural address, President Obama included a reference to the same-sex agenda, stating, "We, the people, declare today that the most evident of truths—

that all of us are created equal—is the star that guides us still; just as it guided our forebears through Seneca Falls, and Selma, and Stonewall" (Obama 2013). This evolution in his rhetorical presentation clearly indicated a full shift toward advocating a same-sex agenda. In the summer of 2013 the Supreme Court decided on the *U.S. v. Windsor* case in which the Court essentially overturned DOMA, ruling that the terms "marriage" and "spouse" were not terms restricted to heterosexual relationships, thus rendering DOMA unconstitutional. The rhetorical timeline presented here maps how Obama's evolutionary progress, which partnered with the repeal of DOMA, advanced the same-sex marriage agenda rapidly in a short amount of time.

REFERENCES

Bumiller, E. 2010. "Forces Pushing Obama on 'Don't Ask, Don't Tell.'" *New York Times,* January 31. Retrieved from http://www.nytimes.com/2010/02/01/us/politics/01military.html?_r=0.

Connelly, M. 2012. "Support for Gay Marriage Growing, but U.S. Remains Divided." *New York Times,* December 7. Retrieved from http://www.nytimes.com/2012/12/08/us/justices-consider-same-sex-marriage-cases-for-docket.html.

Davis, T. 2007. "After Initially Skirting Queries about Morality of Homosexuality, Clinton and Obama Offer Clarifications." *ABC News,* March 25. Retrieved from http://abcnews.go.com/blogs/politics/2007/03/after_initially/.

Erickson, K. V. 2000. "Presidential Rhetoric's Visual Turn: Performance Fragments and the Politics of Illusionism." *Communication Monographs,* 67 (2): 138–157.

Gates, S. 2012. "Gay Marriage Support, 51 Percent of Americans Are in Favor of Marriage Equality, Polls Show." *Huffington Post,* November 14. Retrieved from http://www.huffingtonpost.com/2012/11/14/gay-marriage-support-majority-americans-poll_n_2130371.html.

Goff, K. 2012. "Could Gay Marriage Spur the Black Voter Drop?" *Root,* September 17. Retrieved from http://www.theroot.com/blogs/president-barack-obama/head-cbc-why-gay-marriage-will-cost-obama.

Holder, E. 2011. "Letter from the Attorney General to Congress on Litigation Involving the Defense of Marriage Act." United States Department of Justice, February 23. Retrieved from http://www.justice.gov/opa/pr/2011/February/11-ag-223.html.

Hollar, J. 2010. "Don't Ask Gays about Don't Ask, Don't Tell: Debate on Military Policy Excludes Those Most Affected." *Extra!,* May. Retrieved from http://fair.org/extra-online-articles/don8217t-ask-gays-about-don8217t-ask-don8217t-tell/.

"How the Faithful Voted: 2012 Preliminary Analysis." November 7. Retrieved from http://www.pewforum.org/Politics-and-Elections/How-the-Faithful-Voted -2012-Preliminary-Exit-Poll-Analysis.aspx.

Jakobsen, J. R., and A. Pellegrini. 2009. "Obama's Neo-New Deal: Religion, Secularism, and Sex in Political Debates Now." *Social Research* 76 (4): 1227–1254.

Karimi, F. 2012. "North Carolina's Ban on Same-Sex Marriage Sparks Cheers, Jeers." *CNN,* May 9. Retrieved from http://www.cnn.com/2012/05/09/politics /north-carolina-marriage/index.html.

Klein, R. 2012. "President Obama Affirms His Support for Same Sex Marriage." *ABC News Blog,* May 9. Retrieved from http://gma.yahoo.com/blogs /abc-blogs/president-obama-affirms-his-support-for-same-sex-marriage .html.

Madhani, A., and J. Norman. 2012. "Poll: 51% Agree with Obama's Endorsement of Gay Marriage." *USA Today,* May 11. Retrieved from http://usatoday30. usatoday.com/news/washington/story/2012-05-11/USA-TODAYGallup-poll -Obama-gay-marriage/54905424/1.

Obama, B. H. 2010. "Remarks by the President in State of the Union Address." Speech, January 27. WWTW Chicago Public Television. Debate.

Obama, B. H. 2013. "Inaugural Address by President Obama." Speech, January 21. Retrieved from http://www.whitehouse.gov/the-press-office/2013/01/21 /inaugural-address-president-barack-obama.

O'Keefe, E., and J. Agiesta. 2010. "75% Back Letting Gays Serve Openly." *Washington Post*, February 12. Retrieved from http://www.washingtonpost.com /wp-dyn/content/article/2010/02/11/AR2010021104873.html.

"Part I: CNN/YouTube Democratic Presidential Debate Transcript." 2007. *CNN*, July 24. Retrieved from http://www.cnn.com/2007/POLITICS/07/23/debate .transcript/.

MSNBC. 2008. "*Hardball* with Chris Matthews." Transcript. *Project Vote Smart*, April 2. Retrieved from http://votesmart.org/public-statement/330744 /msnbc-hardball-with-chris-matthews-transcript.

Sudbay, J. 2010. "Transcript of Q and A with the President about DADT and Same-Sex Marriage." *Americablog,* October 27. Retrieved from http:// americablog.com/2010/10/transcript-of-q-and-a-with-the-president-about -dadt-and-same-sex-marriage.html.

Sullivan, A. 2012. "Newsweek's Andrew Sullivan on Barack Obama: The First Gay President." *Daily Beast*, May 13. Retrieved from http://www.thedailybeast.com /newsweek/2012/05/13/andrew-sullivan-on-barack-obama-s-gay-marriage -evolution.html.

"Transcript: George Stephanopoulos's ABC News/Yahoo! News Exclusive Interview with President Obama." 2011. *ABC News,* October 3. Retrieved from http://abcnews.go.com/Politics/transcript-george-stephanopoulos-abc-news -yahoo-news-exclusive/story?id=14659193.

"Transcript: Robin Roberts's ABC News Interview with President Obama." 2012. *ABC News,* May 9. Retrieved from http://abcnews.go.com/Politics/transcript -robin-roberts-abc-news-interview-president-obama/story?id=16316043.

"Vatican Says It Will Never Condone Gay Marriage: Same-Sex Marriage Gains Abroad Strengthen Catholic Church's Opposition." *CBC News,* November 10. Retrieved from http://www.cbc.ca/news/world/story/2012/11/10/wrd-vatican -gay-marriage-opposition.html.

Weisberg, J. 2012. "Obama's Agility on Gay Marriage and Immigration Is Making Romney Look Stodgy and Unprincipled." *Slate,* June 21. Retrieved from http:// www.slate.com/articles/news_and_politics/the_big_idea/2012/06/obama_s _gay_marriage_and_immigration_moves_how_the_president_is_outfoxing _romney_.html.

"Will Obama's Support of Gay Marriage Help Him Politically?" 2012. *US News & World Report: The Debate Club,* May 11. Retrieved from http://www.usnews. com/debate-club/will-obamas-support-of-gay-marriage-help-him-politically.

Yellin, J. 2012. "Biden Apologizes to Obama for Marriage Controversy." *CNN,* May 10. Retrieved from http://www.cnn.com/2012/05/10/politics/obama-same-sex -marriage/index.html.

IV. Voting

Chapter 10

The Predisposing, Motivating, and Constraining Factors of Early Voting
Assessing the Impact of Campaign Strategies and Voting Laws

Lisa Hager, Kent State University

INTRODUCTION

Theoretical models describing the decision to vote weigh individual benefits against the costs of voting (Downs 1957; Riker and Ordeshook 1968). Consequently, studies examining turnout also tend to focus on the costs associated with voting on Election Day (Piven and Cloward 1988; Teixeira 1992; Wolfinger and Rosenstone 1980). Early or convenience voting systems are popular for decreasing the costs of voting by allowing voters to cast their ballots prior to Election Day, thus increasing turnout. Early voting systems have become much more common in the United States with every state utilizing at least one system. Absentee voting by mail, in person, or at a satellite polling place are the most common early voting systems in most U.S. states. Other systems include vote by mail (VBM) in Washington and Oregon, vote by phone in Maine and Vermont, and vote by fax in Montana and Alaska (Gronke et al. 2008).

This chapter seeks to determine the individual, legal, and campaign factors that affected whether citizens voted early in the 2008 presidential election. Investigation into the 2008 election is warranted for three reasons. First, according to the Census Bureau's Current Population Study Voter and Registration Supplement, the 2008 presidential election saw a noteworthy increase in early voting from 20 percent in 2004 to 30 percent in 2008. Second, prior to the 2008 election, numerous states passed same-day voting registration laws and allowed for multiple types of early voting (McDonald 2008). Third, the Obama campaign took advantage of these voting law reforms and included early voting in the campaign's voter registration and mobilization efforts (Luo and Nixon 2008; Saulny 2008; Zeleny 2008).

The analysis in this chapter differs from prior research in three ways. First, the focus will be only on presidential elections rather than gubernatorial, congressional, or a combination of the three, and all types of early voting across all states will be investigated instead of only one form of early voting in one or a few states. Second, previous research has also not tested a full model of early voting including all individual, campaign, and legal factors that have been theorized to influence early voting behavior. Third, no study has sought to determine the impact that the aforementioned factors had in 2008. The study conducted by Gronke, Hicks, and Toffey (2009) tested a limited model and only sought to determine if, in 2008, the Obama campaign was able to mobilize citizens, specifically Southern African Americans, who are not predisposed to vote early. A variety of predictions will be developed and tested to determine if current models of early voting fully explain the 2008 election. It is possible that individual predictors of early voting were less relevant than legal factors because of the recent early voting law reforms in many states. It is also possible that citizens not predisposed to vote early did so because of the Obama campaign's emphasis on early voting and the media coverage the campaign received. This possibility is in direct contrast with existing models predicting that individuals who are highly attentive to the campaign take longer to decide whom to vote for and will vote on Election Day. The results will also be discussed in relation to the 2012 presidential election and the use of early voting as a campaign strategy. The chapter will conclude by discussing opportunities for future research.

DOES EARLY VOTING INCREASE TURNOUT OR VICE VERSA?

Initial research concentrated on whether early voting systems decreased the costs of voting and increased turnout. Results have been mostly mixed, varying based on the method of early voting and the state included in the analysis. For example, an early study by Patterson and Caldeira (1985) analyzed the impact of turnout on in-person and by-mail absentee voting in California and Iowa during the 1978 and 1982 gubernatorial elections. The results indicated that higher turnout only increased early voting consistently in gubernatorial elections in Iowa. The most commonly analyzed state is Oregon because elections are conducted completely by mail and voting by mail (VBM) increases turnout in local and primary elections (Berinsky, Burns, and Traugott 2001; Karp and Banducci 2000; Magleby 1987; Southwell 2010). Since interest is typically low for local and primary elections, voters are less likely to turn out, but VBM decreases the costs of voting in these elections and increases the likelihood that citizens will vote.

Similar studies investigating the relationship between early voting and turnout in midterm and general elections have reported more definitive results at both the state and national levels. In California and Tennessee, increased turnout was not found to produce higher levels of early voting (Dubin and Kalsow 1996; Neeley and Richardson 2001). In a nationwide study spanning 1972–2002, Fitzgerald (2005) found that statewide turnout has not increased following early voting law reform. Additionally, the ease of early voting has not been found to consistently increase the likelihood that voters will vote early (Gronke and Toffey 2008; Kousser and Mullin 2007), but early voting law reform has been found to lead to a brief increase in the number of ballots cast early (Dubin and Kalsow 1996; Oliver 1996). Early voting law reform has been argued to make early voting more accessible to those already predisposed to vote where early voters have been found to use the most convenient method not requiring an excuse (Giammo and Brox 2010; Gronke, Hicks, and Toffey 2009).

While few studies have shown that there is no increase in turnout from early voting, even fewer studies have found that early voting does increase turnout. Studies on Oregon and Texas have found that early voting, particularly VBM, increases turnout (Berinsky, Burns, and Traugott 2001; Southwell 2010; Stein and García-Monet 1997). Increases in nationwide turnout following early voting law reform are very limited. In a study spanning 1980–2004, Gronke, Galanes-Rosenbaum, and Miller (2007) found that VBM is the only form of early voting that increases turnout and this only occurs in presidential elections. Giammo and Brox (2010) found that any increases that are evidenced disappear by the second general election following the early voting law reform. In sum, the literature on early voting and turnout suggests that VBM is the most successful at increasing turnout, but observing an increase in turnout varies by state, type of election, and the law on early voting.

WHO VOTES EARLY?

In addition to determining the impact that early voting has on turnout, research has sought to determine who votes early, which may begin to explain recent increases in early voting. Most studies found that the same sociodemographic characteristics that increase participation on Election Day (education, income, age, race, political knowledge, and political engagement) are also associated with early voting. In other words, early voters are typically white, older, wealthier, and more educated with higher levels of political knowledge and participation than Election Day voters (Barreto et al. 2006; Dubin and Kalsow 1996; Fitzgerald 2005; Gronke, Hicks, and Toffey 2009; Gronke and Toffey 2008; Karp and Banducci 2000, 2001; Oliver 1996; Patterson and Caldeira 1985; Stein 1998; Stein and García-Monet 1997; Southwell and Burchett 2000). However, there is a lack of consensus within the literature because each characteristic does not always directly impact early voting. For example, Neeley and Richardson's (2001) study on Tennessee found no difference between Election Day and early voters for any of the aforementioned sociodemographic characteristics. The lack of consistent results is likely due to the variation in the types of early voting, elections, and states included in empirical analyses.

Despite the lack of consistency on the relationship between sociodemographic characteristics and early voting behavior, there is agreement that these characteristics need to remain in empirical models. However, a lack of consensus exists within the literature regarding political party affiliation, early voting, and turnout. Studies on gubernatorial and presidential elections have found that neither political party benefits from early voting. However, most of the studies focused on only one or a couple of states (Neeley and Richardson 2001; Patterson and Caldeira 1985; Stein 1998). Karp and Banducci's (2001) study of congressional and presidential elections found no advantage for either party except that early voters were stronger partisans. Studies on VBM have also found varying results. In general, no partisan difference was found except for a study by Southwell (2010), who found that more Democrats voted by mail in Oregon (Berinsky, Burns, and Traugott 2001; Karp and Banducci 2000; Stein and García-Monet 1997).

Very few studies have looked at the interactive relationship between sociodemographic characteristics and the ease of early voting, where liberal early voting laws should further accentuate an individual's likelihood of voting early. Using a national sample, Gronke and Toffey (2008) found that ease of early voting did not increase a citizen's likelihood to vote early during presidential elections, except for more educated and politically attentive individuals living in states with liberal early voting laws. Overall, the ease of early voting did not consistently strengthen the relationship between sociodemographic characteristics and the likelihood of voting early. Berinsky, Burns, and Traugott (2001) found that the introduction of VBM in Oregon, in conjunction with age, interest, and level of education, was successful at mobilizing new voters. However, only the ease of early voting alone, and in conjunction with partisan strength, was found to retain voters. The results of these studies confirm the conclusion made by Giammo and Brox (2010) that early voting law reform only makes voting easier for citizens who are already more likely to vote. What remains to be explained is if there are other factors, in addition to early voting law reform, that may influence a voter's decision to vote early.

EXPLAINING EARLY VOTING IN 2008

When seeking to explain early voting in 2008, existing models are incomplete and unable to account for two important dynamics of the 2008 election: the Obama campaign's focus on early voting in voter mobilization efforts and the media's coverage of the Obama campaign. Therefore, the model and theoretical expectations are based on the short-term and long-term forces that influence voting behavior and the length of time it takes for voters to make decisions (Alvarez 1998; Box-Steffens-meier and Kimball 1999; Campbell et al. 1960). Long-term forces are factors that affect the voter prior to the presidential campaign and election such as demographics, partisan identification, political knowledge, and political sophistication, while short-term factors are specific to the campaign and election.

According to Kessel (1968), strong partisans are the first to decide, followed closely by more politically involved and motivated citizens who obtain candidate and issue information early. Indecisive citizens who are heavily influenced by short-term campaign factors and unmotivated citizens are the last to decide (Box-Steffensmeier and Kimball 1999; Campbell et al. 1960; Fournier et al. 2004; Kessel 1968). In general, citizens who are heavily influenced by or attentive to campaigns tend to be more ambivalent and unable to reduce uncertainty and vote on Election Day, not early (Alvarez 1998). However, this would not be expected to be the case in 2008 when highly attentive citizens were probably more likely to vote early because of the media's coverage of the Obama campaign's focus on voter registration and early voting. Overall, the two most important determinants in predicting whether an individual will vote early is the ability to choose between candidates quickly and with certainty where citizens are expected to vote when they are confident in their decision.

Individual Factors

Explaining early voting in 2008 requires that long-term factors typically associated with increasing voter turnout but that have also been linked to early voting be examined. Since previous studies have found that early voters are older, wealthier, highly educated, and white, it is expected that this also would be the case in 2008 (Dubin and Kalsow 1996; Fitzgerald 2005; Gronke and Toffey 2008; Karp and Banducci 2000, 2001; Stein 1998; Stein and García-Monet 1997).

Individuals with strong party identifications and extreme ideological views are expected to vote early because they can choose a candidate quickly and with certainty, which are two of the most important determinants of early voting. These individuals can choose between candidates much faster because vote choice is usually based on a candidate's party identification or ideology (Converse 1962; Fournier et al. 2004;

Gronke and Toffey 2008; Karp and Banducci 2001). These individuals are also more certain in their decision and less likely to change their minds because they view the campaign through a partisan or ideological filter that allows them to reject any opposing partisan or ideological messages (Box-Steffensmeier and Kimball 1999; Zaller 1992).

Politically knowledgeable voters are also expected to vote early because they are able to make decisions quicker and with more certainty (Box-Steffensmeier and Kimball 1999; Gronke and Toffey 2008; Karp and Banducci 2001). Rather than relying on partisan or ideological cues to make decisions, politically knowledgeable voters possess a sufficient amount of information on the parties, candidates, and policies to choose a candidate and feel confident in that decision. In addition to campaign-related political knowledge, voters must understand the process of early voting, such as whether an excuse is needed, when early voting begins, the types of early voting available, and so on. Therefore, it is expected that individuals reporting higher levels of previous political participation at the local, state, and national levels will have the knowledge and skills to vote early. It is important to make a distinction between political skills that indicate that voters are aware of and know how to take advantage of early voting compared to skills that may actually decrease the likelihood of voting early. A good example is whether citizens know where to vote in their neighborhood. Citizens who know their precinct location are probably more likely to vote on Election Day.

Before moving on to legal and campaign factors that are expected to influence the likelihood of voting early, it is important to note that the 2008 presidential election may not conform to models previously used to predict early voting. The Obama campaign's emphasis on early voting and voter registration was not only evident in mobilization efforts, but was also covered extensively by the media (Luo and Nixon 2008; Saulny 2008; Steinhauer 2008; Zeleny 2008). Campaign volunteers canvassed neighborhoods, sent out mailers, and made telephone calls urging citizens to not only register to vote but to vote early (Luo and Nixon 2008). A common way campaigns encourage early voting is by mailing citizens absentee ballot request forms. Due to the amount of exposure that Americans had to the possibility of voting early, and the fact that the Obama campaign mailed citizens voter registration and absentee ballot requests, it is possible that early voters may not differ significantly from Election Day voters on any of the aforementioned individual-level characteristics.

Campaign Factors

Short-term factors are those directly related to campaigns and elections (Campbell et al. 1960). Research on early voting has focused very little on the impact that campaign participation and media campaign coverage can have on early voters; however, this is a necessity when studying the 2008 election. The question of how much of an impact campaigns have on early voters has been approached by how campaigns can influence voter decision making. Even though partisan, politically engaged, and knowledgeable voters tend to have higher levels of campaign attentiveness, they are less likely to be influenced by campaigns in the long run. These individuals will make voting decisions quicker and be more likely to vote early because inconsistent information is rejected and they are more certain with their decision (Box-Steffensmeier and Kimball 1999; Karp and Banducci 2001; Zaller 1992). Gronke and Toffey (2008) found mixed and inconsistent results regarding the impact that campaign attention has on early voters. Such results are also unable to confirm the theoretical expectation that citizens who are highly attentive to the media are uncertain, ambivalent, and unlikely to vote early (Alvarez 1998; Box-Steffensmeier and Kimball 1999; Fournier et al. 2004; Kessel 1968). Due to media coverage of the Obama campaign's efforts to register voters and promote early voting, it is expected that individuals with higher levels of media attentiveness were likely exposed to such stories and are more likely to vote early.

Involvement in a campaign is yet another way to determine an individual's exposure and engagement with election information. Very little focus has been placed on the impact of campaign involvement except for the study by Gronke and Toffey (2008), which did not find campaign activists as more likely to vote early. However, according to Kessel (1968), individuals who report high levels of campaign involvement should be more likely to vote early because they make their voting decisions quicker, especially individuals who are active volunteers or provide campaign donations to parties, candidates, and other campaign organizations. This leads to the prediction that individuals reporting higher levels of campaign involvement, such as posting signs, volunteering, or attending rallies, are more likely to vote early. It is also expected that individuals who make campaign contributions vote early. Campaign involvement is separate from contribution activity because donating to campaigns is heavily dependent on an individual's disposable income, not level of engagement with the campaign.

Political mobilization is another way that campaigns are able to provide citizens with campaign information. In general, research has found that political mobilization efforts increase turnout (Gerber and Green 2000; Goldstein and Ridout 2002; McCann et al. 1996). Prior research has not found evidence that early voters were contacted more than Election Day voters (Gronke and Toffey 2008). However, early voting has increased by half from the 2004 to 2008 elections (McDonald 2008) and the promotion of early voting is regularly used as a campaign strategy to mobilize loyal supporters before focusing attention on undecided voters (Gronke and Toffey 2008; Stein 1998). Since both campaigns sought to secure early voters by sending out absentee ballot request forms and advocating for other forms of early voting, it is expected that respondents who were contacted by either political party were more likely to vote early than respondents who were not contacted.

An individual's campaign interest has been found to increase the likelihood that the individual will vote (Wolfinger and Rosenstone 1980), and has rarely been included in studies of early voting. Berinsky, Burns, and Traugott (2001) did include a measure of campaign interest but found that higher levels of campaign interest did not significantly increase the likelihood that an individual will vote early by mail in Oregon. However, this is not expected to be the case in a nationwide study on all forms of early voting in the 2008 election where early voting was a prominent campaign message. Campaign interest motivates individuals to become politically knowledgeable and pay attention to media coverage of the campaign. Not only does interest motivate an individual to obtain information, but it has been argued that interested individuals make voting decisions sooner. Therefore, interested individuals were probably more likely to be exposed to information regarding early voting in 2008, so it is expected that individuals with higher levels of campaign interest will vote early.

Legal Factors

Previous studies have found that the ease of early voting can heavily influence whether a citizen votes early (Dubin and Kalsow 1996; Giammo and Brox 2010; Gronke and Toffey 2008; Oliver 1996). According to the United States Election Assistance Commission's (EAC) 2008 Election Administration and Voting Survey, there are four different early voting laws states can have:

1. An excuse is needed to vote early in person or by mail.
2. An excuse is needed to vote early by mail, and in person early voting is not allowed.
3. An excuse is needed to vote early by mail, but no excuse is needed to vote early in person.
4. No excuse is needed to vote early by mail or in person.

It is expected that citizens living in states with more liberal early voting laws, where at least one form of early voting does not require an excuse (#3 and #4 above), will be more likely to vote early than citizens living in states with stricter early voting laws (#1 and #2 above).

ANALYZING EARLY VOTING BEHAVIOR IN 2008

A model to explain early voting for the 2008 presidential election was created using data from the 2008 American National Election Studies (ANES) Time Series Study, a survey conducted on a nationally representative sample of voting-aged Americans during the election. Early voting was measured by responses to the question, "Did the respondent vote on Election Day or before Election Day?" Consequently, respondents who did not vote in the election will not be included in the analysis. The majority of the aforementioned individual, campaign, and legal factors expected to predict early voting are also measured using data from the 2008 ANES Time Series Study. To account for the possibility that respondents viewed early voting as a partisan message because of the Obama campaign's emphasis on early voting, partisan identification and vote choice will also be included in the model (Luo and Nixon 2008; McDonald 2008).[1]

The chapter will proceed by examining each individual, campaign, and legal factor included in the model in three separate analyses. First, each factor will be examined alone, without taking any of the other factors into account, to see whether it directly impacts early voting behavior as predicted. Second, all of the factors will be tested simultaneously to determine which factors are the most important in explaining early voting behavior. Finally, separate analyses will be run based on the ease of early voting to show how the different early voting laws can interact with the individual and campaign factors to encourage or impede individuals from voting early. There are two possible results for individuals living in states with liberal early voting laws. The first is that individual and campaign factors will better predict early voting behavior because there are no barriers to early voting. The other alternative is that because early voting does not require an excuse, even citizens who are not predisposed to vote early take advantage of early voting, leading to very few, if any, differences between early and Election Day voters. For residents living in states requiring an excuse to vote early, it is expected that very few differences exist between early and Election Day voters because a vast majority of voters predisposed to vote early will likely not have an excuse to do so.

RESULTS: THE CHARACTERISTICS OF EARLY VOTERS IN 2008

Beginning with the predisposing or individual factors, the individual analysis revealed that each is related to early voting as predicted.[2] The relationships between early voting and age, education, strength of partisanship, strength of ideology, political knowledge, and political skills have all been found to significantly increase the likelihood of voting early. All but one of the campaign-level factors is related to early voting as predicted. Instead of increasing the likelihood of voting early, respondents paying more attention to the campaign in the media are significantly less likely to vote early. This result supports the prior literature arguing that highly attentive voters are uncertain, ambivalent, and less likely to vote early (Alvarez 1998; Box-Steffensmeier and Kimball 1999; Campbell et al. 1960). A few of the campaign factors—campaign involvement, campaign funding, and campaign interest—increase the likelihood of voting early. So too does the ease of early voting where individuals living in states with liberal voting laws are more likely to vote early than individuals living in states requiring an excuse to vote early. It is important to note that Democrats and Obama voters were less rather than more likely to vote early as predicted.

Now that it has been established which individual, campaign, and legal factors significantly impact early voting, all of the factors will be examined together to determine which mattered most in 2008. The results indicate that only voters who were older, made campaign contributions, and were residents of states with liberal early voting laws were significantly more likely to vote early. Beginning with age, Figure 10.1 shows the predicted probabilities of voting early for individuals based on age and type of early voting law.[3] As can be seen, the likelihood of early voting increases at a much higher rate for individuals living in states with liberal early voting laws compared to individuals living in states with strict early voting laws. For example, the likelihood of voting early for individuals aged twenty, forty, sixty, and eighty in states with liberal early voting laws is 36 percent, 44 percent, 52 percent, and 60 percent, respectively; however, the likelihood of voting early for individuals living in states with strict early voting laws is less than 10 percent for individuals aged twenty to fifty and never exceeds 15 percent for individuals older than fifty.

The only campaign factor found to influence early voting behavior in the 2008 election was campaign contribution activity. Respondents making campaign contributions were 6.5 percent, 13 percent, or 19 percent more likely to vote early than individuals not making campaign contributions, depending on how many of the following the individuals contributed funds to: candidates, parties, or other campaign organizations. Overall, the ease of early voting was found to have the most impact with individuals living in states with liberal early voting laws having a 52 percent likelihood of voting early, but with individuals living in states with strict early voting laws having only an 11 percent likelihood of voting early. In this analysis, Democrats were significantly less likely to vote early, underscoring the importance of taking party identification into account when seeking to explain early voting in 2008. The majority of the other factors found to not significantly impact early voting behavior were as predicted, except for income, race, ideological strength, political mobilization, and campaign media attentiveness. In other words, less wealthy, nonwhite, ideologically weak, nonmobilized, inattentive voters were more likely to vote early. This begins to show that no-excuse early

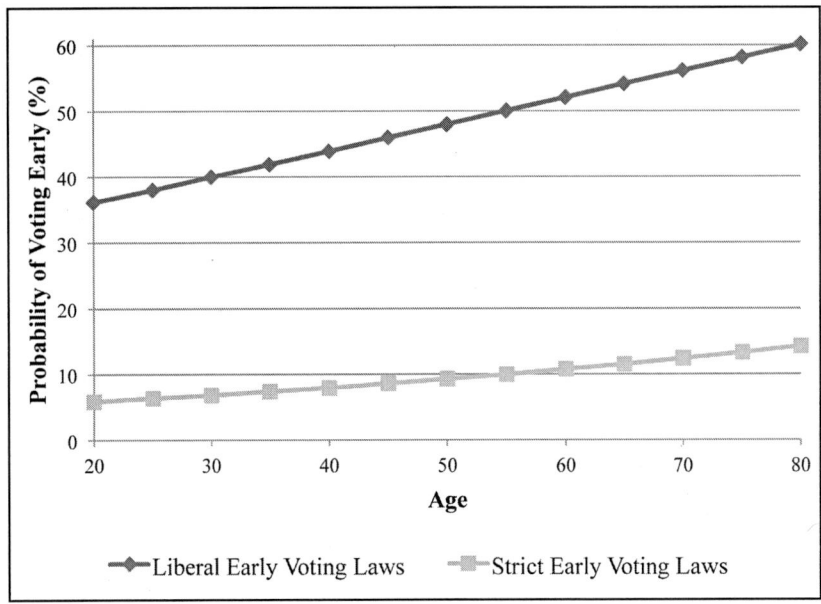

Figure 10.1 Age and Early Voting by Law Type

voting laws may lead more people to vote early (even those who are not predisposed to do so) because of the added convenience of satellite polling places and receiving absentee ballot requests in the mail.

Next, the model is analyzed based on the ease of early voting to show how the early voting law interacts with the individual and campaign factors to either encourage or hinder individuals from voting early. The results for individuals living in states with liberal early voting laws indicate that only age and political skills directly influence early voting behavior. The predicted probabilities for voting early based on age are very similar to those of the full model where the likelihood of voting early for individuals aged twenty, forty, sixty, and eighty is 38 percent, 46 percent, 53 percent, and 60 percent, respectively. With respect to political skills, individuals are 4 percent to as high as 14 percent more likely to vote early than respondents with no reported political skills. It is important to note that, again, Democrats were significantly less likely to vote early, further underscoring the importance of taking partisanship into account when studying early voting in 2008.

Even though no campaign factors were found to significantly impact early voting behavior, campaign donors were just shy of being found significantly more likely to vote early than Election Day voters, as was the case in the previous analysis.[4] Also, most of the associations each individual and campaign factor had with early voting from the previous analysis are found to persist in this analysis. The only differences are that income and campaign media attentiveness are now associated with early voting as predicted where higher levels of both should increase the likelihood of voting early. Overall, the results indicate that there appear to be very few differences between early and Election Day voters in states with liberal early voting laws. This lends support to the idea that even those who are not predisposed to vote early will do so.

For individuals living in states with strict early voting laws, only age and lack of knowledge of precinct location are significant predictors of early voting. Individuals aged twenty, forty, sixty, and eighty have a 3 percent, 5 percent, 8 percent, and 14 percent likelihood of voting early, respectively. These are very similar to the predicted probabilities of the full model seen in Figure 10.1. Neither respondents contributing to campaigns or those possessing political skills were found to be more likely to vote early in states with strict early voting laws as was the case in the previous analyses. However, respondents knowing the location of their precinct were 8 percent less likely to vote early than respondents who did not. Most of the individual and campaign factors were found to be associated with early voting as predicted. However, many of the individual and campaign factors, such as income, race, partisanship strength, political skills, political mobilization, and campaign media attentiveness, were not. Since there are very few differences between early and Election Day voters, this lends support to the idea that strict early voting laws are impeding voters from voting early.

It is also important to note that the model explains early voting behavior much better for individuals living in states with strict early voting laws. The model explains 10 percent of the variation in early voting behavior compared to only 5 percent of the variation in states with liberal early voting laws. As will be discussed in more detail in the next section, such results begin to highlight the possibility that current models are unable to sufficiently explain early voting behavior, especially in states with liberal early voting laws. Furthermore, the use of early voting as a campaign strategy in presidential elections means that more citizens are being exposed to campaign messages urging early voting.

DISCUSSION

In the analyses of early voting behavior for the 2008 election, inconsistent results were evidenced for various campaign- and election-specific characteristics. It is likely that the results are driven by and/or are a proxy for the strength of an individual's party identification, with strong partisans being more likely to be interested in the campaign and donate to candidates, parties, and other political organizations such as PACs. However, the model used to predict the likelihood of voting early did not find these factors to matter significantly. Inconsistency was also evidenced for the impact that political skills have on early voting behavior. Findings that suggest that political skills only significantly increase the likelihood of voting early for individuals living in states with liberal voting laws are not surprising. Neither are the results that political skills are associated, albeit not significantly, with a lower likelihood of voting early for individuals living in states with strict early voting laws. Voting early requires knowledge of the process of early voting, and politically skilled individuals in states with strict early voting laws likely know voting early requires an excuse and is more difficult. Overall, the results of the analyses indicate that age and the ease of early voting mattered most in determining whether an individual voted early instead of on Election Day in 2008.

Age is the only significant individual-level factor found to increase the likelihood of voting early, so the results from this chapter do not confirm the findings of prior research that a host of other individual-level factors increase the likelihood of voting early. There are two reasons for this result. First, the elderly are more likely to vote early because of limited mobility or residing in nursing homes or other assisted care facilities that make it difficult to get to the polls on Election Day. Second, age is the one variable that is unaffected by early voting laws because even if an elderly American lives in a state with strict early voting laws, he or she has the excuse to vote early.

The ease of early voting was found to matter even more than age in predicting whether an individual voted early in the 2008 election. When breaking down the results by the ease of early voting, the results for respondents living in states with liberal early voting laws could still not confirm the results of previous studies. This casts doubt on the ability of current models to describe early voting behavior because there appears to be very little difference between Election Day and early voters on most of the factors tested. However, these results are different from those of Gronke and Toffey (2008) who did not find ease of early voting to be a significant predictor of early voting in presidential elections. The results of this study indicate that the ease of early voting really is what mattered most in 2008, meaning that voters will vote early if it is easy and convenient. In-person early voting at the Board of Elections Office or at a satellite polling place—typically located in shopping malls, grocery stores, and libraries—makes voting more convenient. An article appearing in the *New York Times* talked with early voters in various states and found that early voting is appealing because wait time is reduced and it is more convenient for those who work long hours and may not be able to get to the polls on Election Day, which is best exemplified by the following statement:

> "Voting is always a problem for us nurses," said Donna J. Simmons, 59, who cast a vote in Cleveland, anticipating a 12-hour shift on Election Day. "We're always trying to work out ways to cover for each other so one of us can go and vote. I think this event is the most wonderful thing because voting is always such a challenge for people like me." (Steinhauer 2008)

Similar sentiments were conveyed in a survey conducted by Barreto et al. (2006) in which 37 percent of respondents reported voting early because of the ease and convenience.

Both campaigns advocated for in-person and by-mail early voting by sending out mailings, including absentee ballot request forms, and sending campaign volunteers door-to-door (Luo and Nixon 2008). The Obama campaign went even further by incorporating the message of early voting into campaign speeches and building databases of supporters to identify those with possible obstacles to voting on Election Day, such as long commutes or multiple children (Luo and Nixon 2008). The Obama campaign was also heavily focused on registering and mobilizing voters who identify as Democrats but rarely turn out on Election Day, specifically African Americans (Saulny 2008; Zeleny 2008). Registering voters, informing them of the option of early voting, and/or providing them with an absentee ballot request form increases the likelihood that mobilized citizens will actually cast their ballot (Gronke et al. 2008; Oliver 1996). The strategy of promoting early voting not only worked to help elect Obama, but voter turnout also increased from 60.1 percent in 2004 to 61.6 percent in 2008 (McDonald 2008).[5]

Early Voting in 2012

Considering the success that the Obama campaign had in promoting voter registration and early voting, it is not surprising that Obama continued this strategy during his bid for reelection in 2012. The use of early voting as a campaign strategy has received very little attention in the scholarly literature other than attempting to determine if one party tends to benefit over the other (Karp and Banducci 2001; Neeley and Richardson 2001; Patterson and Caldeira 1985; Southwell 2010; Stein 1998). There is debate on whether liberal early voting laws increase or decrease the costs of running a campaign. Early voting extends the period considered the "final push" by several weeks, which increases how much campaigns spend on "get out the vote" and other mobilization tactics (Gronke 2004; Gronke et al. 2008). However, early voting may actually allow campaigns to be more efficient by focusing first on core, partisan supporters and then moving on to swing or independent voters (Gronke and Toffey 2008; Stein 1998). Typically, candidates will use a different, but not contradictory, message to appeal to the undecided voters. Many states will provide campaigns with lists of voters who have requested absentee ballots, turned in absentee ballots, and voted early in person, which makes it even easier for campaigns to identify voters to target (Gronke et al. 2008).

The push for early voting in the 2012 presidential election did not occur until early voting began on Thursday, September 27, in Iowa, the first of many states allowing no-excuse early voting. At this point, the Obama campaign announced that a new television commercial promoting early voting would begin airing in Iowa, Florida, Nevada, and Colorado (Peters 2012). As was the case in 2008, the media's coverage of early voting has focused heavily on the activity of the Obama campaign. In a *New York Times* article, Obama's campaign manager, Jim Messina, said that he "has built the President's re-election strategy around the growing trend of voting early" (Zeleny 2012). President Obama even voted early himself on Thursday, October 25, in Chicago, making him the first sitting president to vote early in person (Barbaro and Baker 2012; Hennessey 2012; Rutenberg 2012). Prior to Election Day, the strategy appeared to be working. The Iowa Secretary of State's Office reported receiving roughly five Democratic absentee ballot requests for every one Republican request, and similar results were reported in other battleground states (Rutenberg 2012; Zeleny 2012). The Republicans have been slow to embrace early voting; however, the disparity in requests and the prediction that 35 percent to 40 percent of Americans will vote early led the Republicans and the Romney campaign to place more of an emphasis on early voting (Zeleny 2012). Since Republican voters are more likely to show up on Election Day, the Obama campaign recognized the need to mobilize voters early to guarantee that supporters cast their ballots and guard against vote loss from gains made by Romney in public opinion polls (Hennessey 2012).

The Obama campaign's focus on early voting as a tactic to secure votes and guard against late gains by Romney was successful. President Obama was reelected by securing over 300 electoral votes and winning the popular vote (Zeleny and Rutenberg 2012). The role of early voting begins to become apparent as final results from each state are examined. For example, Romney won the popular vote in Iowa on Election Day, but Obama carried the state due to a total of 137,000 early votes (West 2012). Not only did early voting impact the outcome of the election, but the estimate that 35 percent to 40 percent of Americans would vote early appears to be accurate. Roughly 35 percent of Americans voted early, which is an increase from 30 percent in 2008 (West 2012; Zeleny 2012). However, a decrease in overall turnout was evidenced, as roughly 59 percent of Americans voted in 2012 as compared to 61.6 percent in 2008 (McDonald 2008, 2012).

The estimates that more Americans voted in 2008 than in 2012 support the findings of Giammo and Brox (2010) who found that reforming early voting laws only produces a momentary increase in turnout that disappears by the second presidential election after the reform has been in place. It can be inferred that the reforms only make voting more convenient for citizens who are already likely to vote. These results mean that the use of early voting as a campaign strategy is more effective at guaranteeing that individuals more likely to vote will cast a ballot regardless of any unforeseen circumstances arising that impede voting on Election Day. In addition to the comparison between 2008 and 2012, the findings are supported by the difference between 2004 and 2008 that was modest, at best, following early voting reforms in a host of states (McDonald 2008). The results of this study also support Giammo and Brox (2010) where the only differences between early and Election Day voters was that early voters are older and live in states with liberal early voting laws. This means that there is little difference between early and Election Day voters and that campaigns should focus on making early voting as convenient as possible for voters living in states with liberal early voting laws. Campaigns would also benefit if states with strict early voting laws enacted reforms eliminating the need for an excuse.

CONCLUSION

This chapter has analyzed various individual, campaign, and legal factors that influenced the likelihood of early voting in the 2008 presidential election. Analyzing each of the factors separately revealed that many of the factors are significantly associated with early voting; however, very few differences were found between early and Election Day voters when all the factors were analyzed together. The only remaining and consistently significant predictors are age and the ease of early voting, as measured by whether an excuse is required to vote early. These results are quite different from previous studies on early voting that found early and Election Day voters significantly differ from one another on many of the factors included in this study. The most significant finding of this study is that the ease of early voting was not only significant, but had the most impact on whether individuals voted early, which has not been found by prior studies, such as Gronke and Toffey's (2008).

Very few studies have utilized national surveys, opting instead to focus on only one or a few states. Gronke and Toffey's (2008) study reported results where few factors significantly impact early voting when analyzed simultaneously, and argued that this is probably because national survey questions are unable to capture the difference between Election Day and early voters. National surveys only ask respondents if they voted early without asking any follow-up questions as to why. The inclusion of such questions could begin to reveal how early voters differ from Election Day voters. It is most likely that early voters like the added convenience of voting by mail or in person at satellite polling places or at the local Board of Elections Office, which was confirmed by the survey conducted by Barreto et al. (2006). VBM is virtually effortless while in-person early voting options decrease wait times and allow voters to vote when it is convenient. The location of satellite polling places in grocery stores, shopping malls, and libraries allows citizens to vote at locations they would normally frequent. Overall, new survey questions would begin to reveal the reasons citizens vote early.

Data obtained from new survey questions asking early voters why they voted early would provide numerous opportunities for future research. Most importantly, new models need to be developed to explain the differences between Election Day and early voters. If added convenience really is the reason most citizens choose to vote early in states with liberal early voting laws, researchers can begin to determine why some voters forgo voting early in order to vote on Election Day. For example, it may be possible that Election Day voters have flexible work schedules, do not mind waiting at the polls, or there are social norms against voting early. Such social norms were expressed in the following quote from an early voter in Henderson, Nevada, that appeared in an article in the *New York Times*:

> "In New Hampshire where we came from," said Arthur Schuetz, 62, who voted Monday at the community center here in Henderson, "it is not socially acceptable to do anything but go to the polls on Election Day and stand in the snow talking with all your neighbors." (Steinhauer 2008)

Along with creating new and more explanatory models of early voting, future research should also focus on early voting as a campaign strategy. Additional studies can begin to determine if and how early voting was different in 2008 compared to 2012 at not only the individual level but also as a campaign strategy. The outcome of the election shapes the specific research questions that can be asked. Since Obama won, questions can center on how early voting was used similarly to 2008 and helped secure votes before Romney gained momentum.

Future research should not only look at the role that early voting plays in specific elections but how this shapes the campaign strategies of future candidates in both parties. Prior to the Obama campaign in 2008, no other candidate had focused heavily on voter registration and early voting. Future presidential elections will begin to provide evidence of whether this tactic is unique to the Obama campaign or to the Democratic Party. The novelty of early voting should also be taken into account when evaluating whether candidates encourage early voting. Current evidence suggests that early voting is promoted as a way to ensure that voters cast their ballots and secure votes before voters change their minds. However, early voting is also used as a way to try to increase turnout by making voting as easy as possible. Current 2012 turnout statistics have begun to support what Giammo and Brox (2010) suggest: increases in turnout are minimal and early voting reforms only impact individuals already likely to vote. Future research can examine if candidates begin to place less of an emphasis on early voting and more on general campaign messages seeking to persuade voters.

Additional studies may also look at whether early voting is being promoted by candidates in gubernatorial, congressional, and state government elections, and how the messages and tactics are the same and/or different from presidential campaigns. It is possible that candidates in races appearing on the ballots for the 2008 and 2012 elections ran campaigns differently and focused on early voting because the Obama campaign did. Early voting also changes the dynamics of the campaign for these candidates because early voters have decided and are confident with their choice for president, but this may not be the case for the other offices on the ballot, thereby making it even more important for nonpresidential candidates to appeal to and gain support from early voters.

As previously discussed, the topic of early voting provides a vast array of research opportunities for scholars studying a wide variety of actors in American politics. The observations and conclusions that can be drawn currently are somewhat limited by the data available, the status of early voting in some states, and the newness of early voting as a campaign strategy. As advancements in data collection are made and more elections are held, more thorough models can be developed and more concrete conclusions can be made on how early voting is utilized by voters, how early voting campaign messages influence voters, and how early voting aids candidates.

Appendix 10A

Data and Methods

Early Voting	Dichotomous variable with early voters = 1 and Election Day voters = 0. Since the dependent variable is dichotomous, logistic regression analysis will be used.
Age	Self-reported age, ranging from 17 to 90.
Income	Self-reported income, ranging from 1 to 25. The ANES codes income categorically with one indicating zero or less than $2,999 and 25 representing $150,000 and over. The categories do not always increase by the same amount. Near the beginning the categories increase by $2,000, near the middle by $5,000, and near the end by $15,000–$20,000.
Education	Self-reported education, ranging from 1 to 7: 0 = no formal education, 1 = formal education ending during grades K–8, 2 = formal education ending during grades 9–12, 3 = high school diploma or GED, 4 = some college, 5 = associate's degree, 6 = bachelor's degree, and 7 = advanced degree (master's, PhD, MD, etc.).
Race	Dichotomous variable with white = 1 and all other races = 0.
Partisanship Strength	Dichotomous variable with strong Democrats and Republicans = 1 and weak Democrats and Republicans, Independents leaning Democrat or Republican, and Independents = 0.
Ideological Strength	Dichotomous variable with extreme liberals and conservatives and liberals and conservatives = 1 and slight liberals and conservatives and moderates = 0.
Political Knowledge	The number of correct answers to: What job or office does Nancy Pelosi, Dick Cheney, Gordon Brown, and John Roberts currently hold? A total of four questions were used, so the variable ranges from 0 to 4. Since the ANES has not released the coded data from any open-ended items, only the verbatim responses, the coded data were obtained from Martinez and Craig (2010).
Political Skills	The number of reported political and civic skills from the following: attending a community or school meeting, contacting elected officials, and voting in the 2004 election. A total of three items were used, so the variable ranges from 0 to 3.
Know Precinct Location	Dichotomous variable with knowledge of precinct location = 1 and no knowledge = 0.
Political Mobilization	Answers to "Anyone from one of the political parties contact you?" coded as a dichotomous variable with yes = 1 and no = 0.

Campaign Involvement	The reported level of campaign involvement from the following: wearing a campaign button or posting a sign or bumper sticker, attending political meetings, rallies, and/or speeches, working for a party or candidate, and talking to anyone about voting for or against a candidate. Four items were used, so the variable ranges from 0 to 4.
Campaign Funding	The number of political organizations the respondent provided campaign contributions to from the following: a specific candidate, a political party, and any other group for or against a specific candidate. Three items were used, so the variable ranges from 0 to 3.
Campaign Media Attention	The total reported level of campaign media attentiveness to TV, the Internet, radio, and newspapers: none = 0, very little or a little = 1, some or a moderate amount = 2, quite a bit or a lot = 3, and a great deal = 4. Totals were divided by the number of sources the respondent paid attention to, so the variable ranges from 0 to 4.
Campaign Interest	Self-reported interest in the campaign ranging from 0 to 5: no interest = 0, not much interest = 1, slight interest = 2, moderately or somewhat interested = 3, very interested = 4, and extreme or very much interest = 5
Partisanship	Dichotomous variable with Democrats = 1 and Republicans and Independents = 0.
Vote Choice	Dichotomous variable with Obama = 1 and McCain or third-party candidates = 0.
Ease of Early Voting	Dichotomous variable with states not requiring an excuse to vote early in person or by mail = 1 and states requiring excuses to vote in person or by mail = 0. Data obtained from the United States Election Assistance Commission's (EAC) 2008 Election Administration and Voting Survey. Appendix B lists the law of each state included.

Appendix 10B

States and Early Voting Laws

Excuses Needed by Mail and in Person	Excuse Needed by Mail and in Person Not Allowed	Excuse Needed by Mail but No Excuse Needed in Person	No Excuse Needed by Mail or in Person
Alabama	Connecticut	Illinois	Arizona
Delaware	D.C.	Indiana	California
Mississippi	Massachusetts	Louisiana	Colorado
Virginia	Michigan	Tennessee	Florida
	Minnesota	Texas	Georgia
	New York		Kansas
	Pennsylvania		Nevada
	Rhode Island		New Jersey
	South Carolina		New Mexico
			North Carolina
			North Dakota
			Ohio
			Oklahoma
			Wisconsin

Note: Respondents from Oregon and Washington were excluded from the analysis because all elections are conducted by mail (United States Election Assistance Commission 2008).

Appendix 10C

Descriptive Statistics

Variable	Observations	Mean	Standard Deviation	Min.	Max.	Imputed Observations
Early Voting	1,566	.39	.49	0	1	0
Age	1,550	48.48	16.82	17	90	16 (1.02%)
Income	1,454	14.38	6.05	1	25	112 (7.15%)
Education	1,558	4.19	1.55	0	7	8 (0.51%)
Race	1,556	.53	.50	0	1	10 (0.64%)
Partisanship Strength	1,546	.42	.49	0	1	20 (1.28%)
Ideological Strength	1,156	.46	.50	0	1	410 (26.18%)
Political Knowledge	1,563	1.23	.96	0	4	3 (0.19%)
Political Skills	1,566	1.25	.84	0	3	0
Know Precinct Location	1,556	.76	.43	0	1	10 (0.64%)
Political Mobilization	1,566	.47	.50	0	1	0
Campaign Involvement	1,566	.90	.99	0	4	0
Campaign Funding	1,565	.25	.62	0	3	1 (0.06%)
Campaign Media Attention	1,538	1.36	.81	0	4	28 (1.79%)
Campaign Interest	1,566	3.51	.95	0	5	0
Vote Choice	1,552	.65	.48	0	1	38 (2.43%)
Partisanship	1,528	.47	.50	0	1	14 (0.89%)
Ease of Early Voting	1,566	.74	.44	0	1	0

Notes: The percentage of observations imputed is in parentheses. Single imputation is used to predict values for respondents with missing values on a given independent variable based on the values of the other independent variables included in the model. For the index variables of political knowledge, political skills, campaign involvement, and campaign funding, single imputation is used for respondents not answering any of the items used to create the variable. Respondents answering at least one of the questions were recoded as zero when creating the scale with the exception of the political skills variable because the items used were not asked consecutively. Instead, respondents were recoded with the mode. Diagnostics did not reveal any outliers, influential cases, or problems with multicollinearity.

Appendix 10D

Logistic Regression Analysis Results

Variable	Bivariate Model (N = 1566)		Multivariate Model (N = 1566, Pseudo R² = .1418)		Liberal Early Voting Laws (N = 1158, Pseudo R² = .0459)		Strict Early Voting Laws (N = 408, Pseudo R² = .1023)	
	Coefficient (SE)	z score	Coefficient (SE)	z score	Coefficient (SE)	z score	Coefficient (SE)	z score
Age	.012** (.003)	3.97	.016** (.004)	4.34	.015** (.004)	3.64	.030** (.011)	2.70
Income	.015 (.009)	1.63	-.006 (.011)	-0.53	.001 (.012)	0.05	-.038 (.033)	-1.14
Education	.078* (.033)	2.36	.055 (.044)	1.24	.043 (.048)	0.91	.149 (.129)	1.16
Race	.068 (.122)	0.56	-.280 (.153)	-1.83	-.269 (.164)	-1.64	-.039 (.453)	-0.09
Partisanship Strength	.291** (.107)	2.70	.214 (.140)	1.53	.218 (.150)	1.45	-.108 (.430)	-0.25
Ideological Strength	.345** (.115)	3.01	-.008 (.139)	-0.06	-.072 (.149)	-0.48	.626 (.425)	1.47
Political Knowledge	.201** (.054)	3.72	.100 (.072)	1.39	.096 (.078)	1.23	.080 (.207)	0.39
Political Skills	.261** (.063)	4.15	.131 (.082)	1.60	.193* (.088)	2.20	-.323 (.252)	-1.28
Know Precinct Location	-.102 (.126)	-0.81	-.182 (.145)	-1.25	-.094 (.154)	-0.61	-.914* (.440)	-2.08
Political Mobilization	.201 (.105)	1.92	-.073 (.124)	-0.59	-.087 (.134)	-0.65	-.090 (.354)	-0.25
Campaign Involvement	.207** (.054)	3.82	.042 (.070)	0.60	.065 (.076)	0.86	.001 (.200)	0.00
Campaign Funding	.430** (.079)	5.44	.261* (.102)	2.55	.218 (.111)	1.95	.364 (.267)	1.36
Campaign Media Attention	-.157* (.066)	-2.36	-.014 (.084)	-0.17	.036 (.091)	0.40	-.320 (.239)	-1.34
Campaign Interest	.268** (.059)	4.51	.123 (.074)	1.67	.152 (.080)	1.91	.052 (.206)	0.25
Vote Choice	-.181 (.106)	-1.71	.111 (.152)	0.73	.095 (.162)	0.59	.320 (.485)	0.66

	Bivariate Model (N = 1566)		Multivariate Model (N = 1566, Pseudo R² = .1418)		Liberal Early Voting Laws (N = 1158, Pseudo R² = .0459)		Strict Early Voting Laws (N = 408, Pseudo R² = .1023)	
Variable	Coefficient (SE)	z score	Coefficient (SE)	z score	Coefficient (SE)	z score	Coefficient (SE)	z score
Partisanship	-.192 (.110)	-1.75	-.440* (.162)	-2.72	-.475** (.172)	-2.76	.172 (.512)	0.34
Ease of Early Voting	2.070** (.170)	12.18	2.206** (.177)	12.48	-	-	-	-
Constant	-	-	-3.702 (.474)	-7.81	-1.748 (.476)	-3.67	-3.200 (1.229)	-2.60

*p < .05, **p < .01 (two-tailed tests)

Note: The post cross-section sample weight was used as an importance weight to adjust the data because Hispanics were oversampled in 2008.

REFERENCES

Alvarez, M. R. 1998. *Information and Elections*. Ann Arbor, MI: University of Michigan Press.

Barbaro, M., and P. Baker. 2012. "Busy Day on Campaign Trail for Obama and Romney." *New York Times,* October 25.

Barreto, M. A., M. J. Streb, M. Marks, and F. Guerra. 2006. "Do Absentee Voters Differ from Polling Place Voters? New Evidence from California." *Public Opinion Quarterly* 70 (2): 224–234.

Berinsky, A. J., N. Burns, and M. W. Traugott. 2001. "Who Votes by Mail? A Dynamic Model of the Individual-Level Consequences of Voting-by-Mail Systems." *Public Opinion Quarterly* 65 (2): 178–197.

Box-Steffensmeier, J. M., and D. Kimball. 1999. "The Timing of Voting Decision in Presidential Campaigns." Presented at the Annual Meeting of the Midwest Political Science Association, Chicago.

Campbell, A., P. E. Converse, W. E. Miller, and D. E. Stokes. 1960. *The American Voter*. New York: Wiley.

Converse, P. E. 1962. "Information Flow and the Stability of Partisan Attitudes." *Public Opinion Quarterly* 26 (4): 578–599.

Downs, A. 1957. *An Economic Theory of Democracy*. New York: Harper & Row.

Dubin, J. A., and G. A. Kalsow. 1996. "Comparing Absentee and Precinct Voters: A View over Time." *Political Behavior* 18 (4): 369–392.

Fitzgerald, M. 2005. "Greater Convenience But Not Greater Turnout: The Impact of Alternative Voting Methods on Electoral Participation in the United States." *American Politics Research* 33 (6): 842–867.

Fournier, P., R. Nadeau, A. Blais, E. Gigengil, and N. Nevitte. 2004. "Time-of-Voting Decision and Susceptibility to Campaign Effects." *Electoral Studies* 23 (4): 661–681.

Gerber, A., and D. P. Green. 2000. "The Effect of Canvassing, Telephone Calls, and Direct Mail on Voter Turnout: A Field Experiment." *American Political Science Review* 93 (3): 653–662.

Giammo, J. D., and B. J. Brox. 2010. "Reducing the Costs of Participation: Are States Getting a Return on Early Voting?" *Political Research Quarterly* 63 (2): 295–303.

Goldstein, K. M., and T. N. Ridout. 2002. "The Politics of Participation: Mobilization and Turnout over Time." *Political Behavior* 24 (1): 3–29.

Gronke, P. 2004. "Early Voting Reforms and American Elections." Presented at the Annual Meeting of the American Political Science Association.

Gronke, P., E. Galanes-Rosenbaum, and P. A. Miller. 2007. "Early Voting and Turnout." *PS: Political Science & Politics* 40 (4): 639–645.

Gronke, P., E. Galanes-Rosenbaum, P. A. Miller, and D. K. Toffey. 2008. "Convenience Voting." *Annual Review of Political Science* 11 (1): 437–455.

Gronke, P., J. Hicks, and D. K. Toffey. 2009. "N = 1? The Anomalous 2008 Election and Lessons for Reform." Presented at the Annual Meeting of the American Political Science Association, Toronto.

Gronke, P., and D. K. Toffey. 2008. "The Psychological and Institutional Determinants of Early Voting." *Journal of Social Issues* 64 (3): 503–524.

Hennessey, K. 2012. "President Obama Flies to Chicago to Vote Early in Person." *Los Angeles Times*, October 25.

Karp, J. A., and S. A. Banducci. 2000. "Going Postal: How All-Mail Elections Influence Turnout." *Political Behavior* 22 (3): 223–239.

Karp, J. A., and S. A. Banducci. 2001. "Absentee Voting, Mobilization, and Participation." *American Politics Research* 29 (2): 183–195.

Kessel, J. H. 1968. *The Goldwater Coalition: Republican Strategies in 1964*. New York: Bobbs-Merrill.

Kousser, T., and M. Mullin. 2007. "Does Voting by Mail Increase Participation? Using Matching to Analyze a Natural Experiment." *Political Analysis* 15 (4): 428–445.

Luo, M., and R. Nixon. 2008. "More Democrats Casting Early Ballots, Data Show." *The New York Times*, October 22.

Magleby, D. B. 1987. "Participation in Mail Ballot Elections." *Western Political Quarterly* 40 (1): 79–91.

Martinez, M. D., and S. C. Craig. 2010. "Dick Cheney? Didn't He Shoot Somebody? Measuring Political Knowledge in the 2008 American National Election Study." Presented at the Annual Meeting of the American Political Science Association, Washington, D.C.

McCann, J. A., R. W. Partin, R. B. Rapoport, and W. J. Stone. 1996. "Presidential Nomination Campaigns and Party Mobilization: An Assessment of Spillover Effects." *American Journal of Political Science* 40 (3): 756–767.

McDonald, M. P. 2008. "The Return of the Voter: Voter Turnout in the 2008 Presidential Election." *The Forum* 6 (4): 1–10.

McDonald, M. P. 2012. "United States Elections Project: 2012 General Election Turnout Rates." December 11. Retrieved from http://elections.gmu.edu/Turnout_2012G.htm.

Neeley, G. W., and L. E. Richardson, Jr. 2001. "Who Is Early Voting? An Individual Level Examination." *Social Science Journal* 38 (3): 381–392.

Oliver, E. J. 1996. "The Effects of Eligibility Restrictions and Party Activity on Absentee Voting and Overall Turnout." *American Journal of Political Science* 40 (2): 498–513.

Patterson, S. C., and G. A. Caldeira. 1985. "Mailing in the Vote: Correlates and Consequences of Absentee Voting." *American Journal of Political Science* 29 (4): 766–788.

Peters, J. W. 2012. "Obama Unveils New Ad as Early Voting Begins." *New York Times*, September 27.

Piven, F. F., and R. A. Cloward. 1988. *Why Americans Don't Vote*. New York: Pantheon Books.

Riker, W. H., and P. C. Ordeshook. 1968. "A Theory of the Calculus of Voting." *American Political Science Review* 62 (1): 25–42.

Rutenberg, J. 2012. "Obama Campaign Endgame: Grunt Work and Cold Math." *New York Times,* October 25.

Saulny, S. 2008. "Obama-Inspired Black Voters Find Politics Is for Them, Too." *New York Times,* November 2.

Southwell, P. L. 2010. "Voting Behavior in Vote-by-Mail Elections." *Analyses of Social Issues and Public Policy* 10 (1): 106–115.

Southwell, P. L., and J. Burchett. 2000. "Does Changing the Rules Change the Players? The Effect of All-Mail Elections on the Composition of the Electorate." *Social Science Quarterly* 81 (3): 837–845.

Stein, R. M. 1998. "Early Voting." *Public Opinion Quarterly* 62 (1): 57–69.

Stein, R. M., and P. A. García-Monet. 1997. "Voting Early But Not Often." *Social Science Quarterly* 78 (3): 657–671.

Steinhauer, J. 2008. "The Decided Go in Droves to Vote Early." *New York Times,* October 30.

Teixeira, R. A. 1992. *The Disappearing American Voter.* Washington, D.C.: Brookings Institution.

West, P. 2012. "How Obama 'Lost' Key State on Election Day But Won Anyway." *Los Angeles Times,* December 6. Retrieved from http://www.latimes.com/news/politics/la-pn-obama-early-voting-key-victory-20121205,0,7184848.story.

Wolfinger, R. E., and S. J. Rosenstone. 1980. *Who Votes?* New Haven, CT: Yale University Press.

Zaller, J. R. 1992. *The Nature and Origins of Mass Opinion.* Cambridge, MA: Cambridge University Press.

Zeleny, J. 2008. "Obama Plans a Four-Day Hunt for More Democratic Voters." *New York Times,* October 31.

Zeleny, J. 2012. "September, November: 40 Precious Days to Spend on Early Vote." *New York Times,* September 28.

Zeleny, J., and J. Rutenberg. 2012. "Divided U.S. Gives Obama More Time." *New York Times,* November 6.

NOTES

1. For a more detailed discussion of the data and methods used in the analyses, see Appendices A, B, and C.

2. See Appendix D for the results of all of the analyses from this chapter.

3. Predicted probabilities were calculated with all continuous variables and categorical variables set at the mean and all dichotomous variables set at the mode unless specified that certain variables were manipulated to different values.

4. The p value for campaign donors was .051, which is just shy of the .05 cutoff of statistical significance.

5. McDonald uses data from the American Community Survey (ACS) for 2008 and Current Population Survey (CPS) data for 2004 and adjusts the data for overseas citizens at the national level so the turnout rates are consistent with those from previous elections.

Chapter 11

Who Plays the Decider?

Analyzing Key Voters in the 2012 Election: "A Mad Men Party in a Modern Family World"

William J. Miller, Flagler College, and

Sean D. Foreman, Barry University

INTRODUCTION

From a campaign perspective, the 2012 presidential race is relatively easy to summarize into a simple narrative. Mitt Romney, the eventual Republican nominee, fought a prolonged primary battle against a myriad of challengers as he attempted to garner party support and bridge fractures between the more fiscally minded wing of the Republican Party and the Christian conservative base. President Barack Obama, on the other hand, had come off a historic electoral victory in 2008. Despite lagging approval ratings and debatable economic gains, his first term was highlighted by major successful legislative efforts (namely the passage and upholding of the Affordable Care Act) and policy decisions (such as the overturning of the controversial Don't Ask, Don't Tell).

Obama struck first by beginning a series of television ads in anticipated swing states that depicted Romney as being out of touch and unaware of the problems of mainstream America a decade into the twenty-first century. Romney, wanting to demonstrate his international appeal as Obama had done in 2007, went abroad in late summer and seemingly stumbled through a gaffe-filled European trip. The summer culminated for Romney with a lackluster Republican National Convention keynoted by Clint Eastwood carrying on a televised conversation with a chair. By September, it was difficult to tell if Joe Biden or Bill Clinton was Obama's running mate as the latter's presence on the campaign trail helped the president surge in the polls. As the videography of Jimmy Carter's grandson captured Romney's feelings about the 47 percent "who are dependent on government" and "will vote for this president [Obama] no matter what" at a Republican fundraiser, Obama seemed to have a clear path to victory (Madison 2012).

Destined to cruise to a second term, Obama made things difficult for himself by underperforming in the first presidential debate in Denver. All of a sudden, Romney was seen as a legitimate potential president, and independent voters began to view candidate Romney in a different light. Ultimately, Obama regained his 2008 form in the second and third debates before his public, empathetic response to Hurricane Sandy, which battered the northeastern United States. By Election Day, while many pollsters and pundits seemed convinced the race would be tight, Obama's targeted, technologically advanced effort was able to garner him the votes necessary to comfortably claim his second presidential victory. Outside of Indiana, North Carolina, and the eastern congressional district of Nebraska, the Electoral College map looked the same against Romney as it had four years earlier when Obama had faced John McCain.

While the 2008 election will forever be considered more historic, the 2012 election may actually carry more meaning. Whereas 2008 demonstrated a potential change in the American electorate, 2012 showed that our national identity seems to be changing in similar ways as the electorate. As Republican strategist Chuck Warren surmised late on election night, "We're a *Mad Men* party in a *Modern Family* world" (Chapin 2012). If the Republican Party continues to serve as a regionalized party of older, white, evangelical males, its potential for success in coming elections is less than favorable. While the world was aware that the 2012 election would come down to a few key voters in a few key states, most did not expect Romney to fare so poorly across the board with Latinos, women, young voters, and suburbanites as the final margins indicated.

THE RESULTS

If we look to the Electoral College, we see that only two states shifted between the 2008 and 2012 elections—traditional Republican stalwarts Indiana and North Carolina. In addition, the eastern congressional district of Nebraska, whose one electoral vote Obama had carried in 2008, thanks to that state's by-district method of awarding electoral votes, reverted to the Republican candidate in 2012. With the results from Florida released nearly a week after the polls closed, Obama emerged with a 332–206 Electoral College victory over Romney (compared to his 365–173 win over McCain). The popular vote in 2012, however, was far closer than in 2008 with Obama only winning by approximately 2.5 million votes (as opposed to 9.5 million in 2008). There were actually fewer voters in 2012 than in the prior presidential election (just under 127 million in 2012 and 129 million in 2008), and Obama mustered fewer votes than in his first victory (approximately 66 million in 2012 versus 69 million in 2008). These results demonstrate that while Obama garnered slightly less support nationally than in his first campaign, he was still able to largely dominate the Electoral College by winning each of the pre-identified swing states in the election.

Leading up to the election, most pollsters and pundits agreed on nine states that were the most likely to be competitive: Colorado, Florida, Iowa, Nevada, New Hampshire, North Carolina, Ohio, Virginia, and Wisconsin. Of these, four were largely considered to be the most imperative for the two candidates to win given the number of electoral votes associated with each and the perceived competitiveness within their borders: Colorado, Florida, Ohio, and Virginia. Table 11.1 presents the Real Clear Politics polling averages for those states and the actual outcomes.

Ironically, despite many pundits' claim that 2012 was a closer race than 2008, statistical analyses suggest the two margins of victory are nearly identical by state. The correlation between the 2008 and 2012 margins of victory in each state is 0.964. Other than in Utah (where Obama underperformed compared to 2008) and Alaska (where Obama overperformed), the numbers are fairly static.

Table 11.1 Average of Swing State Polls versus 2012 Election Outcome

State	Real Clear Politics Poll Average		Election Outcome	
	Obama	Romney	Obama	Romney
Colorado	48.8	47.3	51.2	46.5
Florida	48.2	49.7	50.0	49.1
Ohio	50.0	47.1	50.1	48.2
Virginia	48.0	47.7	50.8	47.8

While the statewide results paint a telling picture, what really matters for the purposes of predicting future elections is a thorough examination of the key voters within these states and how they pushed Obama to victory. Much of a political campaign focuses on the issues at hand and the efforts of voters at determining which candidate best represents them. What the 2012 election underscores, however, is the way that simple demographic characteristics are playing an ever-increasing role in guiding voters toward a particular candidate whom they then choose to support for numerous potential reasons. For evidence that the 2012 race was heavily impacted by demographics, consider the following series of maps created by the authors but based on those produced by BuzzFeed in the immediate aftermath of the election (BuzzFeed Politics 2012).

Figure 11.1 shows what the electoral map and results would have looked like if the election had been held in 1850 when only white men could vote. For each of the five figures the states in white are "red" states that would have been won by Republicans in 2012 and the black areas are "blue" states that would have been won by Democrats.

Figure 11.2 depicts how the map would have looked if the 2012 outcomes had been transposed to 1870, after the passage of the Fifteenth Amendment when only men could vote.

Figure 11.3 looks at the 2012 results under 1920 rules. With the passage of women's suffrage in the Twenty-Second Amendment, a large population was added to the voting pool. Poll taxes and literacy tests, however, still prevented true universal suffrage. As a result, Figure 11.3 shows only white voters.

Figure 11.1 2012 Election with 1850 Rules

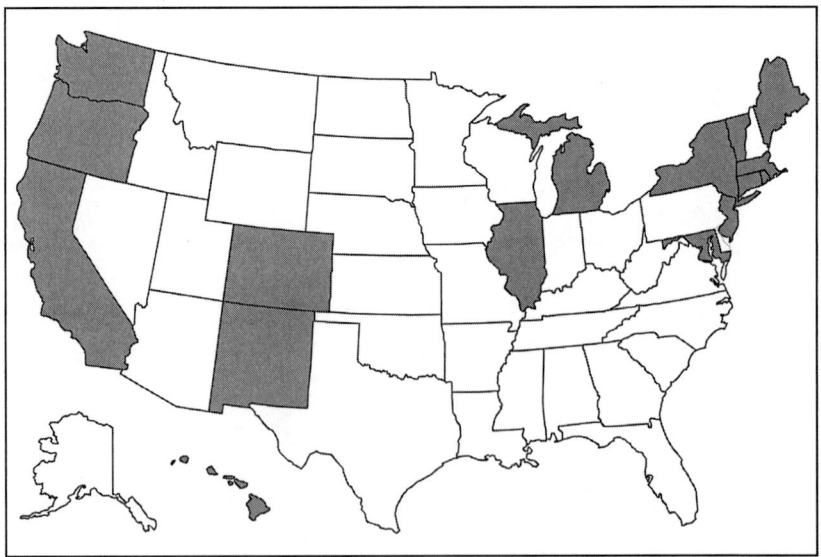

Figure 11.2 2012 Election with 1870 Rules

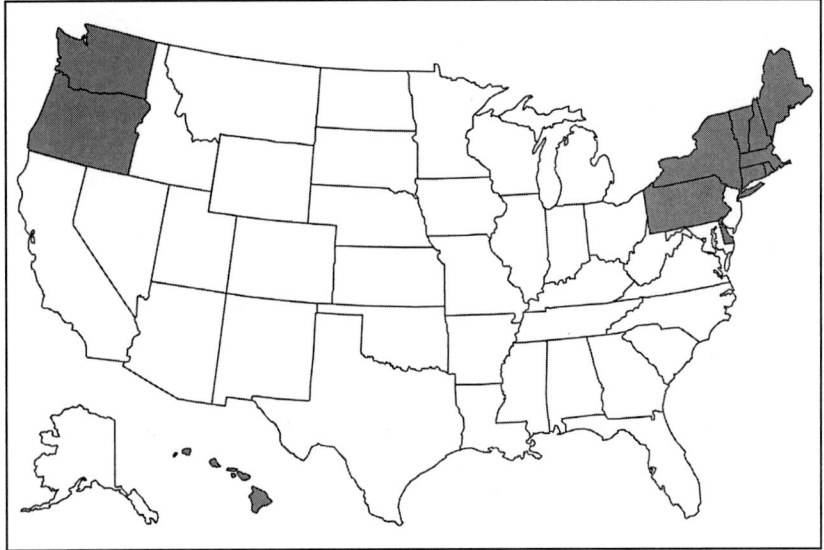

Figure 11.3 2012 Election with 1920 Rules

After the Twenty-Fourth Amendment and the Voting Rights Act of 1965 passed, all voters over age twenty-four were eligible to participate. Figure 11.4 demonstrates the 2012 outcomes under this parameter.

Figure 11.5 removes all of the parameters and presents the actual Electoral College outcome from 2012.

As the maps show, as the electorate expands, Romney's performance weakens significantly. Given the predictions of how particular demographic groups could impact the election, this finding is not surprising; yet the visual effect is still striking.

The Swing Demographics

The Obama victory in 2012 exposed "tectonic demographic shifts" in American society that could alter the political landscape forever (King 2012). Older, working-class white voters have drifted from the Democratic Party to the Republicans. Likewise, former Great Depression–era Democratic stalwarts from rural areas and small towns now lean to the GOP. Cities and many suburbs, however, full of quickly growing minority populations, have become Democratic strongholds. Their strength

Figure 11.4 2012 Election with 1964 Rules

now appears durable and spells potential doom for Republicans in future elections if the party chooses not to alter its appeals.

To describe the outcome of the 2012 election in just a sentence, one could state that while Romney did slightly better with almost every demographic group (by gender, race, ethnicity, and almost all income and education categories) than McCain did in 2008, Obama did much better with two groups, Hispanics and Asian Americans. And Romney's most supportive groups, less educated voters and whites, were not at the polls in large numbers.

Every four years, the media attempts to determine what slice of American voters is most likely to determine the presidential election. From this exercise, we have come to know soccer moms, security moms, NASCAR dads, angry white males, and Joe Six-Packs (Beam 2008). In 2012, however, it was more difficult to determine who this key swing group would be. As a result, CNN opted to trace six undecided voters that belonged to potential swing groups in swing states as they determined for whom to vote (CNN Staff 2012). CNN followed a millennial in New Hampshire, a Catholic in Ohio, a long-term unemployed man in

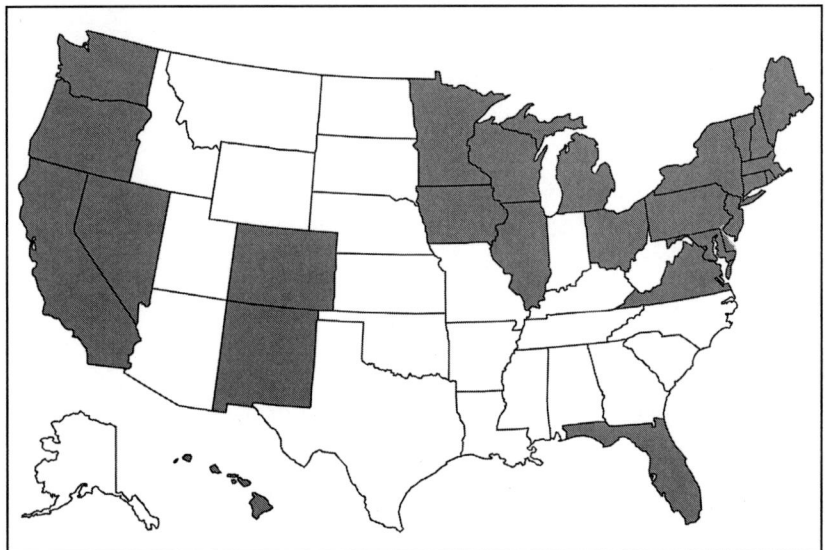

Figure 11.5 2012 Election

Nevada, a Latino in Florida, a single woman in Virginia, and an evangelical in Iowa. While often such journalistic endeavors seem to be more interested in sensationalizing the stories of the individuals, the CNN efforts carefully discussed the decision calculus for each person. No universal swing group ever emerged, but as a prediction of things to come, five of the six indicated (explicitly or implicitly) their status as leaning toward casting a ballot for Obama.

For Romney, the key demographic was white males. Bill McInturff, a Republican pollster, agreed that the white/nonwhite divide was going to be the most critical for Romney and predicted that if the white percentage of the electorate dropped to 72 percent or below that Obama would comfortably win (CNN Political Unit 2012). While polls were showing that Romney would do better with whites than McCain had four years prior, turnout was his problem. Doing four points better (which Romney ultimately did) would be negated by a drop of 2 percent in vote share. For Obama, on the other hand, the key group was his "coalition of the ascendant" (Brownstein 2012). Obama needed to do well with young people, minorities, college-educated women, and blue-collar women. These groups were most likely to relate to Obama's messages of hope and change and to maintain confidence in his goals and policies.

Census 2010 made it clear that minorities were becoming a political force. And Obama and the Democrats created a series of policies aimed at attracting them into the Democratic camp, including broad federal support for medical care, education, and housing (Frey 2012). But turnout has always been the concern. Many of these fast-growing minority groups are too young to vote or less likely to be citizens. Only forty-four of every hundred Hispanic residents are eligible voters (Frey 2012). The Brookings Institution presented three preelection simulations looking at how minorities could determine the next president. In the first scenario, Brookings applied 2008 turnouts and margins to the new Census population. Under these parameters, Obama would win the Electoral College 358–180 and would win ten states (Nevada, New Mexico, Indiana, Ohio, Pennsylvania, New Jersey, Maryland, Virginia, North Carolina, and Florida) due to the minority vote. In the second scenario, Brookings applied 2004 turnouts and margins for all voters. In this case, Romney would win the Electoral College 286–252 and Obama would win eleven states due to minority votes (Oregon, California, Nevada, Wisconsin, Illinois, Michigan, New York, Pennsylvania, New Jersey, Delaware, and Maryland). In the final scenario, Brookings applied 2004 turnouts and margins for whites and 2008 turnouts and margins for minorities. Here Obama would win 292–246 with fourteen states siding with Democrats thanks to minority votes. Through these exercises, we see how important minority voters were poised to be in the 2012 presidential election.

While minorities were important, we know from the previous discussion that other groups played a vital role in the 2012 campaign as well. In the following sections, we will highlight how women, seniors, Hispanics, Catholics, and youths factored into the 2012 presidential election.

Women

While male Republicans talked about transvaginal ultrasounds and legitimate rape, Democrats felt they had safely secured the women's vote (Ball 2012). But when Governor Romney began to surge in the polls during debate season, it was women leading the way as they were seemingly changing their preference. As a result, Obama had to bring the campaign back to women, which he succeeded in doing. For many women, economic issues soured their opinions of Obama. In 2008, Obama won 56 percent of the female vote. By the time all was said and done, he would win 55 percent in 2012. While the one-point drop is notable, we must emphasize that even in 2012, Obama pulled in 4 percent more of the female vote than John Kerry had in his run against George W. Bush in 2004. Looking at the comparative importance of female to male voters in 2012, Obama performed better with females than Romney did with males, and females were 53 percent of the electorate.

Even with the economy souring, most women agreed with Obama on women's rights. When talking to pollsters leading up to the election (especially during Romney's surge), it appeared women were more afraid of appearing to be single-issue voters so they hedged their opinions but did not follow through in the voting booth. Needless to say, Romney's "binders full of women" quip in the final presidential debate likely did not help him convince female voters to come to his side permanently.

In swing states, Obama ran better with "white women without a college education" than generally across the country (Brownstein 2012). These "waitress moms" especially seemed to help in Ohio and Virginia. A strong performance among these women, typically considered to be conservative socially but economically strained, helped pull Obama over predicted margins in these areas. The Obama campaign successfully targeted this group. Advertising was aimed on daytime television shows, such as *Judge Judy* and *Dr. Phil*, which attract large numbers of downscale women. Other ads appeared on networks such as Bravo, Hallmark, and Lifetime. These non-college-educated women were so important to Obama because the particular demographic had gone Republican in every presidential election since 1980 (with the exception of 1996). Alex Bratty, a Republican pollster, spent much of the election season talking to what she coined "Wal-Mart moms." She also felt that Obama held an upper hand with this demographic given how Obama was better able to relate to them (Brownstein 2012).

As Table 11.2 shows, there is clear evidence of a gender gap in presidential voting and it seems to be becoming more constant (Kondik and Skelley 2013).

Table 11.2 Gender Gap in Presidential Elections, 1972–2012

Election	Men			Women		
	Dem %	GOP %	+ Dem	Dem %	GOP %	+ Dem
1972	36	62	-26	37	61	-24
1976	50	48	+2	50	48	+2
1980	36	55	-19	45	47	-2
1984	37	62	-25	44	56	-12
1988	41	57	-16	49	50	-1
1992	41	38	+3	45	37	+8
1996	43	44	-1	54	38	+16
2000	42	53	-11	54	43	+11
2004	44	55	-11	51	48	+3
2008	49	48	+1	56	43	+13
2012	45	52	-7	55	44	+11

Seniors

Senior voters had been stalwarts for Democrats during the 1990s as Medicare and Social Security were prominently discussed. In recent years, however, older voters have started shifting more emphatically toward the Republican Party. As important as who seniors are voting for is the static nature of their vote share in recent years. In 2004 and 2012, senior voters were 16 percent of the total electorate according to CNN national exit polls. Romney did better than McCain or Bush had done with this demographic, defeating Obama by twelve points. This is especially significant given the attention Democrats paid to vice presidential nominee Paul Ryan's alleged plans to obliterate Medicare as we know it, a claim found to be "half true" (PolitiFact 2012).

The problem for Republicans, of course, is that although this is a demographic group that is growing and is supportive of Republican candidates, its members are also quickly perishing. As former Minnesota senator Norm Coleman stated after the election, "What worries me is that the GOP is about to become the WOP—the White Old Party" (King 2012). Likewise, another pundit predicted that "any candidate that wants to run a campaign only at whites is going to lose." The Republican dilemma was simply stated: "Their voters are white, aging, and dying off" (Abdullah 2012). Elderly white men were, after all, Romney's strongest supporters. While seniors do turn out at higher rates than the average

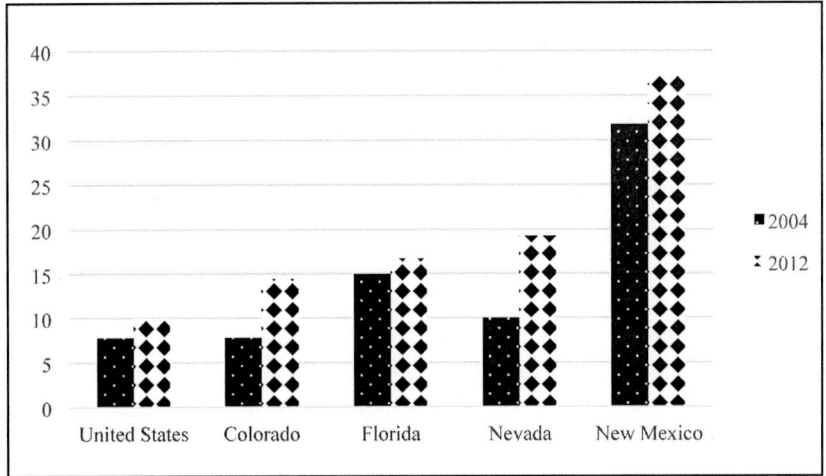

Figure 11.6 Hispanic Portion of the Vote Nationally and in Key Latino States, 2004 versus 2012

voter (61 percent vs. 45 percent on average), the detriment for Republicans is that of the top ten elderly turnout states, only two are swing states: Colorado and Wisconsin (Brandon 2012).

Hispanics

One of the keys of Obama's electoral coalition was Latinos/Hispanics (Latinos in the southwest, and Hispanics in the east, refer to Spanish-speakers). Obama did better in 2012 than in 2008 with Hispanics, a group that was heavily targeted by both campaigns. Hispanics were 16 percent of the population and 10 percent of the registered voters in 2012 (Fox News Exit Polls 2012). We can see in Figure 11.6 how Hispanic populations have increased between 2008 and 2012 (Sabato, Kondik, and Skelley 2012).

At the Univision forum where Obama and Romney took questions from commentators Jorge Ramos and Maria Elena Salinas on two consecutive afternoons, Romney continued to shift his positions to meet the sector of the electorate to whom he was speaking. Obama was hit hard on his perceived failure to deal with immigration in his first term. Romney was not able to capitalize on this weakness due to his own embrace of the Arizona immigration law as a national model during the primaries and for his comment that people in the country illegally should "self-deport" to solve the problem.

Obama won 71 percent of the Hispanic vote to 27 percent for Romney (Pew Hispanic Center 2012). This is four percentage points better than the 67 percent Obama got in 2008. Obama's 71 percent was second only to Bill Clinton's winning of 72 percent of the Hispanic vote in 1996—and a 51 percentage point advantage over Bob Dole with this demographic. Table 11.3 shows the history of Hispanic voting in presidential elections since 1980 (Lopez and Taylor 2012). Obama had a 44 percentage point margin over Romney even after Republicans targeted Spanish-speaking voters.

The Republican National Convention in Tampa highlighted Hispanic rising stars including Florida senator Marco Rubio, Texas Senate candidate Ted Cruz, governors Susana Martinez of New Mexico and Brian Sandoval of Nevada, and former Florida governor Jeb Bush. Democrats also prominently displayed a Hispanic politician with San Antonio mayor Julian Castro giving the keynote address at their convention in Charlotte, NC.

More importantly, however, is how Obama did with Hispanic voters in key swing states. In Florida, he won 58–40 percent; in Colorado, 87–10 percent; in Nevada, 80–17 percent; and in Virginia, 66–31 percent. Thus, in the most important states, Hispanic voters swung overwhelmingly for Obama and helped to assure his reelection.

Cuban Americans, especially in south Florida, traditionally have been strong supporters of the Republican Party. But some exit polls in 2012 showed that Cubans were more evenly split between the two parties and that Obama made large gains with Cuban voters. Fox News Exit Polls even showed Obama won Cuban voters in Florida by 49–47 percent though other organizations had Romney winning Cubans (Fox News Exit Polls 2012). That was compared to 66–34 percent overall with Florida Hispanics.

Obama beat McCain 67–31 percent in 2008 among all Hispanics nationally, which were 8.9 percent of the U.S. electorate (see Table 11.4). The 2012 margin of 44 percent more support for Obama over Romney was telling. The GOP outreach to Hispanic voters was not able to counteract the negative opinions about Romney linked to his hardline position against illegal immigration in the Republican primary and the perception that Romney's wealth put him out of touch with middle- and lower-class Americans.

Table 11.3 Percentage of Hispanic Vote in Presidential Elections, 1980–2012 (Pew Hispanic Center)

Year	Democrat	Republican	Democrat Advantage
1980	Carter—56 percent	Reagan—35 percent	+ 21
1984	Mondale—61 percent	Reagan—37 percent	+ 24
1988	Dukakis—69 percent	G.H.W. Bush—30 percent	+ 39
1992	Clinton—61 percent	G.H.W. Bush—25 percent	+ 36
1996	Clinton—72 percent	Dole—21 percent	+ 51
2000	Gore—62 percent	G.W. Bush—35 percent	+ 27
2004	Kerry—58 percent	G.W. Bush—40 percent	+ 18
2008	Obama—67 percent	McCain—31 percent	+ 36
2012	Obama—71 percent	Romney—27 percent	+ 44

Table 11.4 Percentage of Hispanic Voter Turnout, Hispanic Percentage of Total U.S. Population, and Hispanics in the Electorate, 1980–2012 (U.S. Census Bureau Voting and Registration Data)

Year	Hispanic Voter Turnout	Hispanic Portion of U.S. Population	Hispanic Portion of the U.S. Electorate
1980	29.9%	6.4%	2.8%
1984	32.6%	N/A	3.3%
1988	28.8%	8.1%	3.9%
1992	28.9%	9.5%	4.1%
1996	44%	10.8%	5.1%
2000	45.1%	12.5%	5.8%
2004	47.2%	14.2%	6.5%
2008	50%	15%	7.9%
2012	48%	16.9%	8.9%

As one Republican strategist (who is himself Hispanic) explained, in states such as Colorado Hispanic voters selected along the lines of social class divisions. Many Hispanic voters decided they were going to vote for Obama simply because he was for the little guy while Romney appeared to be for the millionaires (Abdullah 2012).

Ultimately, Hispanics represent a missed opportunity for the Republican Party. George W. Bush was an immigration-friendly Republican who spoke passable Spanish. He gained 40 percent of their vote during his 2004 reelection; McCain won 31 percent in 2008; and then Romney dropped to 27 percent support in the most recent election. If Romney had matched Bush's 2004 percentage, he would have netted one million additional votes nationwide but would not have flipped any of the swing states where Hispanic voters are significant (*Estimados Republicanos* 2012).

Most concerning for Republicans is that the minority groups that carried Obama to victory are projected by the U.S. Census Bureau to become a majority of the nation's population by 2043 (Yen 2012). A statistical analysis by the *Houston Chronicle* and *San Antonio Express-News* has suggested that if trends hold, Texas could end up voting for a Democratic president as soon as 2024 (Dunham 2012).

Religion

Attention to various religious groups appeared to be more pronounced than in recent elections. The selection of Romney (a Mormon) and Ryan (a Catholic) presented a perceived challenge for the Republicans in securing their evangelical base voters. The health care law that mandated insurance coverage for contraception angered many Catholics and even some nonevangelical Protestants. Jewish voters were contested more intensely than in past elections as Republicans saw a chance to make inroads based on concerns over Middle East politics.

Romney won a bruising victory in the Republican nomination race despite opposition from the conservative base of the party. Newt Gingrich, Rick Santorum, Rick Perry, Michele Bachmann, and Herman Cain each tried to appeal to the born-again and evangelical Christian voters. These candidates tried to build on the support Mike Huckabee enjoyed in 2008 when he and Romney challenged McCain for the nomination. Ultimately the moderate and middle factions won the battle for the soul of the party. Romney won the nomination despite scoring low with Southern voters and evangelicals throughout the primaries, largely due to the perceptions that he was more electable, more able to compete with Obama, and better equipped on the issue of the economy.

One question throughout the campaign was whether Romney could inspire the religious right and mobilize the Republican base to vote in large numbers in November. By getting 79 percent of born-again/evangelical voters to 20 percent for Obama, Romney actually did four points better with born-again/evangelical voters than McCain did in 2008. The 79 percent was equal to what George W. Bush got in 2004. A common tale told about this election is that white voters are declining as a percentage of the national voting population. While that may be true, born-again/evangelicals were 23 percent in both 2008 and 2012, up from the 21 percent measured in 2004.

A majority of Catholic voters have backed the winner of every presidential election since Ronald Reagan's first victory in 1980. Catholics have voted for both Republicans and Democrats and have been an important swing bloc. Of course, one problem with categorizing Catholic voters is that there are Catholics of a variety of ethnic and racial backgrounds. There also are conservative Catholics that tend to support Republican candidates and liberal Catholics who favor the Democrats. Republican Catholics tend to be pro-life and favor traditional marriage while Democratic Catholics are more supportive of women's choices and are focused on social justice. It is the moderate Catholics who are the swing voters.

Obama won 54 percent of all Catholics in 2008. In 2012, Obama maintained a slight 50–48 percent advantage with Catholic voters over Romney. But his advantage decreased with white Catholics while it increased with Hispanic Catholics. Obama got 47 percent of white Catholics in 2008 to McCain's 52 percent; in 2012 Obama got 40 percent to Romney's 59 percent, thus losing 7 percentage points with this voting group. The idea that Romney and Ryan targeted white voters and made inroads with white Catholics is not surprising. Ryan, like Vice President Joe Biden, is from an Irish Catholic background. He appealed to the socially conservative voters. But the so-called war on women split Catholics on the issues of abortion and contraception. The Catholic Church sued the federal government over health insurance coverage for contraception. This issue may have helped to close the gap with white Catholics, but it was not enough to make up the deficit with Hispanic Catholics, the growing part of the population.

Obama made great strides with Hispanic Catholic voters just as he did with Hispanics in general. Obama gained 3 percent with Hispanic Catholics, up from 72–26 percent over McCain in 2008 to 75–21 percent over Romney. Obama continued to do well with Mexican Americans and Puerto Rican Americans while making inroads with Cuban Americans, all of which are largely Catholic constituencies.

Romney was the first Mormon candidate for president or vice president on a major party ticket. The Pew analysis found that more Mormons voted for George W. Bush in 2004 than for Romney in 2012. The number was a slight decrease from 80 percent for Bush to 78 percent for Romney. The overall percentage of Mormons voting in 2000 and 2008 elections is not available. One significant factor may have been the Salt Lake City newspaper endorsing President Obama on October 19 under the headline "Too Many Mitts" with a discussion of his changed and unclear positions on a number of issues (Tribune 2012). What is not clear is what percentage of the voting population were Latter-day Saints, as Mormons are less than 2 percent of the total U.S. population.

Obama lost some ground with Jewish voters, but again, held enough of them to maintain the presidency. Obama got 78 percent of the Jewish vote in 2008 over McCain's 21 percent. That was compared to 73 percent for Kerry in 2004 and 79 percent for Gore in 2000. In 2012 Obama got 69 percent of the Jewish vote while Romney got 30 percent. Republicans targeted Jewish voters and wanted to get 40 percent support from Jewish Americans. Romney and Ryan talked about Obama being weak in support of Israel and played the fear card on the Iran nuclear issue. While they did cut into Obama's support with Jewish voters, it was not enough to make a difference on the electoral map.

Youth Voters

Part of the winning coalition for Obama in 2008 was younger voters. The eighteen to twenty-four-year-old voters helped to propel Obama to victory in the Iowa caucus and helped him to win the general election in Indiana and North Carolina (Foreman 2012). However, it was clear that enthusiasm for Obama among younger voters ebbed prior to the 2012 election. Among eighteen to twenty-four-year-olds, voter registration was down from 79 percent in 2008 to 66 percent in 2012 (McKinnon 2012). Obama recognized the concern in registration and polling (where he was predicted to do approximately ten points worse than in 2008) and returned to his touring of college campuses as the race progressed. As a news story from Ohio described, "Three hours later, a second bus pulled into the parking lot, this one carrying 28 students from the nearby campus of Ohio State University. The College Democrats lured them to the polls with cupcakes, chocolate milk and four singing ukulele players" (*Vindicator* 2012). The Obama campaign still knew how to attract its audience of choice.

One study shows that youth voters made a significant impact for Obama in 2012. According to the Center for Information & Research on Civic Learning and Engagement of Tufts University, Obama won the youth vote 67–30 percent nationally. His margin in swing states of Florida, Ohio, Pennsylvania, and Virginia was decisive according to the study (Robillard 2012a). However, Fox News exit polling showed Obama's advantage nationally at 60–40 percent among both eighteen to twenty-four- and eighteen to twenty-nine-year-olds. Fox also showed that Obama won 68–29 percent among eighteen to twenty-four-year-olds in Florida.

While the percentage of eighteen to twenty-nine-year-olds who voted did increase from 18 to 19 percent of the electorate between 2008 and 2012, Obama only got 60 percent of the young voters compared to 66 percent in 2008. Still, while Obama's numbers were lower with young voters, they actually may have been more impactful in 2012 in some key states, according to a Pew study (Pew Research Center 2012b). Obama won more than 60 percent of voters age thirty and under in Florida, Ohio, Virginia, and Pennsylvania, four swing states swept by the incumbent.

CONCLUSION

With all of this information, is it possible to state which group was the most important to Barack Obama's quest for a second term as president? Unfortunately, no. Perhaps the most important demographic group was white America, which failed to achieve the necessary door-busting turnout to turn the election in Romney's favor. As former Bill Clinton advisor turned Republican strategist Dick Morris explained on his website a week after the election: "The mainstream media is pushing the story that a massive turnout among minorities and the young drowned the white male vote as America changes its demography. But the real reason is that the whites who supported Romney didn't turn out to vote" (Morris 2012). Morris used Ohio as an example. Romney lost Ohio by roughly 107,000 votes, but he received almost 100,000 fewer votes than McCain had. Romney simply did not get his people to the polls as effectively as Obama and the Democrats.

What we witnessed in 2012 was a pivot election when the electorate experiences a fundamental shift that is likely to last. If we consider the pro-Obama (and likely pro-Democrat) trends in 2012, 70 percent of Latinos, 73 percent of Asian Americans, more than 90 percent of African Americans, 60 percent of Americans under thirty, and approximately 60 percent of unmarried women supported Barack Obama. And most importantly, all of these groups made up a larger share of the electorate in 2012 than they had in 2008 (Lauter 2012).

Historians and political scientists to come will have to determine if 2008 and 2012 represent critical elections and a realignment of the American electorate similar to 1800, 1824, 1860, 1896, and 1932. Each of these periods marked a shift in the electoral coalition to win the presidency. Since 1968 Republicans held an advantage in winning the White House with their "Southern strategy" of white, conservative, and evangelical voters (Phillips 1970). Bill Clinton, as a Southern, moderate Democratic governor, was able to carve into this constituency in 1992 and 1996. But in 2008 and 2012 this core group of Republican voters could not deliver the presidency for John McCain or Mitt Romney. There may be many reasons for this, not the least of which is that McCain and Romney were viewed more as moderates than true conservatives. But a parallel development has been the rise of the new national electoral coalition of singles, middle-class women, youths, Hispanics, Asians, and African Americans.

Democratic strategist James Carville wrote about a forty-year Democratic Party majority starting with Obama's election in 2008 (Carville 2009). While Republicans won the 2010 midterm congressional elections and captured control of the House of Representatives, they were unsuccessful in unseating Obama in 2012 even with unemployment around 8 percent and uncertainty around the globe. It may well be that as we see the partitioning of the country based on demographic peculiarities, Republicans can remain competitive in House districts but be at a decisive disadvantage in national elections.

Norm Coleman's postelection worries seem legitimate: the GOP cannot survive as the White Old Party—at least not if it wishes to remain relevant to modern presidential politics. Senator Marco Rubio from Florida, and Ileana Ros-Lehtinen, the first Cuban American in Congress, said the party denizens risked becoming dinosaurs if they did not embrace the new demographic realities. Kentucky senator Rand Paul also suggested the Grand Old Party faced extinction unless it adapted to the political environment. "So we need a new type of Republican," Paul said. "I think that involves some of the ideas of libertarian-leaning Republicans—people who believe that we need a less aggressive foreign policy, people who believe that we're not going to deport 12 million Hispanic folks and send them home" (Weiner 2012).

Immediately after Election Day 2012, Republicans did not give signs that they were prepared to cope well with the changing demography. On a conference call with donors on November 14, 2012, Governor Romney stated that Obama had followed the "old playbook" of targeting specific initiatives to swing voters—"especially the African-American community, the Hispanic community and young people" (Parker 2012). "In each case, they were very generous in what they gave to those groups," Romney said, contrasting Obama's strategy with his own of "talking about big issues for the whole country: military strategy, foreign policy, a strong economy, creating jobs and so forth."

Romney cited the forgiveness of college loan interest as "a big gift" for young voters and health coverage of contraceptives as "very big with young, college-aged women." Romney pointed to "Obamacare," the name once derisively given to the Affordable Care Act in 2010 by Republicans but later embraced by Obama as a compliment—and a plan largely modeled after one supported by Romney when he was governor of Massachusetts—as a reason that young voters supported the president. The provision that allows people up to age twenty-six to stay on their parents' insurance plans was another benefit to young voters. "They turned out in large numbers, a larger share in this election even than in 2008," Romney said of youth voters, a development that may have been decisive in some states.

"You can imagine for somebody making $25,000 or $30,000 or $35,000 a year, being told you're now going to get free health care, particularly if you don't have it, getting free health care worth, what, $10,000 per family, in perpetuity—I mean, this is huge," Romney said. "Likewise with Hispanic voters, free health care was a big plus. But in addition with regards to Hispanic voters, the amnesty for children of illegals, the so-called Dream Act kids, was a huge plus for that voting group" (Parker 2012).

Perhaps even more alarming was the reaction of Maine Republican chair Charlie Webster, who stated after the election, "In some parts of rural Maine, there were dozens, dozens of black people who came in and voted on Election Day. Everybody has a right to vote, but nobody in town knows anyone who's black. How did that happen? I don't know. We're going to find out" (Robillard 2012b). This suggests an element of denial among Republicans, who must walk away from 2012 with two pieces of knowledge. First, the GOP has a Latino problem. As Republican strategist Ana Navarro explained, "If we don't do better with Hispanics, we'll be out of the White House forever" (Steinhauser 2012). And second, the white vote is shrinking and will not rebound. Nor, it seems, will the GOP in national elections unless it takes critical steps to better reach out to voters of all walks of life while improving its ground game.

REFERENCES

Abdullah, H. 2012. "With Their Big Political Win, the New American Electorate Has Arrived." *CNN.com,* November 10. Retrieved from http://www.cnn .com/2012/11/09/politics/demographic-political-power/index.html.

Ball, M. 2012. "The Revenge of the Soccer Moms." *Atlantic,* October 10. Retrieved from http://www.theatlantic.com/politics/archive/2012/10/the-revenge-of-the -soccer-moms/263898/.

Beam, C. 2008. "One-Armed Vegetarian Live-In Boyfriends: The Quest for This Year's Sexy Swing Demographic." *Slate.com,* July 16. Retrieved from http:// www.slate.com/articles/news_and_politics/politics/2008/07/onearmed _vegetarian_livein_boyfriends.html.

Brandon, E. 2012. "States with the Best Older Voter Turnout." *U.S. News,* March 19. Retrieved from http://money.usnews.com/money/retirement/slideshows /states-with-the-best-older-voter-turnout.

Brownstein, R. 2012. "Why Obama Is Leading in Swing States." *National Journal* October 1. Retrieved from http://www.nationaljournal.com/2012-presidential -campaign/why-obama-is-leading-in-swing-states-20121001.

BuzzFeed Politics. 2012. "What the 2012 Election Would Have Looked Like without Universal Suffrage." November 9. Retrieved from http://www.buzzfeed.com /buzzfeedpolitics/what-the-2012-election-would-have-looked-like-with.

Carville, J. 2009. *40 More Years: How the Democrats Will Rule the Next Generation.* New York: Simon & Schuster.

Chapin, L. 2012. "The GOP Now a 'Mad Men' Party in a 'Modern Family' World." *DenverPost.com,* November 7. Retrieved from http://blogs.denverpost.com /opinion/2012/11/07/gop-mad-men-party-modern-family-world/28232/.

CNN Political Unit. 2012. "What to Watch for on Election Night." *CNN.com,* November 6. Retrieved from http://www.cnn.com/2012/11/06/politics /what-to-watch-election/index.html.

CNN Staff. 2012. "The Undecided: Have They Made Up Their Minds?" *CNN.com,* November 6. Retrieved from http://www.cnn.com/2012/11/05/politics /undecided-voters-decisions/index.html.

Dunham, R. 2012. "Exclusive Analysis: If Trends Hold, Texas Will Be a Toss-Up State by 2024." *Houston Chronicle,* November 12. Retrieved from http://blog .chron.com/txpotomac/2012/11/exclusive-analysis-if-trends-hold-texas-will -be-a-toss-up-state-by-2024/#4619101=0.

Estimados Republicanos! 2012. *WSJ.com,* November 7. Retrieved from http://online .wsj.com/article/SB10001424127887324894104578104884094510280.html.

Foreman, S. 2012. "Top 10 Reasons Why Barack Obama Won the U.S. Presidency in 2008 and What It Means in the 2012 Election." *Florida Political Chronicle* 20 (1–2), 2009–2012.

Fox News. 2012. "Fox News Exit Polls." Retrieved November 13, 2012 from http:// www.foxnews.com/politics/elections/2012-exit-poll.

Frey, W. H. 2012. "Why Minorities Will Decide the 2012 U.S. Election." *Brookings,* May. Retrieved from http://www.brookings.edu/research/opinions/2012 /05/01-race-elections-frey.

King, N., Jr. 2012. "Vote Data Show Changing Nation." *WSJ.* Retrieved from http:// online.wsj.com/article/SB10001424127887324073504578105360833569352.html.

Kondik, K., and G. Skelley. 2013. "Mind the Gap: Gender Gap Present in Almost All Federal Statewide Races over Last Decade." *Sabato's Crystal Ball,* September 12. Retrieved from http://www.centerforpolitics.org/crystalball/articles/mind-the-gap/.

Lauter, D. 2012. "Nonwhite Voters and Cultural Shifts Make 2012 Election Pivotal." *Los Angeles Times,* November 10. Retrieved from http://articles.latimes.com /2012/nov/10/nation/la-na-election-20121111.

Lopez, M. H., and P. Taylor. 2012. "Latino Voters in the 2012 Election." November 7. Retrieved from http://www.pewhispanic.org/2012/11/07/latino-voters-in-the -2012-election/.

Madison, L. 2012. "Fact-Checking Romney's '47 percent' Comment." *CBS News,* September 18. Retrieved from http://www.cbsnews.com/8301-503544_162 -57515033-503544/fact-checking-romneys-47-percent-comment/.

McKinnon, M. 2012. "Obama's Demographic Worried." *Daily Beast,* October 22. Retrieved from http://www.thedailybeast.com/articles/2012/10/22/mark -mckinnon-on-obama-s-demographic-worries.html.

Morris, D. 2012. "The Real Reason We Lost." *DickMorris.com,* November 15. Retrieved from http://www.dickmorris.com/the-real-reason-we-lost/.

Parker, A. 2012. "Romney Blames Loss on Obama's 'Gifts' to Minorities and Young Voters." November 14. Retrieved from http://thecaucus.blogs.nytimes.com /2012/11/14/romney-blames-loss-on-obamas-gifts-to-minorities-and-young -voters.

PolitiFact. 2012. "Barack Obama Ad Says Paul Ryan's Medicare Plan Could Raise Costs for Medicare Beneficiaries by $6,000 Each." August 17. Retrieved from http://www.politifact.com/truth-o-meter/statements/2012/aug/23/barack -obama/barack-obama-ad-says-paul-ryans-medicare-plan-coul/.

Pew Hispanic Center. 2012. "Latino Voters in the 2012 Election." November 7. Retrieved from http://www.pewhispanic.org/2012/11/07/latino-voters-in-the -2012-election/.

Pew Research Center. 2012a. "An Awakened Giant: The Hispanic Electorate Is Likely to Double by 2020." November 14. Retrieved from http://www .pewhispanic.org/2012/11/14/an-awakened-giant-the-hispanic-electorate-is -likely-to-double-by-2030/.

Pew Research Center. 2012b. "Young Voters Supported Obama Less, But May Have Mattered More." *Pew Research Center for the People & the Press,* November 26. Retrieved from http://www.people-press.org/2012/11/26/young-voters -supported-obama-less-but-may-have-mattered-more/.

Phillips, K. P. 1970. *The Emerging Republican Majority.* New York: Anchor Books.

Robillard, K. 2012a. "Election 2012. Study: Youth Vote Was Decisive." *Politico,* November 7. Retrieved from http://www.politico.com/news/stories/1112/83510 .html.

Robillard, K. 2012b. "GOP Chief: Mystery Black Voters." *Politico,* November 15. Retrieved from http://www.politico.com/news/stories/1112/83895.html.

Sabato, L., K. Kondik, and G. Skelley. 2012. "12 from '12: Some Takeaways from a Wild Election." *Sabato's Crystal Ball,* November 15. Retrieved from http:// www.centerforpolitics.org/crystalball/articles/12-from-12-some-takeaways -from-a-wild-election/.

Steinhauser, P. 2012. "Five Things We Learned on Election Night." *CNN.com,* November 8. Retrieved from http://www.cnn.com/2012/11/07/politics/5 -things-election-night/index.html.

"Tribune Endorsement: Too Many Mitts." 2012. *Salt Lake Tribune,* October 19. Retrieved from http://www.sltrib.com/sltrib/opinion/55019844-82 /endorsement-romney-obama-president.html.csp.

Vindicator. 2012. "Ohio Most Likely to Tip the Balance." October 30. Retrieved from http://www.vindy.com/news/2012/oct/30/ohio-most-likely-to-tip-the -balance/.

Weiner, R. 2012. "Rand Paul: GOP 'in Danger of Becoming a Dinosaur.'" *Washington Post,* November 27. Retrieved from http://www.washingtonpost.com/ blogs/post-politics/wp/2012/11/27/rand-paul-gop-in-danger-of-becoming -a-dinosaur/.

Yen, H. 2012. "Census: Whites No Longer a Majority in U.S. by 2043." *Associated Press*, December 12. Retrieved from http://nbclatino.com/2012/12/12/census -whites-no-longer-a-majority-in-us-by-2043/.

Chapter 12

Constituency Appeals and Group Voting in the 2012 Presidential Election

Mark D. Brewer and Richard J. Powell, University of Maine

INTRODUCTION

In some ways the 2012 American presidential election lacked the excitement of its 2008 predecessor. The newness of an African American candidate (and of course eventual president) was gone, and a good deal of the rock star–like appeal of Barack Obama had been stripped away by the grind of actual governing. The nation continued to suffer economic hard times, with large numbers of Americans worried about their futures and believing that the country was headed in the wrong direction. But what the 2012 contest lacked in glitz it made up for in its instructional utility for understanding presidential campaigns and elections in the present era. The election promised to be close (even if it did not really end up that way), and therefore both Obama and his opponent Mitt Romney were forced to pull out all the stops in the quest for votes. Both campaigns attempted to merge twenty-first-century communications and analytical advances with nineteenth-century boots on the ground organizing and mobilization.

In this chapter we focus on the group-based appeals crafted and exe-cuted by each campaign in the 2012 race. Data mining and sophisticated computer-assisted analytical techniques have increasingly allowed cam-paigns to microtarget their messages and appeals to narrow groups and constituencies. But this does not mean that campaigns can ignore the time-honored practice of making large, group-based appeals. Indeed, American electoral politics largely remains a politics rooted in social groups (Petrocik 1981). Parties identify social and demographic groups that are core elements of their own electoral coalition, groups that are seen as available to either party, or groups that traditionally support the opposition but whose support might be wavering and act strategically to shore up or gain support among these groups (Brewer and Stonecash 2009). The specific targets and particular messages in each election are of course affected by the characteristics of a party's candidate and the conditions of the current political environment, but much of what parties and their candidates do during election campaigns involves trying to gain group-based support in some way, shape, or form. In the 2012 pres-idential election, the most important group-based appeals were rooted in race/ethnicity, sex, age, social class, and religion.

RACE AND ETHNICITY

Race and ethnicity played significant roles in the 2012 presidential campaign, just as they have in most presidential races in recent decades. However, constituency appeals to these groups took on new dimensions in the Obama-Romney campaign, both in terms of a greater sophistica-tion of outreach methods and the degree to which different groups were targeted. Generally, Democrats and Republicans utilized very different strategies in making appeals to these groups. Democratic appeals tended to be rooted in specific governmental policies that were enacted in Obama's first term or proposals for the second term. Republicans, on the other hand, focused less on specific policy appeals, and instead courted these groups with a combination of broad themes and the use of surro-gate speakers matching each demographic group they sought to reach.

Latinos/Hispanics

Of all the highly contested groups of voters in the 2012 election, few received as much attention as Hispanics. This group has comprised one of the most courted groups in American politics in the past several election cycles, in large part because Hispanics represent one of the fastest growing segments of the American electorate. According to the 2010 U.S. Census, Hispanics comprised 16.3 percent of Americans, an increase of over 37 percent since 2000. Some projections indicate that Hispanics will comprise about one-third of all Americans by 2050 (Pew 2008). Moreover, Hispanics tend to have political opinions that do not sort into solely Democratic or Republican categories. The only factor that diminishes the potential impact of the Hispanic vote in presidential elections is the fact that nearly half of all U.S. Hispanics live in the nonbattleground states of California and Texas. Nevertheless, several of the key battleground states in recent elections contain large numbers of Hispanic voters, especially Florida, Nevada, New Mexico, Colorado, and Virginia. Additionally, there is much optimism among Democrats that demographic change will make Texas a battleground state within the next decade (see Battleground Texas—www.battlegroundtexas.com), although Democrats face some difficult work in making such a shift reality (Chozik 2014; Parker 2013).

Latinos have tended to vote Democratic in presidential elections, although at much lower rates than blacks. For example, Obama captured two-thirds of the Hispanic vote in the 2008 election. That showing represented a significant increase over 2004 and 2000, in which George W. Bush made substantial inroads in attracting Hispanic supporters. Bush made extensive appeals to Hispanics a central feature of his campaigns, rooted in his familiarity with Hispanic populations during his time as governor of Texas. Bush supported more liberal immigration policies than normally associated with Republicans and was occasionally known to speak Spanish in ads and campaign speeches. As a result, exit polls indicated Bush carried 44 percent of the Hispanic vote nationally in 2004, although there are some questions regarding the reliability of these data (Leal et al. 2005).

Republicans have long seen the potential to attract a significant percentage of Hispanic voters. For example, Hispanics tend toward a high level of religiosity, which typically indicates a greater likelihood of Republican voting. Similarly, Republicans may attract Latino support based on values appeals in areas such as family, community, religious liberty, and hard work—all values for which Hispanics tend to disproportionately voice support relative to other groups. In addition, Latinos continue to climb the American socioeconomic ladder, a development Republicans believe will eventually lead to increased support by Latinos for the party's support of lower taxes and smaller government. Democrats, on the other hand, have had significant appeal to Hispanic voters in policy areas related to economic improvement, health care, education, and immigration. Democrats believe that Hispanic voters will continue to support a more activist government that provides higher levels of support and opportunity for the less affluent well into the future.

These factors set the stage for a significant amount of political competition between Obama and Romney for the Hispanic vote. Although the Romney campaign knew it was unlikely to win a majority of this group's votes, it hoped to cut into Obama's support. In the end, Romney's appeals proved less effective than Obama's, with the president winning 71 percent of the Hispanic vote, an increase of four points from 2008 and eighteen from John Kerry's 2004 totals. These results are a continuation of a long-running theme: Republican optimism for attracting greater Latino support dashed by strong Democratic support among Latinos on Election Day (de la Garza and Cortina 2007; Leal et al. 2005) (see Tables 12.1a and 12.1b).

Throughout his first four years in office, Obama had sought to strengthen his ties to this key demographic group. For example, in the early months of his presidency in 2009 Obama hired three White House press officers to translate press releases into Spanish. During the 2010 health care debate, the White House created a Spanish-language website to discuss the Affordable Care Act. Obama also touted his appointment of Sonia Sotomayor to the U.S. Supreme Court, the Court's first Latino justice. This extensive outreach from Obama's communications team continued throughout his presidency and into the campaign, which worked extensively on Hispanic voter registration drives and maintained a Spanish-language campaign website (Ross 2012). Obama's courting of Hispanic voters focused on specific policies as well as symbolic appeals. For example, an Obama ad that ran in key swing states in early October featured the president speaking entirely in Spanish and included undocumented immigrants touting his DREAM Act. This effort built on Obama's policy initiatives from earlier in the year. In June 2012 Obama

Change in Obama Vote from 2008 to 2012	Change in Democratic Vote from 2004 to 2012	Change in Share of Voters from 2004 to 2012	Social Group	2012 Obama	2012 Romney	2012 Share of Voters	2008 Obama	2008 McCain	2008 Share of Voters	2004 Kerry	2004 Bush	2004 Share of Voters
			Sex									
-4	1	1	Men	45	52	47	49	48	47	44	55	46
-1	4	-1	Women	55	44	53	56	43	53	51	48	54
			Race & Ethnicity									
-4	-2	-5	White	39	59	72	43	55	74	41	58	77
-2	5	2	Black	93	6	13	95	4	13	88	11	11
4	18	2	Latino/Hispanic	71	27	10	67	31	9	53	44	8
11	17	1	Asian	73	26	3	62	35	2	56	44	2
			Sex & Race									
-6	-2	-2	White Men	35	62	34	41	57	36	37	62	36
-4	-2	-3	White Women	42	56	38	46	53	39	44	55	41
-8			Black Men	87	11	5	95	5	5			
0			Black Women	96	3	8	96	3	7			
1			Latino Men	65	33	5	64	33	4			
8			Latino Women	76	23	6	68	30	5			
			Age									
-6	6	2	18-29	60	37	19	66	32	18	54	45	17
0	6	-2	30-44	52	45	27	52	46	29	46	53	29
-3	-1	8	45-64	47	51	38	50	49	37	48	51	30
-1	-2	-8	65 and over	44	56	16	45	53	16	46	54	24
			Education									
-2	4	-5	No College Degree	51	47	53	53	46	56	47	53	58
-2	3	-3	Some College	49	48	29	51	47	31	46	54	32
-3	1	3	College	47	51	29	50	48	28	46	52	26
-4	0	2	Postgrad	55	42	18	59	40	17	55	44	16
			Party Identification									
-3	0	-5	Republican	6	93	32	9	90	32	6	93	37
3	3	1	Democrat	92	7	38	89	10	39	89	11	37
-7	-4	3	Independent	45	50	29	52	44	29	49	48	26
			Ideology									
-3	2	1	Conservative	17	82	35	20	78	34	15	84	34
-4	2	-4	Moderate	56	41	41	60	39	44	54	45	45
-3	1	4	Liberal	86	11	25	89	10	22	85	13	21
			Type of Community									
-14	-3	-4	Rural	39	59	21	53	45	21	42	57	25
-2	1	1	Suburban	48	50	47	50	48	49	47	52	46
-1	8	2	Urban	62	36	32	63	35	30	54	45	30

Table 12

Sources: All figures are taken from the National Exit Poll conducted by Edison Media Research and Mitofsky International for the National Election Pool (a consortium of ABC News, The Associated Press, CBS News, CNN, Fox News, and NBC News), 2004 data as reported by CNN (available from http://www.cnn.com/ELECTION/2004/pages/results/states/US/P/oo/epolls.o.html) and *The New York Times*, Marjorie Connelly, "How Americans Voted: A Political Portrait," November 7, 2004, p. 4.4; 2008 data as reported by Fox News (available at http://www.foxnews.com/politics/elections/2008-exit-poll); 2012 data as reported by Fox News (available at http://www.foxnews.com/politics/elections/2012-exit-poll). Note: Some numbers do not total to 100 due to rounding.

Change in Obama Vote from 2008 to 2012	Change in Democratic Vote from 2004 to 2012	Change in Share of Voters from 2004 to 2012	Social Group	2012 Obama	2012 Romney	2012 Share of Voters	2008 Obama	2008 McCain	2008 Share of Voters	2004 Kerry	2004 Bush	2004 Share of Voters
			Religious Tradition									
-3	2	-1	Protestant (all)	42	57	53	45	54	54	40	59	54
-4	3	-2	Roman Catholic	50	48	25	54	45	27	47	52	27
-9	-5	-1	Jewish	69	30	2	78	21	2	74	25	3
-5	3	2	None	70	26	12	75	23	12	67	31	10
			Church Attendance									
-7	1	-2	More than weekly	36	63	14	43	55	12	35	64	16
-2	0	2	Weekly	41	58	28	43	55	27	41	58	26
-2	6	0	Monthly	55	44	14	57	42	15	49	50	14
-3	2	-1	Few times per year	56	42	27	59	39	28	54	45	28
-5	0	2	Never	62	34	17	67	30	16	62	36	15
			Family Income									
0	5	4	Under $50,000	60	38	41	60	38	38	55	44	45
-3	-9	-6	$50,000-99,999	46	52	31	49	49	36	55	43	37
-5	3	10	$100,000 and over	44	54	28	49	49	26	41	58	18
			Union Household									
-1	-1	-6	Yes	58	40	18	59	39	21	59	40	24
-2	8	6	No	49	48	82	51	47	79	41	58	76
			Served in Military									
			Yes				44	55	15	41	57	18
			No				54	44	85	50	49	82
			Marital Status									
-5	0	-3	Married	42	56	60	47	52	66	42	57	63
-3	4	3	Not Married	62	35	40	65	33	34	58	40	37
			Children under 18									
-2	6	-1	Yes	51	47	36	53	45	40	45	53	37
-3	1	1	No	50	47	64	53	45	60	49	50	63
			Sexual Orientation									
-4	3	-1	Heterosexual	49	49	95	53	45	96	46	53	96
6	-1	1	Homo- or Bi-Sexual	76	22	5	70	27	4	77	23	4
			Gun Household									
			Yes				37	62	42	36	63	41
			No				65	33	58	57	53	59

Table 12 (continued)

Sources: All figures are taken from the National Exit Poll conducted by Edison Media Research and Mitofsky International for the National Election Pool (a consortium of ABC News, The Associated Press, CBS News, CNN, Fox News, and NBC News), 2004 data as reported by CNN (available from http://www.cnn.com/ELECTION/2004/pages/results/states/US/P/oo/epolls.o.html) and *The New York Times*, Marjorie Connelly, "How Americans Voted: A Political Portrait," November 7, 2004, p. 4.4; 2008 data as reported by Fox News (available at http://www.foxnews.com/politics/elections/2008-exit-poll); 2012 data as reported by Fox News (available at http://www.foxnews.com/politics/elections/2012-exit-poll). Note: Some numbers do not total to 100 due to rounding.

had announced that up to 1.7 million illegal immigrants would get a two-year deferment on deportation under the Deferred Action for Childhood Arrivals program (USA Today 2012).

Romney's goal to broaden Republican appeal to Latinos was fraught with many difficulties, foremost among them that he took a number of hardline stances on immigration issues in order to secure conservative support in the Republican nominating contest. As Senator Marco Rubio (R-FL) observed, "Immigration may not be the No. 1 issue in the Hispanic community, but it is a gateway issue. The way you talk about it matters" (quoted in Barrow 2012). In one high-profile primary debate exchange, Governor Rick Perry (R-TX) lambasted Romney's suggestion that illegal immigrants consider "self-deporting" themselves (USA Today 2012). In another dustup, Romney had to explain away comments he made to a closed audience when a secret videotape emerged in which Romney suggested that he might be more successful if his parents were Mexican, seeming to imply that Hispanics were being given preferential treatment. Further complicating matters for Romney were the inflammatory comments made by other Republicans, such as Representative Steve King's (R-IA) remarks saying illegal immigration was a "slow-motion terrorist attack" and "slow-motion holocaust" (Llorente 2012). Romney's endorsement of King's reelection at an Iowa campaign event in September 2012 drew immediate criticism from the Obama campaign and a Web video from the DNC seeking to explicitly link Romney with King and his views on immigration (Fox News Latino 2012). Romney's strategy to attract Hispanic voters in the general election campaign largely rested on three main components: (1) softening his policy positions from the nominating campaign; (2) appealing to Hispanic voters on economic issues, especially his proposals for small business development; and (3) relying on Hispanic surrogates to deliver his campaign's message. None of these proved effective.

The dramatic Democratic increase in the share of the Hispanic vote represents one of the most important developments in the demographic voting patterns of the U.S. electorate. Between 2004 and 2012, Democrats improved their performance among Latinos by eighteen points. Combined with the fact that they comprise one of the fastest growing demographic segments of the U.S. population, this trend is an ominous one for Republicans. Ceding the Hispanic vote, as Republicans have largely done with blacks, would make it very difficult for Republicans to remain competitive in presidential elections. In recognition of this, numerous postmortems of the 2012 Romney campaign have focused on the necessity of Republicans increasing their appeal to Hispanic voters. Under Obama's leadership, Democrats have been working assiduously to consolidate their support among Hispanics in order to make them a permanent part of the Democratic coalition. The way this plays out will certainly be of central importance to the outcome of future presidential elections in the United States.

Blacks

The campaign for black votes unfolded against the backdrop of the fact that Obama was the first black president in U.S. history. Black voters have played a crucial role in several recent elections, notably in 2008, and were widely regarded as important in 2012 as well. However, the electoral role played by this group is very different from that played by other minority groups. In recent decades, blacks have been the most reliable component of the Democratic coalition, with Kerry winning 88 percent of black votes in 2004 and Obama carrying 95 percent in 2008. As such, black voters received very few direct, persuasive appeals from the Romney campaign. The focus thus entailed the Obama campaign working hard to secure the highest possible turnout rate. Black voters make up 13 percent of the American electorate, and up to 20 percent in some key swing states such as Virginia, so their turnout rate is critical for Democrats.

Ultimately, the 2012 results proved to be consistent with other recent elections as Obama carried 93 percent of the black vote. Although this was a slight drop of 2 percent from 2008, it still represented a five point improvement over Kerry in 2004. Even more importantly, early evidence suggests that black voter turnout remained at levels similar to 2008. Some Republican strategists expected that black voters would be less motivated to vote due to the nation's sagging economy and the fact that Obama was running as the incumbent president rather than the first-ever black nominee of a major party. These predictions turned out to be false as black enthusiasm for Obama remained high.

Whites

Despite the fact that campaign news coverage made frequent reference to Romney's goal of winning at least 60 percent of white voters, this group was not targeted in the aggregate. Instead, the Obama and Romney campaigns made extensive appeals to specific subgroups of white voters based on such distinctions as religion, class, and sex. As a result, our discussion of white voters is largely covered in other sections. It is important to note the future potential for white voters to be targeted explicitly as whites as this group shifts from a majority of the electorate to a plurality. Indeed, George Hawley (2014) argues that the future of American electoral politics will be determined in large part by the actions of non-Latino whites.

One important theme that emerged in the 2012 campaign regarding race was the extent to which some white voters were motivated by latent racism in their opposition to Obama. This issue surfaced, for example, in a YouTube video that went viral in September and showed a black woman claiming that Obama gave her a free cell phone. When this video received attention from Rush Limbaugh, the *Drudge Report*, and other conservative commentators, many observers sensed racial undertones (Reeves 2012). To account for this, in 2008 the Obama campaign developed a sophisticated way of identifying racist voters; this method was further refined for 2012. In its polling, the campaign asked respondents about views "their neighbors" held. The responses were used to predict the extent to which specific types of white voters might be concealing racial sentiments. This enabled Obama to avoid wasting outreach efforts on those groups (Hohman 2012). In the end, Romney won the white vote by twenty points over Obama. However, the aggregate total concealed a great deal of subgroup variation, explored elsewhere in this chapter.

SEX

Women

One of the most glaring trends in recent U.S. elections is the divergent voting patterns of men and women, commonly referred to as the "gender gap." The differences between the partisan voting of men and women continued to widen in the 2012 election. Whereas 55 percent of women voted for Obama, only 45 percent of men did so—a gender gap of ten points. In both 2004 and 2008 this gap was just seven points. The election results were a disappointment for Romney since some October polls showed him pulling even with Obama in the fight for women voters. Women are undoubtedly one of the central components of the Democratic coalition in presidential elections.

Each recent election cycle seems to bring with it a catchy new tag line for the subset of the female electorate that pundits believe is critical to the election outcome. For several cycles, Americans were told that "soccer moms"—married, suburban, mostly white women—were the key to the election. In 2012 popular attention shifted to so-called "Wal-Mart moms" and "waitress moms," comprised of working-class mothers of diverse race and ethnicity, including many single parents (Covert 2012). Indeed, exit polls showed that Obama did very well with this group, while Romney won a solid majority from married, white women.

Since women voters were central to the campaign strategies of both Democrats and Republicans, gender issues were front and center for most of 2012. In the spring, groups aligned with Democrats began a carefully orchestrated attack on what they termed a Republican "War on Women." This line of attack emerged in the aftermath of the dispute over whether the Catholic Church would be required to provide coverage for contraceptives under its employee health insurance plans. Although the issue was originally framed in terms of religious freedom, it morphed into a women's health issue following controversial anticontraception comments by Republican presidential candidate Rick Santorum. Romney seemed to instantly recognize the political dangers of getting drawn into a debate over contraception and tried to deflect attention from the issue. Nevertheless, it became a significant point of discussion in the latter Republican debates. Romney tried mightily to keep the focus on economic issues but was again drawn into women's issues following inflammatory remarks of the Republican Senate candidate in Missouri, Representative Todd Akin, concerning "legitimate rape" and the suggestion that women possessed a mysterious ability to prevent pregnancy when raped. This was followed by the controversial comments of Richard Mourdock, the Republican Senate candidate in Indiana, stating that pregnancies resulting from rape were "something that God intended" (Groer 2012).

The Obama campaign continually sought to link Romney with Santorum, Akin, and Mourdock. Typical of Obama's approach was an all-women town hall meeting in Cincinnati in late September in which he said Romney would cut access to mammograms and contraception (Reinhard 2012a). Obama voiced a similar line of attack in an ad that said Romney would cut access to cancer screenings for women (Easley 2012). This message was interwoven with a sophisticated, well-funded campaign effort by Planned Parenthood, an organization that was particularly motivated by Romney's call to cut off support from the federal government. Planned Parenthood ran numerous ads in key swing states saying Romney was "out of touch" with women and developed the online campaigns #askMitt and "This is Personal" website that focused on a GOP "War on Women" (Viebeck 2012). Similarly, the National Abortion Rights Action League engaged in microtargeting of women that were potential "Obama defectors" in battleground states, sending over 1.2 million pieces of mail, as well as extensive phone banking, social media use, and targeted cable television ads (Stanage, Parnes, and Easley 2012).

Romney's attempts to attract the support of women voters were similar to his outreach efforts with other highly contested groups. In general, his campaign relied on a two-pronged strategy: (1) attempt to show how Obama's economic policies had damaged women and their families, and (2) enlist the help of high-profile women surrogates to speak on his behalf. The economic appeals proved to be attractive to married, white women. Although this group of women may have largely agreed with Obama on reproductive issues, they saw those issues as secondary to the economy (Davis 2012). A typical appeal made to women by Romney was in his widely run ad with footage of a newborn girl and narration that said, "Dear Daughter. Welcome to America. Your share of Obama's debt is over $50,000. And it grows every day. Obama's policies are making it harder on women. The poverty rate for women—the highest in seventeen years. More women are unemployed under President Obama. More than 5.5 million women can't find work. That's what Obama's policies have done for women" (Sink 2012a).

Of course, both campaigns relied heavily on female surrogates to spread their message. The Obama campaign deployed women such as First Lady Michele Obama, Sandra Fluke, Lilly Ledbetter, and Nancy Pelosi. The Romney campaign established a touring group of supporters dubbed "Women for Mitt" that included former Hewlett-Packard CEO

Carly Fiorina, as well as Governor Nikki Haley (R-SC), Governor Susana Martinez (R-NM), former Labor secretary Elaine Chow, Senator Kelly Ayotte (R-NH), and former secretary of state Condoleezza Rice. Romney's wife, Ann, who polled very well with independents and women, also made numerous media and campaign appearances, including as guest host of ABC's *Good Morning America* (Cillizza and Blake 2012).

The period surrounding the second presidential debate proved to be decisive in the battle for women voters. In response to polls showing Romney pulling even with Obama among women, Obama initiated a mid-October offensive on abortion issues. For example, in an interview with ABC News, Obama said Romney was being deceptive in saying "there's no legislation with regards to abortion that I'm familiar with that would become part of my agenda." This culminated in Romney's damaging response to a question in the second debate in which he awkwardly referred to receiving "binders full of women" when he was hiring staffers as Massachusetts governor. In the end, the central problem for Romney was that polls consistently showed women supporting government actions to help people in need. Although Romney made extensive attempts to strike a moderate tone during the fall campaign, Romney was unable to overcome the perception that Republicans would damage the social safety net in ways that women largely disliked (Kranish 2012).

Men

As with white voters, male voters were not generally targeted in the aggregate by the Obama and Romney campaigns. Instead, appeals were made to men based on other characteristics, especially religion and class. Romney won the male vote by a margin of 52–47, but there was substantial variation in totals across different subgroups of men. Those differences are explored in other sections of this chapter.

AGE

One of the truisms of the American elections in recent decades is that voters of different age blocs differ significantly in their vote choice as well as their likelihood to vote. Senior citizens, for example, typically have the highest rates of voting participation of any age group, and they have tended to support Republicans in recent decades. Young people, on the other hand, have voted at a significantly lower rate and their vote has often been up for grabs between the two major parties based on the circumstances of the times.

In 2008, much of Obama's campaign was focused on attracting the youth vote. This was done through a well-coordinated campaign of issues appeals, innovative use of social media, as well as marketing the candidate as being more in tune with younger Americans. Obama was rewarded at the polls for his efforts, winning the youth vote by a margin of 34 percentage points over John McCain. This represented an improvement of twenty-five points over Kerry's total in 2004. Moreover, the youth vote increased slightly as a share of the overall electorate, in large part due to Obama's intensive mobilization efforts. With senior citizens, however, Obama failed to make significant inroads. In 2008 McCain won with this group by eight points over Obama, which was the same advantage that Bush had over Kerry in 2004.

As the 2012 campaign got underway, it quickly became apparent that the Obama and Romney campaigns once again considered both groups to be crucial voting blocs in determining the election's outcome. As a result, both groups received extensive campaign appeals from the candidates.

Seniors

Due to the aging of the Baby Boomer generation, older voters have been increasing in numbers in recent years. This is true in most states, but the senior vote has been especially important in the critical swing state of Florida due to its attractiveness as a retirement destination. Thus, issues important to seniors were a significant part of the campaign appeals, especially in Florida.

Typical of Obama's efforts to attract seniors was a bus tour he took through Florida in early September. During that trip, Obama spoke repeatedly about the risks to seniors of the Republican plan to reform Medicare. That plan was a signature issue of vice presidential candidate Paul Ryan's career in Congress. The Ryan plan, which was widely touted by Romney, sought to convert Medicare into a voucher program for people under the age of fifty-five. Even though Ryan's proposal did not affect current seniors, the Obama campaign sought to sow fears among seniors that Republicans would damage the popular federal program (Cooper

2012). This line of attack was a frequent theme throughout the Obama campaign. For example, in a satellite appearance before the convention of the American Association of Retired Persons (AARP), the country's largest organized interest group, Obama repeated his line of attack against the "risky" Republican plan (Goldman and Brower 2012). Obama also ran extensive advertising in key swing states that simultaneously touted Obama's record on Medicare while criticizing the Romney-Ryan plan (Sink 2012c). Vice President Joseph Biden reinforced these messages, often telling seniors that Romney would raise their Social Security taxes (Cohn and Becker 2012).

Despite the controversies surrounding the Romney-Ryan plans for Medicare and Social Security, Obama continued to face an uphill fight in attracting this typically Republican voting bloc. For example, a national poll conducted in late September showed that seniors were more concerned with the general state of the U.S. economy than just the narrow issues of Medicare and Social Security. Moreover, seniors were disproportionately opposed to the controversial "Obamacare" health reforms (Associated Press 2012). As a result, Romney's general campaign messages on economic issues were widely appealing to senior voters. Romney and Ryan also sought to neutralize the Medicare issue by repeatedly saying that Obamacare resulted in drastic cuts to Medicare, a charge that many fact-checking organizations found to be misleading (Sink, 2012c). In the end, Romney's targeting of senior voters turned out to be more effective than Obama's; Romney not only improved on McCain's performance with seniors, but did better than Bush in 2004 as well, beating Obama by twelve points among seniors.

Youth Vote

The youth vote has been a particularly volatile segment of the electorate across different elections because it is largely influenced by the circumstances of the times. "Millennials," the current generation of young voters, were a significant part of the Obama coalition in 2008 due to their widespread dissatisfaction with George W. Bush's presidency as well as the sense that Obama's candidacy was historic. Indicators throughout the campaign continued to point to a Democratic advantage with young voters, but as with blacks the key question was whether their waning enthusiasm would result in lower turnout rates. Outreach to the youth vote normally focuses on college campuses, but the campaigns also recognized the need to target working-class young people since there were about eighteen million young people in the United States who had not attended college. This bloc tends not to be very engaged, but it is highly persuadable (Saulny 2012a). Thus, the Obama campaign worked especially hard to mobilize the youth vote again in 2012. The Republicans did not completely concede the youth vote, but it was not an important part of the Romney campaign's appeals.

Much of Obama's efforts with young people were based on voter registration drives. He also made numerous appearances on college campuses, many with celebrities such as Beyoncé, Jay-Z, and Katy Perry (Mendelson 2012). Illustrative of these rallies was an early October event at the University of Wisconsin–Madison with over thirty thousand attendees in which he spoke about education and student loans. By requiring attendees of these rallies to give email addresses to get an electronic ticket, Obama built an extensive database of young voters that may continue to bear fruit in the years to come (Stein and Marley 2012). This was combined with continued innovations in the use of social media. For example, after Romney's controversial "47 percent comment" leaked, the Obama campaign started a "For All" effort in which it encouraged young voters to post their picture on Instagram or Twitter.

The Romney campaign created a group called Young Americans for Romney that largely sponsored campaign appearances by Romney's younger adult children and youthful surrogates such as George P. Bush (Rubino 2012). Romney also made many appeals to non-college-enrolled young people on economic and social issues. In the end, Obama won the youth vote by twenty-three points over Romney, although waning enthusiasm due to the nation's ongoing economic problems decreased his vote total with this group by six points from 2008. Nevertheless, the long-term trend continues to favor Democrats when it comes to young voters.

SOCIAL CLASS

The place of class in American society has long been a contested and complicated topic, a situation that is perhaps even more true when one considers the role of class in American politics. Arguments about how class factors into the American political arrangement have been around longer than American political science itself, and these arguments show no signs of abating any time soon (see, e.g., Bartels 2008). Indeed, even the question of how one should measure class in order to investigate its effects within the American polity is the subject of relatively heated debate (Bartels 2008; Brewer and Stonecash 2001; Stonecash 2000).

One thing that has become increasingly clear over the past few years is that the significance of social class is alive and well in American politics. Rather than fading away in a postmodern, postindustrial, postmaterialist world dominated by political divisions rooted in noneconomic issues, class still matters in American politics in a variety of ways (Bartels 2008; Fiorina et al. 2011; Stonecash 2000). Some of these effects have lengthy histories in the American context, while others are quite new. The 2012 presidential election provides ample evidence of this. Indeed, one could argue that class-related themes were front and center in the 2012 presidential election in a way that had not been seen since at least the 1992 contest. The two presidential candidates came from opposite ends of the American class spectrum, Obama with his decidedly modest early family life and upbringing and Romney as the scion of a wealthy and powerful family who was afforded all of the advantages that such circumstances allow. While both men are today in what anyone would term the upper class, there is still a substantial gap between their respective net worths (with Romney obviously much wealthier), and it is also the case that Obama's ascent into the upper class is quite recent while Romney has been there his entire life. Obama discussed his class background at every opportunity, while Romney was forced to defend his great wealth as the product of his own individual talents, hard work, and initiative.

The larger political and economic environments in which the 2012 campaign was conducted also lent themselves to a heavy focus on issues and ideas related to class. Economic inequality in the United States is at very high levels (Stiglitz 2013). The effects of the 2008–2009 recession were still being felt by millions of Americans, and the economy was far and away the top issue on the minds of voters. President Obama and Republicans in Congress had been prominently at odds over how to deal with the still struggling economy throughout much of 2011 and 2012, and many of these disagreements had clear class elements to them. These partisan differences only became sharper and more well known after the party conventions ended and the rush to Election Day commenced. As the general election campaign unfolded, it became clear that for both campaigns the crucial groups in play in terms of class were the working class and the middle class. Both Obama and Romney devoted serious time, energy, and other resources toward attracting the votes of Americans in these groups.

Deciding to go after working-class and middle-class voters is one thing. Determining how well the respective campaigns did in their quests is another. A big difficulty faced by analysts of class in American politics is trying to define what the various classes are in any meaningful way. A large majority of Americans consider themselves to be part of the middle class, regardless of what their income or education levels are. At the same time, the concept of the working class has achieved somewhat of a mythic (in a positive way) status in American society, and many Americans claim at least working-class roots if not current membership in the working class, again regardless of education and income levels. These facts leave analysts in a sticky situation, one that cannot be addressed in an entirely satisfactory manner. Fortunately, we do not have to engage in too much class parsing here. The two presidential campaigns often, indeed most of the time, wrapped these two groups together in their class-based appeals. Even when the campaigns did attempt to speak or appeal explicitly to one of these groups, it was generally presented that what was good for one of these groups was also good for the other.

At least since the New Deal, certain class divisions have been taken as givens in American politics, namely that lower class voters (aka the poor, the less affluent) are going to favor the Democratic Party and its candidates for office and the upper class (aka the rich, the wealthy, the most affluent) will do the same for the GOP and its candidates. The levels of support vary marginally from election to election, but the pattern holds in almost all cases, although there have been a few exceptions (one of which was 2008). Neither party seriously contests the other party's advantage with the lowest and highest income groups, at least not on class or economic grounds. This was the case in 2012. Although Romney occasionally mouthed words indicating that his policies would help the poor, they were not backed up with any specifics and they were generally delivered with little enthusiasm. Obama did even less in terms of courting rich voters as a group, at least on the basis of their wealth. In fact, Obama was very open during the campaign that he strongly supported raising taxes on the very wealthy (the so-called "1 percent") while Romney regularly referred to such Americans as "job creators" and argued that raising taxes on these Americans would hurt the overall American economy (Freeland 2012). In the end, voters with 2011 family incomes less than $30,000 (the lowest income bracket reported by the 2012 Exit Poll) favored Obama over Romney 63 percent to 35 percent, while voters in families earning $250,000 or more (the highest income bracket reported) favored Romney 55 percent to 42 percent. Rather than trying to overturn the long-standing vote patterns of low-income individuals and high-earners, Obama and Romney set their sights on working- and middle-class voters.

Two related but distinct phenomena provide crucial context for all of the working-class and middle-class appeals made by both sides during the campaign. Both are negatives for Romney, one that was carried out against him and one that was self-inflicted. Let us begin with the former. During the Republican primary season Romney's opponents (most notably Newt Gingrich and Rick Perry but eventually Rick Santorum as well) harshly criticized Romney for his tenure as the head of the venture capital firm Bain Capital (Sonmez 2012; Zeleny 2012). Calling Romney a vulture capitalist who made millions by benefiting from and/or causing the suffering of others, his primary opponents attempted to portray Romney as a man whose fantastic gains were ill-gotten, who was out of touch with and opposed to the interests of hard-working, normal Americans. Romney was Wall Street, and as such could never understand and would certainly not sympathize with Main Street. Although clearly stung by such criticism, Romney was able to overcome it and secure the GOP presidential nomination. He was damaged by these attacks, however, and during the summer months (well before the party conventions) the Obama campaign went on the attack to reopen and in many ways enlarge Romney's wounds. The Obama camp aired a series of ads in critical battleground states attacking Romney for his time at Bain, painting Romney as an out-of-touch rich guy who could not possibly understand the needs and problems of average Americans, who are of course all members of the middle class with working-class roots. Romney never responded, thus allowing the Obama camp to define him. It seemed as though the Romney people had not learned anything from the Swiftboat attacks on John Kerry in 2004. These attacks cut deep and stuck with Romney all the way through to Election Day.

Now for a wound of the self-inflicted variety. The dynamic of the 2012 presidential campaign changed dramatically and permanently on September 17 when liberal magazine *Mother Jones* released an undercover video of Romney speaking to a crowd of wealthy donors at a May 2012 fundraiser. This event is of course the source of the infamous "47 percent" comment. The full text of the comment, along with the question that elicited Romney's remarks (taken from the full transcript published by *Mother Jones* on its website on September 19, 2012), is presented below:

> *Audience member:* For the last three years, all everybody's been told is, "Don't worry, we'll take care of you." How are you going to do it, in two months before the elections, to convince everybody you've got to take care of yourself?
>
> *Romney:* There are 47 percent of the people who will vote for the president no matter what. All right, there are 47 percent who are with him, who are dependent upon government, who believe that they are victims, who believe that government has a responsibility to care for them, who believe that they are entitled to health care, to food, to housing, to you name it. That that's an entitlement. And the government should give it to them. And they will vote for this president no matter what. And I mean, the president starts off with 48, 49, and 48—he starts off with a huge number. These are people who pay no income tax. Forty-seven percent of Americans pay no income tax. So our message of low taxes doesn't connect. And he'll be out there talking about tax cuts for the rich. I mean that's what they sell every four years. And so my job is not to worry about those people—I'll never convince them that they should take personal responsibility and care for their lives. What I have to do is convince the 5 to 10 percent in the center that are independents that are thoughtful, that look at voting one way or the other depending upon in some cases emotion, whether they like the guy or not, what it looks like.

Never before has a presidential candidate of a major political party declared, on tape complete with the tinkling of silverware, that almost half of all Americans see themselves as victims who have completely abrogated hard work and personal responsibility, who now look to the government to feed them, house them, and provide their health care. Never before has a presidential candidate called about half of Americans a bunch of lazy moochers. In an entry entitled "Thurston Howell Romney," *New York Times* columnist David Brooks (2012) nicely captured the impact of the video: "But, as a description of America today, Romney's comment is a country club fantasy. It's what self-satisfied millionaires say to each other. It reinforces every negative view people have about Romney."

The recording, directed to *Mother Jones* journalist David Corn by a grandson of former Democratic president Jimmy Carter, provided the Obama campaign with an enormous opportunity. The campaign and its allies did not whiff. Appearing the next day on the *Late Show with David Letterman*, Obama criticized Romney's remarks as off base and inappropriate for someone who wanted to be president, saying "My expectation is that if you want to be president, you have to work for everyone, not just for some" (Daly 2012). Democratic Senate majority leader Harry Reid opened Senate business on September 19 by stating, "This rare look at the real Mitt Romney proves one thing: that he is completely out of touch with average Americans" (Lerer and Davis 2012). Within days of the video's release the Obama campaign had featured it in two different commercials airing in swing states. Soon after, Obama's Super PAC Priorities USA Action and a labor PAC (AFSCME) were doing the same. The video was, to use the words of *Los Angeles Times* journalist Matea Gold, "the gift that keeps on giving for the Democrats" (Gold 2012). Beltway publication *National Journal* queried political insiders on both sides of the partisan aisle as to how damaging Romney's 47 percent comments were. Out of 101 Democrats, 78 percent thought the remarks were very damaging and 22 percent felt they were damaging. Note that not a single Democrat saw them as nondamaging. As one would expect, the numbers were different among the ninety-seven Republicans polled, but even here 18 percent saw the remarks as very damaging to Romney and 68 percent evaluated them as damaging. Only 14 percent viewed them as not damaging (Roarty et al. 2012). If possible, Romney made the situation even worse by standing by his comments for over two weeks, only going so far as to say they were "ineloquently worded." Finally, on October 4 in an interview with Sean Hannity on Fox News, Romney capitulated and apologized for the remarks, telling Hannity: "In this case, I said something that's just completely wrong." But much damage was already done. Romney had reinforced the image of him as an out-of-touch member of the ultra-wealthy who did not care about average Americans that his opponents—first within the GOP and then the Obama campaign and its allies—had worked so hard to create.

With these two elements heavily influencing the parameters of class-based appeals in the campaign, the fights for middle- and working-class voters are relatively easily understood. The Obama team sensed it had the edge and moved aggressively to take advantage. Appearing before suburban audiences and in other venues likely to have significant chunks of middle-class voters, Obama routinely promised that he would keep taxes low for the middle class throughout his second term while at the same time claiming that Romney would raise taxes on the middle class (often specified as ending popular tax deductions) in order to preserve or even extend tax cuts for the wealthy (Gardner 2012; Memoli 2012). One Obama campaign video cut right to the chase, stating, "In fact, Romney's plan would cut taxes even more for millionaires like himself and raise them on the middle class" and "Mitt Romney on tax fairness: Tax cuts for millionaires and billionaires, tax hikes (and insults) for the middle class" (Sink 2012d).

Romney tried hard to counter such claims and attract middle-class support. Shortly after assuming a greater role in the Romney campaign, senior adviser and top-level Republican strategist Ed Gillespie made the campaign more assertive in claiming its candidate and his plans were much better for middle-class voters (O'Keefe and Rucker 2012). Romney went after middle-class voters extremely hard during the first debate in Denver, and followed that up with numerous ads trying to woo valuable middle-class votes. Romney, playing off a 1998 video clip uploaded to YouTube and publicized by the Drudge Report and Fox News in which then–Illinois state senator Obama had voiced his belief in redistribution of wealth, hammered away on Obama as a "redistributor" of wealth who would take from the middle class to give to those who were less than deserving (Lerer and Davis 2012; Sink 2012b).

The battle for working-class support was just as intense. The Romney campaign knew that working-class support was critical to their hopes of victory on Election Day. Obama and the Democrats knew this as well, and one could make the case that the second night of their national convention was focused largely on appealing to the working class (and in keeping with this campaign, the middle class as well). Then–Senate candidate from Massachusetts Elizabeth Warren spent her speech beating up on the GOP for its complete disdain for working Americans, telling the crowd, "The Republican vision is clear: 'I've got mine, the rest of you are on your own'" (Hughes 2012). Former president Bill Clinton, the keynote speaker at the convention that evening, emphatically defended Obama's economic performance during his first term in office and made the case that Obama fully understood the needs of and looked out for the interests of average, working people (Haberman 2012). Clinton as an Obama surrogate to the working class, especially the white working class, was a scene repeated again and again throughout the campaign.

Romney attempted to make the case that he had real plans to help the working class. He attacked Obama relentlessly for being too soft on trade with China, claiming that doing so had cost countless blue-collar workers their jobs (Landsberg 2012a). Romney played up his support for the coal industry, especially its miners, and criticized Obama for being against the industry. Vice presidential candidate Paul Ryan was dispatched to address working-class audiences across the Midwest, where he spoke fondly of his working-class roots and his understanding of working-class needs and concerns (Prendergast 2012).

The Obama campaign countered each of these moves. Vice President Biden was even more prominent than Ryan in front of working-class audiences and was generally very well received by such crowds (Beaumont 2012; Klein 2012; Prendergast 2012). Reports surfaced that coal miners who appeared in a Romney campaign ad had been forced to attend at no pay (Gomez 2012). Obama defended his record on trade actions against China as more aggressive than those of his predecessor, Republican George W. Bush, and actually filed a complaint against China with the WTO (over illegally subsidized automobiles and auto parts) in September (Puzzanghera and Memoli 2012).

But again, in another instance of a self-inflicted wound for the Romney campaign, the most damning portrait of Romney being opposed to working-class interests was painted by Romney himself. In October

2008, Romney had published an op-ed in the *New York Times*, entitled "Let Detroit Go Bankrupt," in which he outlined his opposition to the federal government's bailout of General Motors and Chrysler then being discussed and eventually enacted in Washington, DC in the waning days of the Bush administration. This opposition came back to haunt Romney at every turn throughout the campaign as Obama and surrogates too numerous to count pointed to this stance as evidence that Romney did not care about the working class (Healey 2012; Rutenberg and Peters 2012). Yet again, Romney exacerbated this problem when late in the campaign Romney released ads claiming that bailed-out Chrysler was going to outsource Jeep production to China. Chrysler immediately stated that the charges were untrue, and Obama and many union allies pounced all over Romney (Kessler 2012; Rutenberg and Peters 2012; Shepardson 2012). Speaking in Ohio, Obama said of the ads, "You don't scare hardworking Americans just to scare up some votes. That's not what being president is about" (Shepardson 2012).

So, how did all of these class-based appeals and criticisms play out on Election Day? As noted above, there are multiple ways in which one might measure social class, all of which have their strengths and weaknesses and none of which is entirely satisfactory on its own. The 2012 exit polls allow us to utilize two of these measures—family income levels and educational attainment. Of all of the possible class measures out there, family income is perhaps the cleanest. It comes to us already quantified, possesses a continuous range, and is easily interpretable. In addition, family income gives one a relatively good idea as to how much ease or difficulty one has in meeting life's day-to-day needs and also about the opportunities available to the individuals within the family unit. The 2012 exit polls present family income sliced in a number of different ways; all show pretty much the same picture. Among those Americans with 2011 family incomes of less than $50,000 (41 percent of voters), Obama bested Romney 60 percent to 38 percent. Among voters in the $50,000–$99,000 range (31 percent of voters), Romney edged Obama 52 percent to 46 percent. Finally, among voters with incomes over $100,000 (28 percent), Romney notched a convincing, but not overwhelming, 54 percent to 44 percent win. The latter two figures for Romney were significantly better than John McCain had done in 2008. But they were not enough to overcome Obama's huge edge among less affluent voters. Educational attainment presents a somewhat different picture. If one cuts the electorate into two simple groups of no college degree (53 percent of the electorate) or college degree (47 percent), the results look remarkably similar: a 51 percent to 47 percent edge for Obama among the former group and a 50 percent to 48 percent margin among the latter. But if one looks at the lowest education attainment group—no high school diploma (3 percent of the electorate)—Obama scores a convincing 64 percent to 35 percent win. The same is true with the highest group—postgraduate study (18 percent of the electorate)—55 percent to 42 percent for Obama. The middle three groups—high school grads, those with some college, and college grads—are all incredibly closely divided between the two candidates. All of these divisions are quite similar to 2008 divisions. In one final class-related note, Obama bested Romney 58 percent to 40 percent among voters who lived in union households (18 percent of the electorate). Organized labor held strong for the Democrats.

It appears that the middle-class vote is up for grabs and that the traditional low income/upper income divide remains relevant in American electoral politics, but with a newly emerging twist. Those Americans with the highest levels of educational attainment have now gone strongly for the Democratic candidate in the last three presidential elections. When one combines this with high levels of Democratic support among the least affluent Americans and union voters, it appears that the current playing field on social class favors the Democrats. But the middle class—however one defines it—still looms large as a target for both parties moving forward.

RELIGION

Arguing against the importance of religion in American electoral politics is always tricky, and doing so in the context of the 2012 presidential contest is no exception. Religion was an important element in this campaign, but for a variety of reasons religion was a less contested sphere in the 2012 race (at least during the general election), and therefore the place of religion in the public narrative of this presidential race was more low-profile than it had been in any contest since 1996. Part of this certainly had to do with the religious affiliations of the two candidates and the public's beliefs about those affiliations. Despite almost five years of Obama publicly identifying himself as a practicing Christian, only 49 percent of respondents in a July 2012 Pew survey classified him as such. Seventeen percent of respondents said that Obama was a Muslim, while 31 percent said they did not know the president's religious affiliation (Pew 2012a). These figures clearly presented a problem for the Obama campaign, at least among some voters. It is difficult to mount a broad-based religious appeal in search of votes when less than half of voters believe that you belong to the nation's historically dominant faith tradition, and almost a fifth of voters believe that you belong to a religious tradition that at present is viewed quite negatively by the populace. Even if more Americans were able to correctly identify Obama's religious identity, it is unlikely that the president would have been in any hurry to interject religion into the campaign given some of the tenets of black liberation theology (Cone 1969, 1970) and the controversial nature of his former pastor, Jeremiah Wright.

Romney found himself in a very similar situation. Romney, of course, was the first member of the Church of Jesus Christ of Latter-day Saints (known popularly as the Mormon Church) to gain the presidential nomination of a major political party in the United States. Mormonism has been quite controversial during its short history, and the faith has been the victim of much discrimination and distrust (Ostling and Ostling 1999). The same Pew study referenced above shows that 60 percent of respondents could correctly identify Romney as Mormon in July 2012. Of those 60 percent, 22 percent were uncomfortable with Romney's Mormonism, a somewhat lower figure than many expected but still relatively high. Furthermore, only 50 percent of the Pew respondents felt that LDS was a Christian religion, and 61 percent said that the Mormon religion was very different from their own beliefs (Pew 2012a). Given the circumstances, it is not surprising that both candidates were somewhat reluctant to discuss religious specifics on the campaign trail (Hagerty 2012; Rozell 2012).

But just because the two presidential candidates were at least somewhat reluctant to engage in so-called "God talk" does not mean that religion was relegated to the sidelines in 2012. Religion mattered in this campaign—but it mattered in much the same way that it mattered in 2008, and really along the same lines that have been in place since the mid-

1980s and early 1990s. Each party has religious groups that it can expect strong support from, and both the Democrats and the Republicans have come to rely heavily on these groups for success at the polls. The parties then hotly pursue voters who fall into a handful of religious groups that are viewed as up for grabs. These patterns held in 2012.

Looking first at the Republican side of the ledger, it is clear that over the past twenty to thirty years the GOP has come to rely heavily on two religious groups: those for whom religion is highly salient (generally measured by worship service attendance or the importance of religion in one's life) and white evangelical Protestants (Layman 2001). These groups are obviously not mutually exclusive. Both of these groups more than pulled their weight for Romney and the Republican Party in 2012. As Frank Newport, editor-in-chief of Gallup, pointed out in analysis of pre-election polling data, religiosity was a huge predictor of support for Romney (Newport 2012). This carried through to Election Day. Americans who attend worship services more than once a week (14 percent of voters) chose Romney over Obama 63 percent to 36 percent, and those who attend once a week (28 percent) favored Romney 58 percent to 41 percent. These figures are very similar to those achieved by Bush among these groups in 2004 and represent an improvement over the numbers recorded by McCain in 2008.

The degree to which white evangelicals would support Romney was a hotly debated question as the candidate secured the GOP nomination and geared up for the general election. Some believed that Romney's Mormonism—which many evangelicals view in a very negative light—would result in decreased support from this critical group. Few thought that these voters would turn to Obama in any significant way, but rather that at least some would choose to stay home instead of casting a ballot for Romney. These fears were unwarranted. Although many white evangelicals did indeed oppose Romney during the nomination phase, they quickly fell in line behind him once he secured the nomination. They also turned out on Election Day, accounting for 26 percent of the electorate, a figure that was up from both 2008 (24 percent) and 2004 (23 percent). Romney's success among evangelicals did not happen without cause or effort. White evangelicals may not have loved Romney, but many were genuinely fearful of a second term for a president who had already endorsed same-sex marriage, was a strong supporter of abortion rights, ended the policy of Don't Ask, Don't Tell, and included mandatory coverage of contraception in his signature health care reform package (Schultheis 2012; Sherry 2012). In addition, it is highly possible that the phenomenon of "negative partisanship" was in play among evangelicals, where their distaste for Romney was superseded by a longstanding commitment to never vote for a Democratic candidate (or perhaps an African American candidate?) for president (Medeiros and Noël 2014). There was also a huge effort to sell Romney to evangelical leaders in particular and to evangelicals in general. Mark DeMoss, an evangelical leader who served as a key adviser to Romney in the campaign, was crucial in these efforts, as were others such as Jim Daly, president of the powerful group Focus on the Family, and Ralph Reed, back in the spotlight as the founder of the Faith and Freedom Coalition (Landsberg 2012d; Kucinich 2012). Meetings between and events with Romney and white evangelical Protestant icons such as Billy Graham and Pat Robertson were carefully planned and highly publicized (Funk 2012; Hunt 2012; Kucinich 2012; Landsberg 2012d; Politi 2012). The removal of references to Mormonism as a cult from Graham's website and the full-page newspaper ad Graham placed in newspapers around the country urging Americans to "vote for biblical values" were seen as crucial tacit endorsements of Romney by evangelical Protestantism's biggest name. Reed's group was also important in microtargeting over seventeen million religiously conservative voters and urging them to support Romney (Becker 2012; Reinhard 2012b). Romney's pledge to end funding for Planned Parenthood was placed front and center for evangelicals (Funk 2012). At the end of the day all of these efforts paid off. White evangelicals supported Romney 78 percent to 21 percent, higher than 2008 (74 percent to 24 percent) and identical to 2004.

The religious element of the Democratic Party's coalition looks very different from that of the GOP. The largest religion-based element of the Democratic base is actually a group that is increasingly referred to as the "nones," but is more accurately demarcated by those who identify themselves as having no religious affiliation, agnostic, or atheist. This group has grown steadily in recent years, reaching 20 percent in 2012. Almost one-third of those Americans ages eighteen to twenty-nine fall into this category (Pew 2012b). Preelection analysis by the Public Religion Research Institute

(PRRI) found that this group was likely to be crucial to Obama's chances of victory on Election Day (Markoe 2012; PRRI 2012), and the exit polls bear this out although they also point to the fact that nonreligious individuals are less likely to vote than those for whom religion is a strong influence. Religiously unaffiliated Americans made up 12 percent of the electorate in 2012 and favored Obama over Romney 70 percent to 26 percent, figures that represent a 5 percentage point drop from Obama's performance with this group in 2008 but a three point increase from Kerry's support levels in 2004. To a certain extent, those for whom religion is not important would tend to be Democratic almost by default given the central place of religion within the contemporary Republican Party. But at the same time, one can certainly see that throughout his presidency Obama has consistently included those who have no faith in his public rhetoric in such a way that identifies such a view as perfectly legitimate.

Two additional religious groups are generally found at the center of the Democratic coalition, although in each case one could make the argument that their Democratic proclivities have as much or more to do with race and ethnicity as with religion. The first of these groups is African American Protestants. Some worried that Obama's endorsement of same-sex marriage would hurt him among this group, and a few black Protestant ministers did publicly oppose Obama on the basis of this issue (Parker 2012; Zoll 2012). But such ministers were a distinct minority among African American clergy. Far more black ministers urged their flocks to take advantage of early voting and support Obama in what were labeled "souls to the polls" efforts (Jonsson 2012; Saulny 2012b; Zoll 2012). A coalition of black clergy members in the swing state of Virginia went so far as to produce and distribute over one hundred thousand pro-Obama voter guides offering what was presented as a comparison of the respective religious beliefs of Obama and Romney (Wallsten 2012). While the exit polls do not allow us to determine how black Protestants voted in 2012, we do know that the overwhelming majority of African Americans are Protestant, and that blacks favored Obama over Romney 93 percent to 6 percent.

Jews are the final religious group that consistently aligns with the Democrats. However, Republicans have long been attempting to increase their support among Jewish voters, and we can see that both campaigns went after Jews hard in 2012. The Obama campaign regularly dispatched

Chicago mayor and former Obama chief of staff Rahm Emanuel to speak to Jewish audiences (where he often used his middle name, Israel) (Sweet 2012) and employed high-profile Jewish celebrities such as Barbra Streisand in support of the president (Cohn 2012). The Obama campaign also earned what was labeled an "unprecedented" statement of support by the powerful American Israel Public Affairs Committee (AIPAC) on Rosh Hashanah (Jewish New Year) (European Jewish Press 2012), endorsements from popular current and former Jewish mayors of New York City Michael Bloomberg and Ed Koch (Farrell 2012; Scherer 2012), and ran a campaign ad touting the administration's support of Israel in general and its role in helping Israel to develop its new Iron Dome antimissile defense system (Sink 2012e; Sweet 2012).

The Romney campaign attempted to counter these appeals to Jews in a number of ways (Alvarez 2012). Throughout the campaign Romney argued that Obama was seriously endangering Israel by being too soft on Iran and that country's nuclear program (Jerusalem Post 2012). Romney also attacked Obama for failing to meet with Israeli prime minister Benjamin Netanyahu while both leaders were in New York City to attend the United Nations General Assembly, and an outside group called Secure America Now released a pro-Romney television ad in Florida featuring Netanyahu (Marcus 2012; Spetalnick and Fisher-Ilan 2012; Sullivan 2012). The Romney camp also went after Obama for refusing to acknowledge Jerusalem as the capital of Israel (Cleveland Plain Dealer 2012), and Romney personally criticized Obama for not visiting Israel on what he labeled as Obama's "apology tour" of the Middle East (Scherer 2012). Finally, staunch Israel supporter and casino magnate Sheldon Adelson spent millions of dollars of his own money to mobilize Jewish voters in support of Romney (Gur 2012). When all was said and done, Jewish voters continued their longstanding pattern of Democratic support, but at somewhat lower levels than in the past. Obama bested Romney 69 percent to 30 percent among Jews, down from his 78 percent to 21 percent advantage over McCain in 2008 and Kerry's 74 percent to 25 percent win over Bush among Jewish voters in 2004. This development merits monitoring in future contests.

Dispensing with the religious bases of both parties leaves us with those religious groups whose support has been more evenly divided between the parties in recent elections, and whose support is also seen as at least somewhat up for grabs during the campaign: white mainline Protestants and Roman Catholics. Unfortunately, we will not be able to say much of anything with regard to mainliners in this chapter. The 2012 exit polls did not report separate results for white mainline Protestants, so any analysis of the voting patterns of this group will have to wait until additional exit poll data are available to researchers. But even if such data were currently available, it is unclear what insight we could offer regarding this religious group. In our monitoring of the campaign we did not detect any appeals from either side aimed explicitly at mainline Protestants, nor did we see any commentary on the candidates or the parties coming from the mainline. In our view it is possible that as mainline Protestantism has lost its central and in some ways privileged place in American society it has also lost some of its distinction, thus making appeals to the mainline as a whole less doable and less important.

We have no such difficulties with Catholics. The exit polls provide data for this group, and there was no shortage of attention and appeals to Catholics on the part of both candidates during the campaign. Catholic leadership in the United States was very active and vocal during the 2012 contest, as were other Catholic organizations and groups. Over the past few election cycles Catholics have emerged as quintessential swing voters, and both campaigns competed fervently for Catholic support. Both parties had Cardinal Timothy Dolan, archbishop of New York and president of the U.S. Conference of Catholic Bishops, give the closing benediction at their national conventions, and in a first, both Obama and Romney chose regularly practicing Catholics as their running mates. After this, however, the similarities regarding how the campaigns attempted to attract Catholic votes ended.

For the most part, the differences in the respective campaigns' appeals to Catholics followed the lines of a significant division that exists within the American Catholic Church. Labeled by some as a pre-Vatican II and a post-Vatican II divide, by others as a split between conservative and liberal Catholics, by some as a division between traditionalist and progressive Catholics, and perhaps most recently by PRRI as a cleavage between "social justice" Catholics and "right to life" Catholics, the current split of American Catholics fits quite well with existing partisan divides. Traditionalist Catholics tend to place more emphasis on the necessity of conservative stances on social issues. Therefore, these Catholics tend to be quite strongly Republican. Progressive Catholics tend to focus on more heavily on economic-related issues and favor issue positions that in their view promote fairness and care for the less fortunate. As such these Catholic voters more closely align with the Democrats. As Landsberg (2012b, 2012c) noted, this division was represented almost to perfection by the vice presidential candidates in this campaign, with Republican Paul Ryan playing the part of the traditionalist Catholic and Democrat Joe Biden representing the progressive Catholic. Both men were deployed by their respective campaigns to speak in Catholic areas and to Catholic audiences throughout the campaign. Biden appeared in an ad talking about the relevance of Catholic social doctrine to the Obama administration's positions (May 2012), and Ryan appeared in video specifically directed to Catholic voters making the case for the Romney/Ryan ticket as best prepared to represent their views and interests. Ryan specifically noted religious freedom in this video, saying that a Romney administration would protect religious freedom where the Obama administration had trampled on it (NCR 2012). This referenced the element of the Obama health care law that required religious institutions other than churches to cover contraception for their employees. Romney also made this argument in an ad directed at Catholics. During the summer months, the Catholic Church held a Fortnight for Freedom event in which it tried to bring attention to the religious freedom issue; in the final days of the campaign the U.S. bishops reminded Catholics in a voter guide distributed at masses that Catholics should not vote for a candidate who supports acts that are "intrinsically evil" (a list that has abortion at the very top); and numerous Catholic bishops spoke openly on both subjects in a way that clearly directed Catholics that they should vote for Romney over Obama (Baklinski 2012; Erickson 2012; Gibson 2012; USCCB 2007; Zito 2012).

Initially, it would seem that all of this effort to attract Catholic votes was a wash: Catholic voters (25 percent of the electorate) favored Obama over Romney by a slim 50 percent to 48 percent margin. But this only tells a very limited part of the story. The exit polls do not allow us to say anything regarding the divide between traditionalist and progressive

Catholics. The best we can do here (and it is a very poor proxy) is to look at differences between Catholics who attend mass weekly and those who do not. Here, weekly attenders favored Romney over Obama 57 percent to 42 percent, while those Catholics who did not attend weekly favored Obama 56 percent to 42 percent. Finally, the exit polls also do not allow us to examine differences between white, non-Latino Catholics and Latino Catholics, something that is necessary to present a full picture of the Catholic vote. But what we can say at this point is that the Catholic vote as a whole is closely divided between the parties, and that both parties will surely continue to compete strongly for Catholic support.

CONCLUSION

In terms of group-based appeals and outcomes, the 2012 presidential election results point to a bright future for the Democratic Party at the presidential level and the need for at least somewhat of a shift of direction for the Republicans. The Democrats did very well among nonwhites (especially Latinos) and young voters. We know nonwhites are going to continue to increase as a percentage of the electorate, and voters aged eighteen to twenty-nine in the 2012 presidential election have a good many presidential contests in their futures. The Democrats also performed well among Americans with postgraduate education, and one can assume that this group will continue to increase in size as well. Women will not decline as a percentage of the electorate, and unfortunately, the less affluent are unlikely to, either. Finally, while it is always dangerous to bet against religion in the American context, the percentage of unaffiliated Americans is rising. All of these elements combined bode well for the Democratic Party. The GOP, on the other hand, needs to recognize that the days of an America where a majority of the population was comprised of white Christians are over, and that those of an America that is majority white soon will be as well. The party will soon lose voters in its strongest age group by attrition, and the religious tides are not currently in its favor. Republicans also need to be concerned about their growing difficulties among Americans with postgraduate education, which is likely reducing their traditional advantage among wealthier voters. Without an incumbent on the ballot, the 2016 presidential contest will provide an interesting laboratory in which to examine these developments, and undoubtedly others as well.

REFERENCES

Alvarez, L. 2012. "Republicans Intensify Drive to Win Over Jewish Voters." *New York Times,* September 26.

Associated Press. 2012. "Looking Past Entitlements, Senior Voters Ask How They Will Fare in an Obama or Romney Economy." *Associated Press,* September 27.

Baklinski, T. 2012. "Green Bay Bishop: Voting for Pro-Abortion/Gay 'Marriage' Candidate Could Put Your Soul in Jeopardy." *LifeSiteNews,* October 29.

Barrow, B. 2012. "Out of Reach Today, Minorities a Key to GOP Future." *Associated Press,* November 2.

Bartels, L. M. 2008. *Unequal Democracy.* New York: Russell Sage / Princeton.

Beaumont, T. 2012. "Vice President Biden Hits Blue-Collar Towns in Southeast Iowa, Keys for Obama in Swing States." *Associated Press,* September 18.

Becker, J. 2012. "An Evangelical Is Back from Exile, Lifting Romney." *New York Times,* September 22.

Brewer, M. D., and J. M. Stonecash. 2001. "Class, Race Issues, and Declining White Support for the Democratic Party in the South." *Political Behavior* 23 (2): 131–155.

Brewer, M. D., and J. M. Stonecash. 2009. *Dynamics of American Political Parties.* New York: Cambridge University Press.

Brooks, D. 2012. "Thurston Howell Romney." *New York Times,* September 17.

Chozik, A. 2014. "For Democrats, Texas Push Gets an Early Shove." *New York Times,* May 16.

Cillizza, C., and A. Blake. 2012. "Is Ann Romney Saving Her Husband's Campaign? She Just Might Be." *Washington Post,* October 10.

Cleveland Plain Dealer. 2012. "Republican Jewish Coalitions Says Obama Refuses to Acknowledge Jerusalem as Israel's Capital." September 24.

Cohn, A. M. 2012. "Streisand Urges Jewish Voters to Support Obama." *Hill,* November 2.

Cohn, A. M., and B. Becker. 2012. "Biden Tells Florida Seniors Romney-Ryan Will Raise Their Social Security Taxes." *Hill,* September 28.

Cone, J. H. 1969. *Black Theology and Black Power.* New York: Seabury Press.

Cone, J. H. 1970. *A Black Theology of Liberation.* Philadelphia: Lippincott.

Cooper, H. 2012. "Obama, Stumping in Florida, Tries to Turn Focus to Medicare from Jobs." *New York Times,* September 8.

Covert, B. 2012. "Working Class Women, Slammed by Job Loss, Pull Away from GOP." *Forbes,* October 2.

Daly, M. 2012. "What Did Obama Say on the 'Late Show with David Letterman'?" *Associated Press,* September 19.

Davis, J. H. 2012. "Swing-State Moms Trust Romney on Economy, Obama on Women." *Businessweek,* October 9.

de la Garza, R. O., and J. Cantina. 2007. "Are Latinos Republicans But Just Don't Know It? The Latino Vote in the 2000 and 2004 Presidential Elections." *American Politics Research* 35 (2) (March): 202–223.

Easley, J. 2012. "New Obama Campaign Ad Calls Romney 'Dangerous' for Women's Health." *Hill,* September 11.

Erickson, D. 2012. "In the Spirit: Catholic Vote a Moral Calculation." *Wisconsin State Journal,* September 16.

European Jewish Press. 2012. "Obama's Standing with Jewish Voters Given Boost with Unprecedented AIPAC Tribute to His 'Steadfast' Support of Israel." September 21.

Farrell, J. A. 2012. "Bloomberg's 'Warm Hug' of Obama Arrives at Opportune Moment." *National Journal,* November 1.

Fiorina, M. P., S. J. Abrams, and J. C. Pope. 2011. *Culture War? The Myth of a Polarized America,* 3rd ed. New York: Longman.

Fox News Latino. 2012. "Romney Endorses Immigration Hardliner, Drawing Criticism from Obama Camp." September 9.

Freeland, C. 2012. "The 1 Percent vs. President Obama." *Reuters,* July 12.

Funk, T. 2012. "Romney Reassures Conservatives in N.C." *Charlotte Observer,* October 11.

Gardner, A. 2012. "Obama Reaches Out to Middle Class Voters in Colorado Visit." *Washington Post,* September 13.

Gibson, D. 2012. "Catholic Bishops Make Last Minute Pitch for Romney." *Washington Post,* November 1.

Gold, M. 2012. "Pro-Obama 'Super PAC' uses '47%' Comment to Strafe Romney." *Los Angeles Times,* September 27.

Goldman, J., and K. A. Brower. 2012. "Obama Hits Romney on Medicare as Ryan Vows 'Honest Answers.'" *Businessweek,* September 21.

Gomez, H. J. 2012. "Romney Campaign Targets Eastern Ohio Voters with Two New Ads Emphasizing Coal Industry." *Cleveland Plain Dealer,* September 19.

Groer, A. 2012. "Indiana GOP Senate Hopeful Mourdock Says God 'Intended' Rape Pregnancies." *Washington Post,* October 24.

Gur, H. R. 2012. "Obama's Rosh Hashanah Gift: A Bump in Jewish Support." *Times of Israel,* September 16.

Haberman, M. 2012. "Clinton's Effective Obama Embrace." *Politico,* September 6.

Hagerty, B. B. 2012. "Both Candidates Leave God off the Campaign Trail." *NPR,* October 2.

Hawley, G. 2014. *White Voters in the 21st Century.* New York: Routledge.

Healey, J. 2012. "Romney Swings at Obama's Auto Bailout, Hits Himself." *Los Angeles Times,* October 30.

Hohman, J. 2012. "Obama Camp Figured Out How to Test for Racism." *Politico,* September 11.

Hughes, B. 2012. "Warren Makes Blue-Collar Pitch at DNC, Rails Against Wall Street." *Washington Examiner,* September 5.

Hunt, K. 2012. "Romney Meets with Rev. Billy Graham." *Associated Press,* October 11.

Jerusalem Post. 2012. "Poll: Obama Pulls Ahead Among Jewish Voters. September 17.

Jonsson, P. 2012. "In Blow to Romney, Court Says Ohio Can't Restrict 'Souls to the Polls' Voting by Blacks." *Christian Science Monitor,* October 6.

Kessler, G. 2012. "4 Pinocchios for Mitt Romney's Misleading Ad on Chrysler and China." *Washington Post,* October 29.

Klein, K. 2012. "Biden Makes Obama Campaign Appeal to Working-Class Voters." *Voice of America,* August 22.

Kranish, M. 2012. "Mitt Romney Shifts Tone to Try to Win Over Women." *Boston Globe* October 7.

Kucinich, J. 2012. "Evangelicals Mobilize for Romney Campaign." *USA Today,* October 17.

Landsberg, M. 2012a. "Romney Ad Hits Obama's China Policies, Says They Cost U.S. Jobs." *Los Angeles Times,* September 24.

Landsberg, M. 2012b. "Biden-Ryan Debate Highlights Nation's Catholic Political Divide." *Los Angeles Times,* October 9.

Landsberg, M. 2012c. "Catholic Bishops Chide Biden over Contraception Mandate Comments." *Los Angeles Times,* October 12.

Landsberg, M. 2012d. "Evangelical Support Grows for Romney." *Los Angeles Times,* October 25.

Layman, G. 2001. *The Great Divide.* New York: Columbia University Press.

Leal, D. L., M. A. Barreto, J. Lee, and R. O. de la Garza. 2005. "The Latino Vote in the 2004 Election." *PS: Political Science and Politics* 38 (1) (January): 41–49.

Lerer, L., and J. H. Davis. 2012. "Romney on Offense, Says Obama Can't Help Middle Class." *Businessweek,* September 20.

Llorente, E. 2012. "Romney Camp Distances Itself from Congressman's Hardline Immigration Views." *Fox News Latino,* September 12.

Marcus, L. L. 2012. "Netanyahu Bashing Obama's Appeasement in Campaign Ad Showing Today in Florida." *Jewish Press,* September 20.

Markoe, L. 2012. "The Biggest Slice of Obama's Religious Coalition? The Unaffiliated." *Washington Post,* October 23.

May, C. 2012. "'Practicing Catholic' Biden Makes a Play for Catholic Vote in New Campaign Ad." *Daily Caller,* October 29.

Medeiros, M., and A. Noël. 2014. "The Forgotten Side of Partisanship: Negative Party Identification in Four Anglo-American Democracies." *Comparative Political Studies* 47 (7) (June): 1022–1046.

Memoli, M. A. 2012. "New Ad Says Romney Has 'Tough Luck' Attitude Toward Middle Class." *Los Angeles Times,* September 18.

Mendelson, W. 2012. "Obama Looks to Woo Young Voters." *United Press International,* October 11.

National Catholic Register. 2012. "Paul Ryan Video for Catholic Voters Highlights Religious Freedom Pledge." October 5.

Newport, F. 2012. "Religiosity Continues to Power Presidential Vote Choice." *Gallup.com,* September 13.

O'Keefe, E., and P. Rucker. 2012. "Mitt Romney Refocuses Campaign on Economy and Policy Details." *Washington Post,* September 17.

Ostling, R. N., and J. K. Ostling. 1999. *Mormon America.* San Francisco: Harper Collins.

Parker, L. O. 2012. "Black Preacher Spreads the Word … Against Obama." *Washington Post,* November 4.

Parker, R. 2013. "Lone Star Blues." *New York Times,* February 19.

Petrocik, J. R. 1981. *Party Coalitions: Realignments and the Decline of the New Deal Party System.* Chicago: University of Chicago Press.

Pew Research Center. 2008. "US Population Projections, 2005–2050." Retrieved from http://www.pewhispanic.org/2008/02/11/us-population-projections -2005-2050

Pew Research Center. 2012a. "Little Voter Discomfort with Romney's Mormon Religion. July 26. Retrieved from http://www.pewforum.org/uploadedFiles /Topics/Issues/Politics_and_Elections/Little-Voter-Discomfort%20-Full.pdf.

Pew Research Center. 2012b. "'Nones' on the Rise: One-in-Five Adults Have No Religious Affiliation." October 9.

Politi, D. 2012. "Romney Suggests Obama Has Plans to Remove God from Currency." *Slate,* September 8.

Prendergast, J. 2012. "Biden vs. Ryan: A Battle to Be More Blue-Collar." *Cincinnati Enquirer,* October 11.

Public Religion Research Institute. 2012. "The 2012 American Values Survey." October 23.

Puzzanghera, J., and M. A. Memoli. 2012. "U.S., China File Dueling Complaints as Trade Tensions Heat Up." *Los Angeles Times,* September 18.

Reeves, E. 2012. "No, You're the Racist, or Blogging About Obama Phones." *Atlantic Wire,* September 28.

Reinhard, B. 2012a. "Romney Faces a Formidable Gender Gap." *National Journal,* September 30.

Reinhard, B. 2012b. "Evangelicals Will Vote for Romney, but the Passion Isn't There." *National Journal,* November 3.

Roarty, A., N. Khan, and P. Bell. 2012. "Political Insiders Poll: How Much Has Mitt Romney's '47 Percent' Comment Hurt His Candidacy?" *National Journal,* October 4.

Ross, J. 2012. "Latino Voter Outreach Breaks New Ground, Putting Obama Ahead." *Huffington Post Latino Politics,* September 17.

Rozell, M. J. 2012. "Presidential Election: Religious Voting Groups Could Determine the Winner." *Washington Post,* October 31.

Rubino, J. 2012. "Josh Romney Stumps for His Dad at Boulder's University Hill." *Boulder Daily Camera,* September 13.

Rutenberg, J., and J. W. Peters. 2012. "G.O.P. Turns Fire on Obama Pillar, the Auto Bailout." *New York Times,* October 29.

Saulny, S. 2012a. "Struggling Young Adults Are Question Mark for Campaigns." *New York Times,* September 19.

Saulny, S. 2012b. "With Less Time for Voting, Black Churches Redouble Their Efforts." *New York Times,* October 28.

Scherer, R. 2012. "Can Mitt Romney Sway Jewish Voters with 'Apology Tour' Quip?" *Christian Science Monitor,* October 23.

Schultheis, E. 2012. "Obama 'Fear' Drives Social Conservatives." *Politico*, September 16.

Shepardson, D. 2012. "Obama Attacks Romney in Ohio on Jeep Claims." *Detroit News*, November 2.

Sherry, A. 2012. "Faith Voters Onboard for Mitt Romney." *Denver Post*, October 16.

Sink, J. 2012a. "Obama Campaign: Romney Using 'Failed Playbook' of Sarah Palin, Joe the Plumber." *The Hill*, September 18.

Sink, J. 2012b. "Obama, Romney Compete with Ads for Female Voters." *Hill*, September 18.

Sink, J. 2012c. "Latest Obama Ad Says Romney Welfare Plan Raises Costs for Seniors." *Hill*, September 20.

Sink, J. 2012d. "Obama Video Targets Romney on Tax Fairness." *Hill*, September 25.

Sink, J. 2012e. "New Obama Ad in Florida Touts Ties to Israel." *Hill*, October 26.

Sonmez, F. 2012. "Rick Santorum's Camp Hits Romney on Bain Tenure." *Washington Post*, March 19.

Spetalnick, M., and A. Fisher-Ilan. 2012. "In Unusual Snub, Obama to Avoid Meeting with Netanyahu." *Reuters*, September 12.

Stanage, N., A. Parnes, and J. Easley. 2012. "Obama Fights Erosion of Female Voters with Attacks on Romney over Abortion." *Hill*, October 10.

Stein, J., and P. Marley. 2012. "Obama Urges Crowd in Madison to Vote, Says He Can Beat Romney." *Milwaukee Journal Sentinel*, October 4.

Stiglitz, J. E. 2013. *The Price of Inequality*. New York: W. W. Norton.

Stonecash, J. M. 2000. *Class and Party in American Politics*. Boulder, CO: Westview Press.

Sullivan, A. 2012. "In Obama's Trip to New York, There's Whoopi but No 'Bibi.'" *Reuters*, September 25.

Sweet, L. 2012. "Campaigns Battle for Critical Jewish Votes." *Chicago Sun Times*, October 28.

United States Conference of Catholic Bishops. 2007. "The Challenge of Forming Consciences for Faithful Citizenship."

USA Today. 2012. "Romney Won't Revoke Visas for Young Illegal Immigrants. October 2.

Viebeck, E. 2012. "Planned Parenthood Targets Romney in New Swing-State Ad." *Hill*, September 25.

Wallsten, P. 2012. "Romney's Mormon Beliefs Featured in Pro-Obama 'Voter Education' Brochure." *Washington Post*, November 5.

Zeleny, J. 2012. "For Romney, Attacks on Bain Career Have Upside." *New York Times*, January 14.

Zito, S. 2012. "Pennsylvania Bishops Urge Voters to Be Guided by Faith." *Pittsburgh Tribune Review*, November 1.

Zoll, R. 2012. "African-American Christians Waver over Vote." *Associated Press*, September 16.

Contributors

Douglas M. Brattebo is Associate Professor of Political Science and Director of the James A. Garfield Center for the Study of the American Presidency at Hiram College. Among the courses Brattebo teaches are Ethics in U.S. Foreign Policy, Introduction to American Government, The American Presidency and the Executive Branch, The Virtues, Leadership, and Legacy of Abraham Lincoln, and Engaged Citizenship. One of his most recent publications is a chapter, "Closed for Repairs So It Can Reengage with the World: Prospects for Reforming the Republican Party," in *The American Election 2012: Contexts and Consequences*, edited by R. Ward Holder and Peter B. Josephson.

Tom Lansford is a Professor of Political Science. His research interests include foreign and security policy, and the U.S. presidency. Dr. Lansford is the author, coauthor, editor, or coeditor of more than forty books, and the author of more than one hundred essays, book chapters, and reviews. His books include *A Bitter Harvest: U.S. Foreign Policy and Afghanistan* (2003), *The Historical Dictionary of U.S. Diplomacy Since the Cold War* (2007), and *9/11 and the Wars in Afghanistan and Iraq: A Chronology and Reference Guide* (2011). His more recent edited collections include *America's War on Terror* (2003; 2nd ed., 2009), *Judging Bush* (2009), and *The Obama Presidency: A Preliminary Assessment* (2012).

Jack Covarrubias is the Director of the Center for Policy and Resilience and a member of the governing board of the National Social Science Association. His experience bridges academia and the military where he has focused on the American foreign policy experience and homeland security. His most recent works include the edited volume *The Obama Presidency: A Preliminary Assessment* (2012) and the co-authored work *Fostering Community Resilience: Homeland Security and Hurricane Katrina* (2010).

Robert J. Pauly, Jr. is Associate Dean for Gulf Coast Operations of the College of Arts and Letters and Tenured Associate Professor of International Policy and Development at The University of Southern Mississippi. His research interests focus broadly on the fields of U.S. foreign policy, national security, and homeland security, with emphasis on American policy toward the states of the greater Middle East. He is the author of five books and nearly forty academic articles, essays, and book chapters, including, most recently, *The Ashgate Research Companion to US Foreign Policy* (2010). He analyzes U.S. foreign policy and national security issues during a weekly appearance on the *Gulf Coast Mornings* radio show on 104.9 FM in Biloxi, MS.

Mark D. Brewer is Associate Professor of Political Science and member of the Honors College faculty at the University of Maine. His research interests focus generally on political behavior, with specific research areas including partisanship and electoral behavior at both the mass and elite levels, the linkages between public opinion and public policy, and the interactions that exist between religion and politics in the United States. Brewer is the author or editor of a number of books and articles in academic journals, with the most recent being The Parties Respond, 5th ed. (with L. Sandy Maisel, Westview Press, 2013), Parties and Elections in America, 6th ed. (with L. Sandy Maisel, Rowman & Littlefield, 2012), Party Images in the American Electorate (Routledge, 2009), and Dynamics of American Political Parties (with Jeffrey M. Stonecash, Cambridge University Press, 2009). He is also the editor-in-chief of the New England Journal of Political Science.

Graham G. Dodds is an Associate Professor of Political Science at Concordia University in Montreal. He has worked as a legislative assistant and speechwriter for a member of the U.S. House of Representatives and as a Research Fellow at the Brookings Institution. His primary expertise is in American political development, particularly the U.S. president's use of unilateral directives, but he has also published work on governmental apologies, U.S. political culture, and political theory.

Sean D. Foreman is an Associate Professor of Political Science in the Department of History and Political Science at Barry University in Miami Shores, FL. He was president of the Florida Political Science Association in 2012–2013 and is the Chair of the Education Committee for the Greater Miami Chamber of Commerce. Foreman is co-editor of The Roads to Congress 2010 (Lexington Press, 2011), where he wrote about the 2010 midterm elections and about Marco Rubio's election to the U.S. Senate, and co-editor of The Roads to Congress 2012 (Lexington Press, 2013) in which he also wrote about the Florida District 26 campaign (Rivera vs. Garcia). His article "Top 10 Reasons Why Barack Obama Won the Presidency in 2008 and What It Means in the 2012 Election" was published in the Florida Political Chronicle in August 2012.

Lisa Hager earned her BA from Wartburg College in 2009 and her MA in 2013 from Kent State University where she is currently ABD in the Department of Political Science. She also serves as the President of Kent State University's Political Science Graduate Student Association. Her research interests primarily focus on the behavior of and interactions between American political institutions, particularly the Supreme Court and Congress. She is currently researching the dynamics of congressional Court-curbing bill sponsorship for her dissertation. Additionally, she is interested in how the law impacts the political process and voting behavior.

Casey Malone Maugh (PhD, Pennsylvania State University, 2007) is Assistant Professor of Communication Studies at the University of Southern Mississippi, Gulf Coast. Her research interests include visual rhetoric, cultural studies, rhetorical theory and criticism, political communication, and public memory studies. Recent publications include "Blogging for Peace: Realistic Job Preview Strategies from the 21st-Century Peace Corps Volunteer" in Volunteering and Communication: Studies from Multiple Contexts; "Seeing the World through Their Eyes: How Peace Corps and Their Volunteers Confront the Universalism/Particularism Continuum" in the American Journal of Communication; and a chapter in The Obama Presidency entitled "Rhetoric and Image."

Matthew R. Miles is a Professor in the Department of History, Geography, and Political Science at Brigham Young University–Idaho. His research on the presidency and the information environment in the United States has been accepted for publication in the journals Environmental Politics and The International Review of Press and Politics.

William J. Miller is Director of Institutional Research and Effectiveness at Flagler College. He is the editor of Tea Party Effects on 2010 U.S. Senate Elections: Stuck in the Middle to Lose (Lexington, 2012), Taking Sides: Clashing Views on Public Administration & Policy (McGraw-Hill, 2012), The Political Battle over Congressional Redistricting (Lexington, 2013), The 2012 Nomination and the Future of the Republican Party: The Internal Battle (Lexington, 2013), and Handbook on Teaching and Learning in Political Science and International Relations (Edward Elgar, forthcoming). His research appears in Journal of Political Science Education, Journal of Political Marketing, Studies in Conflict & Terrorism, International Studies Quarterly, Nonproliferation Review, Afro-Americans in New York Life and History, Journal of South Asian and Middle Eastern Studies, American Behavioral Scientist, PS: Political Science and Politics, and Journal of Common Market Studies.

Douglas Mock is an Adjunct Professor of Political Science at University of New England. He regularly teaches courses on American Elections and the Presidency, as well as Introduction to Political Science.

William D. Pederson (PhD, University of Oregon) is Professor of Political Science, American Studies endowed Chair, and Director of the International Lincoln Center at Louisiana State University, Shreveport. He is the author or editor of thirty books on American politics and the presidency, most recently Lincoln Lessons (Southern Illinois University Press), Lincoln's Enduring Legacy: Perspectives from Great Leaders, Great Thinkers, and the American Experiment (with Robert P. Watson and Frank J. Williams; Lexington), The FDR Years (Facts on File), and A Companion to Franklin D. Roosevelt (Wiley-Blackwell).

Luke Perry is the Chair of the Department of Government and Politics and Associate Professor of Government at Utica College in New York. Perry earned a PhD in Political Science from the University of Massachusetts at Amherst and worked previously as Assistant Professor of Political Science at Southern Utah University from 2008 to 2011. In 2012 Perry served as a Fulbright Scholar at Vilnius University in Lithuania. Perry's research focuses on the presidency and politics and religion. His recent books include Mormons in American Politics: From Persecution to Power (Praeger, 2012) and Mitt Romney, Mormonism, and the 2012 Election (Palgrave-Macmillan, 2014).

Richard J. Powell is Associate Professor of Political Science and Director of the Institute for Leadership and Democracy at the University of Maine. He is the author or editor of Changing Members: The Maine Legislature in the Era of Term Limits (with Matthew Moen and Kenneth Palmer) and Legislating Without Experience: Case Studies in State Legislative Term Limits (with Rick Farmer, Christopher Mooney, and John Green), as well as numerous academic journal articles and book chapters on the U.S. presidency, Congress, state politics, elections, and public opinion.

Max J. Skidmore is University of Missouri Curators' Professor of Political Science, and Thomas Jefferson Fellow. He teaches at the University of Missouri–Kansas City and has been Distinguished Fulbright Lecturer in India and Senior Fulbright Scholar at the University of Hong Kong. He specializes in the presidency, American political thought, and the politics of Social Security, Medicare, and health care, and is founder and president of the Caucus on Poverty, Inequality, and Public Policy of the American Political Science Association. He edits the journal Poverty and Public Policy and is a member of the Scholars' Strategy Network and the

National Academy of Social Insurance. He is the author of more than one hundred articles and book chapters, and of approximately two dozen books, including Securing America's Future, Presidential Performance, After the White House: Former Presidents as Private Citizens, Legacy to the World: A History of America's Political Ideas, and Hong Kong and China: Pursuing a New Destiny. His PhD is from the University of Minnesota.

Justin S. Vaughn is an Assistant Professor of Political Science at Boise State University. He has published several studies of presidential politics, including Gendering the Presidency: Gender, Presidential Politics, and Popular Culture (University Press of Kentucky, 2012) and The Rhetoric of Heroic Expectations: Establishing the Obama Presidency (Texas A&M University Press, 2014), as well as articles in Presidential Studies Quarterly, Political Research Quarterly, Social Science Quarterly, International Journal of Public Administration, Review of Policy Research, Administration & Society, and White House Studies. Dr. Vaughn is co-editor of the Presidents & Executive Politics Report and has previously been a member of the Executive Council of the Presidency Research Section of the American Political Science Association, Executive Politics Section Chair for the Western Political Science Association, and a Fellow at the Center for the Study of the Presidency.

Index

Romney, Mitt (continued), as governor of Massachusetts, 50, 52; as head of Bain Capital, 49, 256; "Let Detroit Go Bankrupt" op-ed of, 261; as a Mormon, 49, 50–53, 64–65, 232, 263; as portrayed on the cover of *Newsweek* on June 13, 2011, 42; underscoring of his commitment to God by, 73; unflattering comparisons of to fictional wealthy characters, 79. *See also* Romney, Mitt, 2008 presidential campaign of; Romney, Mitt, 2012 presidential campaign of

Romney, Mitt, 2008 presidential campaign of, 50–54; campaign slogan, 104

Romney, Mitt, 2012 presidential campaign of, 54–66 *passim*, 216–17; "47 percent" comment of, 79, 217, 253, 257–59; acceptance speech of at the Republican National Convention, 108–9; African American votes for, 266; Americans' perceptions of Mormonism at the time, 55–56, 72–73; Americans' unwillingness to vote for a Mormon presidential candidate, 62–64, 65, 72; belittling of the Obama campaign's slogan, 84; and Big Bird, 81; campaign slogan, 82; casting of as a "vulture capitalist" by his Republican opponents, 256; Catholic votes for, 60–61, 231, 269, 279; commencement address of at Falwell's Liberty University, 36, 73; and early voting, 202; and economic issues, 78–79; European trip of, 217; evangelical/fundamentalist votes for, 230–31; Hispanic votes for, 228, 230; and immigration issues, 227–28, 245; Jewish votes for, 61, 232, 267; key demographic of, 223; male votes for, 250; and microtargeting, 123; Mormon votes for, 232; portrayal of by the Obama camp, 79, 256–57; post-election comments of, 235; refusal of to release most of his past tax returns, 79; religiously active votes for, 62, 264;

religiously unaffiliated votes for, 266; senior votes for, 226, 252; social class votes for, 261–62; strategy of to attract Hispanic voters, 245; strategy of to attract women voters, 249; use of Obama's "you didn't build that" quote by, 103, 109; white evangelical votes for, 60, 73, 264–65; white votes for, 247; and "Women for Mitt," 249–50; and Young Americans for Romney, 253; youth votes for, 253. *See also* 2012 presidential debates; 2012 presidential election; 2012 Republican National Convention (RNC)

Roosevelt, Franklin, 9, 11; co-optation of Lincoln into the Democratic Party, 11; leadership style of, 16; and national health care, 15; as an outsider, 11; self-actualization of through politics, 12

Roosevelt, Theodore, 97; identification of with Lincoln, 10; and national health care, 15; as an outsider, 10–11

Ros-Lehtinen, Ileana, 234

Ross, A. Larry, 39

Rove, Karl, 71

Rubio, Marco, 228, 234, 245

Rushdoony, Rousas John, 29–30, 32; as the father of "Dominionism" or "Re-constructionism," 29

Ryan, Paul, 34, 73; acceptance speech of at the 2012 Republican National Convention, 109–10, 112; as a Catholic, 35, 231, 269; influence of Rand on, 35; Medicare plan of, 226, 251–52; and working-class audiences, 260

Salinas, Maria Elena, 227

Sandoval, Brian, 228

Santorum, Rick, 59, 230, 256; anti-contraception comments of, 248; as a Catholic, 35; criticism of Kennedy's famous 1960 speech, 35, 72

Saralegui, Cristina, 111

Scalia, Antonin, 76